PRAIS
A PRECAUTI

"An inspiring tale of citizen science and community action."
— RAJ PATEL, author of *Stuffed and Starved:
The Hidden Battle for the World Food System*

"Ackerman-Leist tells the story of how a small town took on the powerful forces of chemical agriculture and not only won, but created a template that anyone seeking a poison-free environment anywhere in the world can follow."

—BARRY ESTABROOK,
author of *Tomatoland* and *Pig Tales*

"Climate change, xenophobia, war, hunger, madmen and autocrats running the world. It's easy to feel paralyzed when faced with the enormity of our modern dilemma. Philip Ackerman-Leist's *A Precautionary Tale* gives us hope, and provides us with a real-life tale of regular folk who stood up to the Goliath that was about to swallow their community, and succeeded. This book is living proof that even against overwhelming odds we have enormous power in and around the places where we live."
— MICHAEL ABLEMAN, farmer; author of *Street Farm:
Growing Food, Jobs, and Hope on the Urban Frontier*

"*A Precautionary Tale* is the hopeful message we all need! Philip Ackerman-Leist shows us that we still have the power, as citizens, to gather and change the reality of our daily lives. The people from Mals could be you and me. They have proven that working for empowerment is not in vain. Indeed, they have managed to defeat giant corporations. And they remind us that we can't let despair or sadness paralyze us, that we can trust the strength of community, and that we must do our part and act."
— PERRINE AND CHARLES HERVÉ-GRUYER,
authors of *Miraculous Abundance*

"Many, many thanks to Philip Ackerman-Leist for telling us the wonderful story of Mals, the town in Italy that decided to ban the use of pesticides! This story is extremely inspiring for us all. It shows that there is a way out of the actual dependency of our agriculture on pesticides, and that a group of informed and active citizens, together with brave local politicians, can change the world for the better. May this excellent book inspire communities all around the world — and our politicians, too!"

— FRANÇOIS VEILLERETTE, chair,
Pesticide Action Network Europe

A
Precautionary
TALE

Also by Philip Ackerman-Leist

Rebuilding the Foodshed:
How to Create Local, Sustainable, and Secure Food Systems

Up Tunket Road:
The Education of a Modern Homesteader

A Precautionary TALE

How One Small Town Banned Pesticides, Preserved Its Food Heritage, *and* Inspired a Movement

PHILIP ACKERMAN-LEIST

foreword by Vandana Shiva

Chelsea Green Publishing
White River Junction, Vermont

Editor: Joni Praded
Project Manager: Angela Boyle
Copy Editor: Laura Jorstad
Proofreader: Paula Brisco
Indexer: Shana Milkie
Designer: Melissa Jacobson

Printed in Canada.
First printing October 2017.
10 9 8 7 6 5 4 3 2 1   17 18 19 20 21

Our Commitment to Green Publishing

Library of Congress Cataloging-in-Publication Data
Names: Ackerman-Leist, Philip, 1963- author.
Title: A precautionary tale : the story of how one small town banned pesticides, preserved its food heritage, and inspired a movement / Philip Ackerman-Leist ; photographs by Douglas Gayeton ; foreword by Vandana Shiva.
Description: White River Junction, VT : Chelsea Green Publishing, [2017] | Includes bibliographical references and index.
Identifiers: LCCN 2017024437 | ISBN 9781603587051 (pbk.) | ISBN 9781603587068 (ebook)
Subjects: LCSH: Farms, Large--Italy--Malles Venosta. | Farm corporations--Italy--Malles Venosta. | Protest movements--Italy--Malles Venosta. | Pesticides--Government policy--Italy--Malles Venosta. | Malles Venosta (Italy)
Classification: LCC HD1471.I82 A25 2017 | DDC 338.10945/383--dc23
LC record available at https://lccn.loc.gov/2017024437

Chelsea Green Publishing
85 North Main Street, Suite 120
White River Junction, VT 05001
(802) 295-6300
www.chelseagreen.com

To my Brunnenburg family —
Mary, Sizzo, Brigitte, Patrizia, Graziella, Michi, and Nik
— and in memory of Boris and Lois

CONTENTS

FOREWORD

Mals, a small village in South Tirol, has shown once again the truth in the famous words of Margaret Mead: "Never doubt that a small group of thoughtful, committed citizens can change the world; indeed, it's the only thing that ever has."

I feel honored that I had a chance to support the movement for Mals to become pesticide-free, and also to write the foreword to Philip Ackerman-Leist's book, *A Precautionary Tale*, about the courageous and creative citizens of Mals.

For more than a century, a poison cartel has experimented with and developed chemicals to kill people, first in Hitler's concentration camps and the war. These chemicals were later sold as inputs for industrial agriculture.

The poison cartel I refer to here is the handful of global corporations that push chemicals and genetically modified organisms (GMOs) in farming — Bayer/Monsanto, Dow/Dupont, Syngenta/ChemChina. Killing is their expertise.

In India, a country of small farmers, the assault of the poison cartel has driven millions off the land and pushed 300,000 farmers to suicide due to debt for costly seeds and chemicals. The genetically modified (GM) seeds have failed to control pests and weeds. Instead they are creating super pests and super weeds, trapping farmers deeper in debt.

And it is not just farmers who are dying. Our soil organisms and pollinators are dying. Our soils are dying. Our societies are dying. Our children are dying — because of diseases caused by food loaded with toxics.

Pesticide pollution knows no boundaries, and the pesticide sprays contaminate entire ecosystems, our food, our water. These corporations take away our right to be free from harm.

They do not poison just people, our farms, and our food; they poison regulatory systems and science. Corruption of science, of regulation, of centralized governments is their expertise.

A Precautionary Tale

The agrochemical industry and its new avatar, the biotechnology industry, do not merely distort and manipulate knowledge, science, and public policy. They also manipulate the law and the justice system.

That is why the movement for freedom from poisons in our food and agriculture is the most important freedom movement in our times. It is a movement for the rights of the Earth, the rights of all species, of all peoples to be free from harm, to be healthy. It is a movement to protect the diversity of species, of cultures, of economies, of knowledge, of decision making from the local to the global.

It is the movement for justice, for the right to life and livelihood. It is the right to know about the potential harm from poisons and poison-producing plants — GMOs. It is freedom from manipulated alternative facts and post-truths, which hide truth and try to bury it, as we are witnessing in the case of glyphosate and GMOs .

The World Health Organization (WHO) categorized Monsanto's glyphosate (Roundup) as a probable carcinogen. Monsanto attacked WHO and has deployed its lobbyists to block its ban.

Philip's book, based on real stories about the courage of real people, provides touching human details of how the movement evolved in Mals and reminds us that this is what freedom looks like. This is what Earth Democracy looks like. It is like a seed. It begins small. It grows from the ground up. It spreads its roots deep, its branches wide. In the soil the mycorrhizal fungi and billions of microorganisms spread life and nourishment. From the flowers, pollinators spread life and nourishment.

Every place is a Mals waiting to spread its wings of freedom.

In India since 1999 we have been creating living democracy villages to be free of poisons and GMOs, to protect our biodiversity, our seeds, our forests, our land, our waters.

Democracy has to begin where people are. It cannot be hijacked by the poison cartel, corrupting one, two, three, and so many more men behind closed doors of opaque decision making. That is not democracy. It is the dictatorship of those who make and sell poisons.

My own journey to create a pesticide-free world began in 1984 with the tragedies in Punjab and Bhopal in India.

The Green Revolution, which began in Punjab, was given a Nobel Peace prize based on the narrative that new seeds and chemicals would create prosperity and hence peace. But by 1984, Punjab was a land of violence and war. Thirty thousand people had been killed.

It was this divergence between the Green Revolution myth and the reality of violence that compelled me to conduct research on what was happening in Punjab. That is when I wrote *The Violence of the Green Revolution*.

The Bhopal gas tragedy was the worst industrial disaster in human history. Twenty-five thousand people died, 500,000 were injured, and the injustice done to the victims of Bhopal over the past 25 years will go down as the worst case of jurisprudence ever.

The gas leak in Bhopal in December 1984 was from the Union Carbide pesticide plant that manufactured carabaryl (trade name Sevin) — a pesticide used mostly on cotton plants. It was, in fact, because of the Bhopal gas tragedy and the tragedy of extremist violence in Punjab that I woke up to the fact that agriculture had become a war zone. Pesticides are war chemicals that kill: The United Nations estimates that 220,000 people are killed every year by pesticides worldwide.

After research, I realized that we do not need toxic pesticides that kill humans and other species that maintain the web of life. Pesticides do not control pests: They create pests by killing beneficial species. We have safer, nonviolent alternatives such as neem. That is why at the time of the Bhopal disaster I started the campaign "No more Bhopals, plant a neem." The neem campaign led, in 1994, to challenging the biopiracy of neem. At that time, I discovered that US-based, multinational W. R. Grace had patented neem for use as pesticide and fungicide and was setting up a neem-oil extraction plant in Tumkur, Karnataka. We fought the biopiracy case for eleven years and were eventually successful in striking down the biopiracy patent.

Meanwhile, the old pesticide industry was mutating into the biotechnology and genetic engineering industry. While genetic engineering was promoted as an alternative to pesticides, Bt cotton was introduced to end pesticide use. But Bt cotton has failed to control the bollworm and has instead created major new pests, leading to an increase in pesticide use.

The high costs of GM seeds and pesticides are pushing farmers into debt, and indebted farmers are committing suicide. Adding the 310,000 farmer suicides in India to the 25,000 killed in Bhopal, we are witnessing a massive corporate genocide — the killing of people for super profits.

To maintain these super profits, lies are told about how, without pesticides and GMOs, there will be no food. In fact, the conclusions of the International Assessment of Agricultural Knowledge, Science and Technology for Development, undertaken by the United Nations, show that ecologically organic agriculture produces more food and better food at a lower cost than either chemical agriculture or GMOs.

In my book *Who Really Feeds the World?*, I have shown how neither corporations nor their pesticides feed the world. It is small farmers who feed the world. Our work in Navdanya over the past thirty years has shown that we can grow enough nourishing food for two Indias through biodiversity and agroecology.

The process of holding the poison cartel accountable is the culmination of thirty years of scientific, legal, social, and political work by movements and concerned citizens and scientists. These movements and people make up the coalition that came together to organize the Monsanto Tribunal and People's Assembly in October 2016.

The tribunal both synthesized the existing crimes and violations for which Monsanto and Bayer have been brought to court across the world — in India, Europe, the United States, Mexico, Argentina — and expanded the scope of criminal activity to include the crime of ecocide, the violation of the rights of nature.

Crimes against nature are connected to crimes against humanity. Corporate crimes have become visible everywhere. The corporations become bigger, claiming absolute power, absolute rights, absolute immunity — and deploying more violent tools against nature and people. The ongoing process of supporting People's Assemblies will not just take stock of the past and present crimes. It will also look at future potential crimes, with the aim of preventing them.

The introduction of GMOs, by the poison cartel, has accelerated the crisis of disease and death.

But movements for GMO-free and poison-free food have also been growing. The chemical corporations had expected to take over all seed by the year 2000 through GMOs, patents, mergers, and acquisitions. But most seed is still not genetically modified, and most countries do not recognize seeds and plants as corporate inventions, which would make them patentable. Monsanto's crimes have become so well known that it now wants to disappear itself through the Bayer acquisition. The movements against Monsanto have already won. Now we need to shut down the poison cartel.

While GMOs fail, a new generation of genetic engineering based on CRISPR, gene editing, and gene drives is being promoted to grab more patents and wreck the planet faster for the benefit of a few toxic billionaires.

While courts can investigate crimes of the poison cartel, and this is important for justice, people have the power to change the way we grow our food. That is why hundreds of People's Assemblies, being organized everywhere, will make commitments to create a healthy future of food and of the planet. From the People's Assemblies, we are launching a boycott campaign to liberate our seeds and soils, our communities and societies, our planet and ourselves from poisons and the rule of the poison cartel.

As the poison cartel undemocratically tries to force its poisons and GMOs across the world, more and more communities and countries are making the democratic choice to become poison-free and GMO-free.

Mals stands out as a community that decided to create toxic-free food and agriculture systems through real democracy, democracy based on the active participation of citizens.

Read the story of Mals to get inspired. And *act*.

And let us join hands, minds, and hearts to create a healthy, happy world, free of poisons and the poison cartel. Seed by seed, farm by farm, community by community, let us make this beautiful Earth a garden of diversity and abundance, of well-being and freedom for all people and all beings.

DR. VANDANA SHIVA
JUNE 2017

CHAPTER 1

Drift

It wasn't the first time that the small town of 5,300 inhabitants had come under siege. Far from it. Situated at the intersection of three countries and two historic passes over the Alps, the town of Mals had a long history of being caught in the middle of various turf battles waged by warring tribes, bishops, counts, emperors, and even nations. But this newest turf battle was a little more literal — it was about hayfields.

Medieval watchtowers still dot the landscape, springing up from promontories and village centers, while castles in various states of glory and disrepair cling to valley edges. Fortified village walls and massive iron-clad doors are now part of the local charm, drawing in tourists from regions that were once rival territories. Concrete pillboxes erupt ever so slightly from the ground in the broad, tilting upper reaches of the valley, most of them shrouded with grassy sod spilling over their rounded tops like unkempt hair, given away only by the narrow slits that hid all but the watchful eyes of the World War II gunners sent to guard the relatively new borders of modern-day Italy, Austria, and Switzerland.

With this newest incursion, though, there were no warnings or obvious outsiders. No screams, bells, or sirens. Even though vigilance seemed embedded in the cultural DNA of the locals, they weren't quite sure whether the dangers were real or simply the delusions of alarmists, people who wanted to deny the new economic order and live in the past. Watchtowers, binoculars, cutting-edge night-vision goggles — none of it was any help in detecting the newest interlopers. Safe in quiet café corners or at home among family and close friends, some locals would talk quietly about the imminent threat when they first suspected it, but every time they tried to pinpoint it, the enemy in question had a way of vaporizing, literally.

This invasion wasn't anything like the last war, which had taken the lives of a number of Malsers — a proud but simple people eking out a living from the steep slopes but caught between the Fascists of the south and the Nazis of the north. This time it was completely different. In the valley below them, the pounding of mortars was replaced by the pounding of concrete posts, and barbed wire was traded for trellis wire. Laser beams were cutting through farm fields along established coordinates, providing the precision needed to commandeer the terrain and turn hay- and grain fields into fruit factories. The new orchards followed a combination of laser-straight lines and tilted topography, taking over strategic positions for capturing maximum sunlight and avoiding the coldest of temperatures.

The incursion itself was no secret. It was years in the making; the people of Mals had watched the gradual march of the orchards up the slopes, directly toward them, with a few infiltrators already ensconced in the town's network of villages. But the biggest threats were hidden in the enveloping mists blasted from the spray machines mounted on the back of the advancing tractors. Even after the tractors passed and the mists dissipated, the stench would linger in the air, permeating a landscape with more than five thousand years of documented agricultural traditions in this high Alpine valley. It was all up for grabs.

Big Apple was rolling into town. And it seemed like nobody was going to stop it.

Tucked up next to the Swiss border, Laatsch is one of eleven villages making up the town of Mals. Most of the locals refer to their township as Mals (pronounced *maltz*), its historic German name, while Italian officials and tourists typically use the lilting Italian version, Malles (*MAH-less*). The twin names of the town are but one reminder of a long history of power plays evident everywhere around the Alpine outpost. Before becoming a part of the Italian autonomous province of South Tirol, Mals was a proud part of *das Land Tirol*, a region ruled for centuries by the Hapsburgs but known today primarily for its seminal role in the development of winter sports. In return for their allegiance in protecting the strategic mountain territories, the Hapsburgs had always treated the Tirolean farmers more as compatriots than lowly peasants. The royal family depended upon the farmers' fierce loyalty and vigilance.

If you enter Laatsch by way of the Swiss border — presuming you successfully evade the Italian border guards in search of your cache of Swiss chocolates — it's not the speed limit signs that will slow you down as much as the architecture plopped directly in your trajectory. Laatsch is a village of twisting passages, not roads. The flared foundations of its medieval buildings are the reason the structures are still standing, but their angled bulk creeps into the streets. Farmers' and merchants' wagons were well accommodated in the days of yore, but there was clearly no anticipation of modern-day cars, much less milk trucks and tractors.

When you drive into Laatsch, the initial warning of impending vehicular doom comes in the ironic form of a church. As you round one of the first curves entering the village, the road suddenly splits, with oncoming traffic going through two narrow stone arches underneath the church while you are forced to swerve to the right and around the church before entering the narrow main thoroughfare through the village. The steady plod of oxcarts might have at one time ensured the safe simultaneous passage of two vehicles through the winding thoroughfare, but the precision steering of modern vehicles is compromised by our penchant for speed: There is no room for four-wheeled velocity in Laatsch. The wisest travelers use two feet or two wheels for safe and speedy passage. That said, the farmers on tractors do not necessarily operate under any basic laws of physics other than velocity × mass = victory. It should be no surprise: Farmers have long been the driving force in the area.

The main route through the village opens up slightly where a torrent of water shoots its way through a stone-lined channel that used to power a number of the village's mills. Only one of those mills remains, conveniently and not coincidentally set just across the street from Bäckerei Schuster, the local bakery. A few hundred feet uphill past that waterway and near the opposite end of the village is another, larger flume that races its way down toward the Adige River. If you drive over the wooden bridge crossing the brook in the warmer months, you might notice a cow patty or two. But chances are Günther Wallnöfer already shoveled up any deposits left by his cattle. He doesn't think a farmer should leave messes that someone else has to clean up.

Günther is adept at putting a halt to anything rolling his way when he maneuvers his two dozen cows through the crooked streets of his village and across the bridge twice each day, escorting them from barn to pasture and back. However, he never thought he would be the first in Mals to slow the growing momentum of Big Apple as it came his way, much less become a figure who would inspire organic markets and social justice movements in Europe and beyond.

No matter what time of day or night you might meet him, your lasting impression of Günther is likely to be of a man in motion. Tall, lean, and equipped with a strong stride accustomed to craggy hills, he is adroit at leaping into and out of his tractor cab. The velocity of Günther's local dialect matches his pace, and his hand gestures tend to be the only punctuation in his high-speed commentary. Chances are, if you're talking to him, it's while he's doing something else, and his hands are constantly shifting between completing the task at hand and conveying a point of emphasis.

With an ever-present hat tilted to deflect the intensity of sun, wind, or cold from his receding hairline, Günther tends to keep his head down and his long gait in motion, focusing on everything that has to happen within the constraints of a twenty-four-hour day — a time frame obviously devised without any consideration for how much a dairy farmer has to achieve in the allotted time span. A dairy farmer anywhere in the world is up against the odds, but the steep slopes and short summers of the Alps make the life of a mountain farmer an even greater challenge. Günther's fast clip, no matter the means of locomotion, is a constant reminder that there's no time to slow down when you have to be one step ahead of what some call progress.

Inheriting a family business, much less a farm, can be as much a weight as it is a gift, and the local inheritance practices don't make it any easier. As a young man, Günther began managing his family's dairy farm in Laatsch. Unlike many other places in the region, the farmers in Laatsch and the other villages of Mals tended to have their houses and main barns inside the village proper, with the buildings huddled tightly around the inevitable spire of the village church. The surrounding fields were used for hay, grains, vegetables, and pastures. It was, by design, a means of countering the vulnerability of the coveted valley with a tight collective identity and a stone-fortified armory to protect their livestock and winter stores.

However, that design meant that each farm family, even up to this day, has managed a patchwork of very small, scattered fields, many of them less than an acre or two in size. Crops that needed to be brought to the barn for winter storage were grown close to the village, while most livestock were sent to the high mountain pastures for summer grazing so that hay from the nearby fields could be readily transported to the barn. This scattering of exceedingly small parcels, at least by modern standards, would ultimately play a key defensive role for the locals in their newest onslaught — one that no one could have predicted.

Günther was fortunate enough to inherit a relatively large assortment of fields. With 47 acres (19 ha) to divide among hay, pasture, grains, and even some vegetables, he had the ecological base to support about twenty-five milking cows and seven to eight calves, along with pigs and a small poultry flock. However, a sound ecological base doesn't automatically translate into a manageable income.

Whereas his ancestors had struggled simply to subsist through the seasonal cycles of each year, Günther had to endure not just the Alps' temperamental seasons but also the tempestuous markets that dictated whether he was in debt or on modest economic footing. As he gradually took over his family's farm, he continued to manage it conventionally and sell to the local dairy processor, much as his father had. However, the consistently meager economic return created by the combination of market plunges and increased costs forced him to question whether he would be the last in his family's long line of diversified farmers if he kept going that route.

That long lineage stretched far beyond just three or four generations. Archaeologists have discovered the relics of several settlements in the area that date back as far as the Stone Age. They have even unearthed a variety of grains in the carbonized remains, including some strains that are still grown in the area for the hearty traditional breads and dishes. The rich diversity of the Upper Vinschgau was coveted long before it ever appeared on a map.

A Precautionary Tale

After too many nights long on worry and short on sleep, Günther eventually came to the conclusion that the only way he could ensure the economic viability of his family's farm was to certify it as organic and tap into those more lucrative and stable markets, earning him 20 to 30 percent more for his milk. He could also diversify his products, adding organic poultry, grain, and vegetables, and capitalize on those added income streams. In 2001 he went *bio* (pronounced *BEE-oh*) and became certified organic. In the end it wasn't such a radical decision: Going organic was, for him, a return to the traditional ways. He would be managing livestock, crops, and the landscape the same way his ancestors did. It turned out, however, that his decision to go organic put him directly in the path of progress. Big Apple was on its way up the Vinschgau Valley, and he could see it coming. He just didn't realize how quickly he would be surrounded.

The Vinschgau Valley, known by the Italians as Val Venosta, forms the westernmost corner of the autonomous province of South Tirol in Italy. The driest valley in the Alps, with an average of 16 to 20 inches (40–50 cm) of rain and nearly 300 days of sun per year, it is ideal for growing apples, grapes, cherries, pears, and other fruits. Since moisture and cloudy weather create optimal conditions for the spread of plant diseases, the sunny slopes, good air drainage, and deep valley soils in the Vinschgau combine to create a Paradise for fruit growers. And nothing is more tempting than an apple in Paradise.

While apples had a long history in the lower reaches of the Vinschgau Valley, they weren't a big part of the traditional agricultural economy of the Upper Vinschgau. Because neither climate nor custom was conducive to growing apples in the eleven high-elevation villages of Mals, which range from 3,300 to 5,600 feet (1,000–1,700 m) in elevation, inhabitants of the region have relied upon livestock and crops well adapted to the intensity of weather and topography in the area at least since the Stone Age.

Mals is flanked on three sides by some of the highest mountains in the South Tirol, including the Ortler, the highest at 12,812 feet (3,905 m). The Adige River gathers its force from the downward-flowing waters of the surrounding mountains and pushes its way eastward through the valley and into the city of Meran, then veers southward toward Verona, eventually dumping into the Adriatic Sea. Despite the constraints of elevation, the inhabitants of the higher reaches of the Vinschgau long ago discovered ways in which to optimize slope and turn it into a useful variable for agriculture.

Cattle, goats, sheep, and even pigs traditionally followed the greening of the grass as it gradually moved up beyond the tree line and then back down, essentially following the rise and fall of the mercury through the course of the year. With much of the livestock sent to the high pastures, farmers could use the lower fields to grow grains, vegetables, and the linchpin of the system: hay. In such a risky growing environment, farmers grew fruits for subsistence but not extensively for commercial purposes. Milk products, cold-hardy vegetables, and grains were a better bet for market. Even as modern markets evolved and fruits began commanding higher prices and better incomes than the other high-elevation products, the farmers of the Upper Vinschgau generally stuck by the traditions and conservative wisdom that had served them well for millennia.

That aversion to risk began to melt away not too long ago, virtually in sync with the shrinking of the glaciers in the mountains high above the valley. Suddenly a warming climate and hardier fruit varieties conspired to create not just new but also more lucrative market opportunities for farmers. The sweet possibilities were hard to resist, and in the course of a few short years locals found themselves watching what looked like a big game of tic-tac-toe progress up the valley, with farmers weighing their options before filling the patchwork grid of open fields with trellised apples, grapes, and cherries. Günther was just one of many farmers about to find themselves caught in a game they'd never agreed to play.

Emboldened by the ever-earlier retreat of winter, Big Apple's avantgarde began to brazenly take up position in a few fields in Mals. In a township covering just over 90 square miles (233 sq km), it would seem that there was plenty of land to spare, and a few apple and cherry orchards wouldn't matter. However, fruit growers and livestock farmers both preferred the flatter fields in the broad valley floor, and those areas were in limited supply.

In 2010 Günther noticed the first concrete posts and trellis wire delivered to his neighbor's adjacent fields. Soon the reverberations of the post driver seemed to pound the fear of what was coming deeper and deeper into his consciousness. Workers came in to stretch the trellis wires and anchor them to the posts before installing the drip irrigation system. Only after the engineering was complete did the planting begin. More workers planted the young apple whips about 3 to 9 feet (1–3 m) apart so that each row of apples would become a highly efficient production line: Pruning, anchoring, watering, spraying, and harvesting could all be done with relative ease and consistency.

Although Günther wasn't so keen on the intrusive aesthetics of the intensive trellising system, that was the least of his worries. The real intrusion wasn't visible, but it put everything that he had worked so hard to build at risk.

As Günther and his cows wove their way through Laatsch, a beeping horn stopped him. He turned around, spreading his arms to slow the bovine promenade behind him, and let the car slip by before he and his cows stepped back into the main thoroughfare for their jaunt from the barn to pasture. The driver had Swiss plates and a business suit. Someone in a rush to make money, he surmised, while he headed out to his fields to seal his own financial fate in several plastic bags.

He crossed the street, with the boss cow and her entourage following. Then he stepped aside and let her lead the herd — she knew where she was headed — while he waited for the inevitable straggler, gave her a firm slap on the haunch, and watched her leap forward to catch up with the rest. Günther then sprinted along the edge of the paved bike path and past the last of the ambling cows to the pasture gate, where the cows were calmly filing in before rushing to the new strip of ungrazed grass that he had opened up earlier that morning. His portable electric fencing allowed him to carefully manage his small pastures, maximizing their regrowth and nutritional value by giving the cows access to fresh grass every day but preventing them from overgrazing any one spot.

A cow's milk production is directly correlated to what she eats, and what she eats depends upon the farmer's management. There was only one thing more important to Günther than fresh grass: high-quality hay. Fresh grass in lush pastures made him money, but good hay meant survival. For his livestock, it was the bridge between seasons; for his family it was the difference between a healthy future and financial ruin.

Günther made his way up to where his neighbor's new apple trees bordered one of his hayfields. Were it not for the apple trees on one side and the hay meadow on the other, the boundary between the two parcels probably wouldn't be discernible to the ordinary passerby. He had just cut the leafy mixture of grasses, legumes, and other broad-leafed herbs. It was a task he usually enjoyed, watching the diverse green bounty fall to the ground in tidy swaths and feeling like he had winter under control. Most years he would pass through each hay meadow three times. Although it varied by year, the first cut tended to have more grasses and carbohydrates while the latter cuts usually had more legumes and higher protein levels. With the variety of cuttings, Günther could give his cows, calves, steers, and other livestock what best fit their nutritional needs. The one thing that couldn't vary, however, was whether the hay was pesticide-free.

It was that concern that had slowed his stride and distracted him in his chores all morning. He made his way up through the hayfield, kicking the toppled grasses and legumes to check their dryness, wishing that this year's crop would give him the age-old sense of security he'd always known before. He walked toward to his first sampling location, shaking his head with frustration at the laughable 10-foot (3 m) buffer between his hay and the outer row of apples, a distance that was supposed to protect his hay from his neighbor's pesticides.

He knelt down to collect the first sample and put it in one of the sterile plastic bags he'd brought with him. He was nervous enough about the results, but to make matters worse, he had to pay 250 euros per bag (about $300 at the time) out of his own pocket simply to have each bag tested for pesticide residues — pesticides used by someone else.

He felt like he was gathering the tea leaves for his entire future and sending them off to a white-coated technician who would place them in a laboratory cocktail and read them before sending him a verdict on the future of his farm. Whether or not he could make sense of the analysis when it came was another question. He was accustomed to dealing with tons, hectares, and liters, but "parts per million" and "tolerances" were things he and other organic farmers had always intended to avoid.

Hay had long been the linchpin of Tirolean agriculture. Günther describes it as "the most important thing that we have here." Whereas some other areas of the South Tirol have higher levels of protein in their hay, the Upper Vinschgau is comparable to a semiarid steppe region, with a diversity of herbs stemming from the dry substrate. Those herbs create what Günther and others there consider pastures and hay meadows of an exceptional quality that are essential to the healthy livestock of the region. If he lost his organic certification due to a confirmation of pesticide residues in his hay, he would lose more than his feed. He would also have to give up his farm and the traditional farming practices that were the foundation of the local culture. And he would simply be the first domino to fall.

Any sense of solitude in the Alps usually comes by way of feeling diminutive in the presence of mountains. In a small Alpine village, however, one seldom feels alone. But when Günther answered the phone on that fateful day and heard the voice of the toxicologist deliver the results of his hay sample analyses, he had never felt quite so isolated, despite being in the middle of the village that had nurtured him for his entire life. There was no silver lining in the report. Every sample that he had sent in had tested positive for residues of multiple pesticides. He'd been kicked and rammed around by cattle his whole life, but he'd never been knocked breathless by a phone call. The follow-up email detailing the results only added to the darkening reality.

The lab results might have been conclusive, but Günther felt like they generated more questions than answers. How was he going to explain the results to his neighbors who had sprayed the pesticides? What was he going to do with the contaminated feed? What substances were detected and what did they mean for the health of his animals and his land?

Günther spent the rest of the day and most of the night on the phone and sending out emails. Even if it was unclear to him at the time, this was the first sign that his life as a dairy farmer was about to change, and he was about to be dialed into more people and networks than he'd ever imagined. Phone calls, emails, and letters were about to fill every narrow crevice of his daily schedule, and the village's image of him as the gangly young farmer with the ever-present hat would soon include him holding his cell phone to his ear.

However, none of the conversations helped alleviate the feelings of isolation and fear. If anything, the consequences of the analyses were becoming ever clearer, even if they were bewildering. His first call after receiving the results was to his certifier at Bioland, the organic cooperative to which he belonged. He'd long believed that the membership fees he paid to the cooperative were ultimately an investment in the betterment of his own farm. It wasn't simply a contractual relationship. Bioland also held farm tours and seminars and offered a social network for farmers who too often felt like they were going it alone in their farming ventures. Günther was about to find out if Bioland also provided a safety net for its members.

It didn't feel so positive at first. His certifier at Bioland informed him that in order to keep his organic certification — the keystone to his farm's economic success at the moment — he would have to dispose of the entire first cutting of hay that he'd harvested in areas adjacent to the new orchards. Winter had never looked bleaker.

However, summer seemed just as bad. He would have to take samples from his next two hay harvests, too, and it seemed all too likely that they would also test positive. To boot, he would have to pay for even more analyses while also buying organic hay from another farmer at a premium price, if anyone had any surplus for sale. It was a coveted commodity.

Finally, there was the ironic reality that illuminated the absurdity of the whole situation. In order to maintain his certification, he had to dispose of the tainted hay crop and document that it had left the farm. He actually had to find a buyer for it — someone who would take the hay, despite the fact that it contained pesticide residues. Ordinarily he would walk out of his house and be down at the local bar, the Gasthaus Lamm, to have a drink to commiserate with his friends. For the time being, though, he had to figure out his best course of action. A turf battle in a small town is guaranteed to get personal, but to Günther the issue seemed much bigger than him alone. And if it didn't get resolved now, in a good way, he was sure that it would turn into an ugly battle that would stretch far past his generation.

The people of Mals had just elected a new young mayor who seemed much different from the usual politicians in the South Tirol. Günther decided to reach out to him first to see if he had any insights. Little did he know that he was inviting the mayor to join him in careening down a path that neither could have expected — in fact, it would turn out to be a path that no town had ever gone down before.

A striking but soft-spoken figure, Ulrich Veith — known by most locals as Uli — isn't anyone's image of a stereotypical mayor. Perfectly comfortable in a crisp Italian suit and fashionable footwear, he can play the part of mayor in traditional table-and-chair ways. However, he seems most at home when he is casually walking the streets of Mals, greeting virtually everyone he bumps into with a fitting salutation, be it in Tirolean dialect, Italian, or on one knee, for the smallest of his patrons.

Though he's in his midforties, Uli's trim physique and casually groomed wavy hair give the impression that he is a decade younger. His slightly bronze, fit appearance isn't an artifice created in a spa but rather on the hiking paths, bike trails, and ski slopes in and above Mals, often in pursuit of his super-athlete wife, Marian, with their young son in tow. Neither unaware of custom nor flippant about cultural expectations, Uli is nonetheless just as likely to appear at an appointment in fashionable athletic wear as he is in a suit. He always seems ready to take advantage of the best that Mals has to offer in year-round outdoor activities — or perhaps he is in constant training to keep up with Marian, an avid rock climber and mountain biker who is at least as nontraditional in her mother-athlete role as Uli is in politics.

After more than a decade of traveling the world for business, Uli had returned to his native Mals with no real political aspirations — in fact, he was not even registered with a political party at the time. He did, however, have a deep desire to see the Upper Vinschgau make its way forward into the twenty-first century, building upon the best the region had to offer. That desire eventually led him to a victorious run for mayor of Mals in 2009, and he was eager to represent his townspeople as well as he possibly could. So when Günther called to set up a meeting about a problem he was having, Uli immediately invited him to his office in the town hall.

You would be hard-pressed to find a better measure of contrasts in Mals than Uli and Günther. Günther will show up to almost any function in a T-shirt, work pants, and heavy leather farm boots, while Uli will appear looking fresh and dapper, if not aerodynamic, in his perfectly tailored suit or formfitting running outfit. Günther's handshake will feel like he's about to squeeze milk out of your four fingers while Uli's firm but uncallused squeeze is a testament to his habit of making acquaintances from all walks of life. In a moment of uncertainty, Günther might run his hand over the tingle of his buzz cut while Uli slips his hand through his wavy hair during a pensive pause. Günther will insist that he can speak only Tirolean dialect and high German while Uli will shift fluently between both before jumping in with English or Italian.

But they always shared one thing in common: a deep passion for what they both dubbed a sustainable future for Mals. Before long, they would both add another descriptor to the future they envisioned for their town — *healthy*.

Dairy farmers don't tend to embrace politicians or meetings very readily, but as far as he could tell, Günther had limited options for people who would comprehend the full scope of the dilemma, much less have the means to help address the looming issues. When he met with Uli, he described the problem as succinctly as he could, framing it as not just his issue but a quandary facing all of the 5,300 citizens in the eleven villages of the Mals township.

With the small field sizes that dominated the Mals landscape — usually just a few acres — and the renowned *Vinschgerwind*, the legendary wind of the valley blowing for days or weeks at a time, the drifting of pesticides applied by any single farmer onto other farmers' fields was inevitable. In addition, with the town's waterways, bike paths, playgrounds, and schoolyards in such close proximity to fields that might be converted to intensive fruit production, the health of the people and the environment was in peril.

Mals was going green but the future was looking gray, at best. With organic farms, traditional grain growing, bike touring, agritourism, herbal products, and even the region's first organic hotel all in the works and on the rise, an influx of pesticide-dependent fruit "plantations" could mean the collapse of so many collective dreams.

Günther was adamant: Farmers should be able to manage their farms the way they wanted to, but only up to the point at which their decisions negatively impacted others. If the situation he faced was just the beginning, which certainly seemed to be the case, then any hope of Mals being the last regional bastion of sustainable and diversified agriculture seemed doomed.

Uli concurred and agreed to help find a solution. Neither quite realized what they were agreeing to. They were about to challenge the way things were done not just in the orchards and vineyards of the South Tirol but also in the ballot box. Stirring things up is a messy business.

CHAPTER 2

Roots of a Rebellion

Fully armed and having traded the burden of hand-forged armor and mail for impenetrable rubber, I was a battle-ready American mercenary, waging war to protect the bounty of a medieval castle in Italy. Located on the crumbling edge of a promontory sticking out over the entrance to the Vinschgau Valley, Brunnenburg Castle has maintained the ideal position to keep an eye on what is happening below since the thirteenth century. With its commanding view and southern exposure atop a heap of glacial till, it's also an ideal location to grow grapes, apples, pears, and a host of other fruits for which the South Tirol region of Italy is famous.

However, things weren't going so well on this particular day. I ripped off the respirator and jumped from the tractor, pulling hard at the cuffs of each sleeve, eager to shed the impermeable rubber raincoat. It was like shedding a reptilian skin as it peeled away from my sweaty body. I was one of the only guys in the Alpine village opting to wear any kind of real protection, but even on days like this one, with temperatures well into the 90s and the sun beating down, I questioned my sanity, wondering if I was just an overly cautious American ninny.

I'd just driven the tractor back up through the vineyard and to the shaded comfort of the castle, eager to grab a drink of water at what I hoped was the end of my workday, or at least the end of my unsavory task of spraying the vineyard with its biweekly dose of pesticides. I ducked into the earthy coolness of the wine cellar, stooping to avoid the bruisingly low stone lintel of the medieval doorway, and filled a glass with water from the bottle-washing sink, resting for a moment amid barrels, tubs, and tools.

The smell of wine-soaked wood and gravel emanated from every crevice and corner. But any hope of a new harvest seemed to depend on me getting back to work to protect the terraced flanks of the castle with whatever armaments I had, so I downed a last glass of water and went back out to the tractor. An orange Goldoni tractor, small by American standards but with a low center of gravity, it articulated in the middle, easily negotiating the treacherous paths and tight curves of the castle farm, as long as you paid careful attention to the positioning of heavy loads.

I popped the black rubber lid off the stainless-steel sprayer tank on the back of the tractor and checked inside to see how well I'd calculated on this round. With the sun almost directly overhead as the noon hour neared, a shaft of circular sunlight lit up a portion of the frothy blue potion beginning to settle after the rough uphill ride from the bottom of the vineyard.

Damn it! I still had about a fifth of a tank left. It was bad enough to start in the cool of the early dawn and spend five to seven hours dragging around a hose and brass-tipped spray pistol, dousing the entire vineyard once. I really hated the idea of donning all that hot and smelly gear again and going back down to spray a second coating of the copper-based fungicide somewhere, just to empty the tank. My other option was much simpler but less palatable: I could open the drain on the bottom of the tank and let the leftovers disappear through the steel grate of the drainage pipe at the wash station, eventually making their way to the Adige River down below.

A portion of what I was spraying would eventually end up downstream anyway, so it seemed like I was just prolonging the inevitable. Spraying on the precarious slopes of a mountainside in the Alps lends a certain drama to any notion of "downstream impact." In this case, I could simply look out from under the grape trellises and see the Adige River churning its way through the valley, gradually winding its way toward the Adriatic Sea many miles away. In the end, even though I dreaded donning my modern armor one more time and dosing a section of vines with another round of chemicals, my misery was ultimately a result of my own miscalculation.

It was always a challenge to estimate the liters of pesticide needed to cover the upper and lower leafy surface area of the vines spread out on the elaborate trellises tracing the mountainside below. In shed-roof fashion, the pergola trellises followed the contours of the irregular terrain below the castle, sending the vines up and over each trellis, sprawling outward to catch the sun and movement of the air while protecting the large clusters of grapes from hail and intense winds with a green roof. The pergolas offered just enough clearance for me to spend the day walking slightly hunched under beautiful bunches of ripening grapes, waving my magic wand in the hope of vaporizing any evil spores or multi-legged creatures intent on turning the leafy Paradise into an operations base for wreaking havoc on the wine harvest.

The pergolas were so low and the paths so narrow that I had to park the tractor and sprayer at the end of each row and unreel more than 150 feet (46 m) of blue hose to access the farthest reaches of each row. Once there, I would begin spraying the upper canopy of the vines, then walk backward, retracing the path of the hose as I sprayed up into the leafy roof, making sure to thoroughly coat the dangling bunches of grapes. It seemed I could never back my way out of the rows fast enough. Once the underside of the canopy was doused, the pesticides would drip off the foliage and grapes and onto my hat and coat, inevitably finding their way inside my sleeves and down my neck. No matter how careful I was, some exposure was inevitable, and one gust of wind could ruin a day's worth of caution in a second or two.

Eager to find my way to the shower and a double lathering of soap and shampoo, I suited back up and drove down to an area of vines that I hoped would appreciate an extra dousing. If an ounce of prevention was worth a pound of cure, perhaps a liter of prevention would yield sixteen more liters of fine South Tirolean wine.

But when I peered anxiously through the murky blue concoction for the bottom of the spray tank on that sweltering August day in 1994, only one thing seemed clear. I was deciding between two bad choices — and two bad choices never yield a good solution. Both had far-reaching consequences, whether examined on a map or on a time line.

After three years of spraying, I couldn't do it anymore. It was time to leave the South Tirol, the place where I'd found the kind of diversified agriculture I'd never quite encountered in the cropland of the American South. I'd first come to the South Tirol as a college student at the Brunnenburg Castle and Agricultural Museum semester-abroad program in 1983, and I was immediately smitten with the carefully tended gardens, manicured hayfields, Alpine pastures, medieval architecture, and blended wafts of woodsmoke and manure. Even though most of my time living and working there involved orchards and vineyards — familiar realms for me thanks to my own grandparents' fruit operation — I was particularly attracted to the lives of the *Bergbauern*, the mountain farmers whose holdings clung to the mountainsides with a tenacity seldom found in our modern world. They tended fields of hay, grains, and vegetables near their steep mountainside farms and in the valleys below, and they sent many of their cattle, goats, and pigs up to the *Almen*, the high pastures above tree line. Under the watchful eye of an *Almmeister*, the head shepherd at each pasturage, the animals would graze the protein- and mineral-rich Alpine grasses between 5,000 and 8,000 feet (1,524–2,438 m) in elevation.

My vista of those precarious lifestyles was often from the passenger seat of a variety of Italian straight-drive vehicles driven by Siegfried de Rachewiltz, my boss and mentor, the owner of the castle. Gears would wind out as centrifugal forces pulled me left and right, leaving me to make a human triangle for safety, left hand gripping the edge of my seat and right hand latched in a death grip on the overhead handle, when there was one. One of the best-respected ethnographers in the region, Siegfried would graciously take me along for his interviews and film productions with mountain farmers or to heft and haul donated tools back to the castle's agricultural history museum, which he had founded. It gave me a window into a disappearing world that few Americans would ever see — but it was a white-knuckle view that framed the fragility and resilience of the mountain farmers all in one glance. Fortunately for me, the Vinschgau and its side valleys were his favorite destination, and the valley became my classroom, first as a student and later as a teacher.

It was always a relief to leave the intensively managed landscape of orchards and vineyards and escape to the upper reaches of the Vinschgau Valley, where life seemed richer but less profitable, less predictable but more diverse. The mountain farmers' wisdom and lore on how to survive — indeed, thrive — on those steep slopes had me completely hooked, and it seemed much more aligned with the ebb and flow of the surrounding ecosystem than the constant battles in the vineyard. Somehow the farmers of the valley had endured not just for hundreds of years but for millennia. And they'd even done it without pesticides.

It was a contrast in agricultural systems that I would ponder for the next few decades, although I never expected that that same valley would later become the setting for a standoff between those low-input and chemical-intensive systems. Ultimately surprising even themselves with their successes — despite the odds and obstacles — a troupe of unlikely small-town activists in Mals raised the curtain on the problematic plots of industrial agricultural interests and, in the process, set an international precedent for the role of community mobilization and direct democracy in creating a pesticide-free future.

———————

When I unhooked the spray machine from the Goldoni tractor for the last time in 1994, I felt relieved but not decoupled, either from pesticides or the South Tirol. It was simply time to try to find an agriculture that made sense, on my terms, although my next step seemed, at first glance, completely contrary to that intent. In the supportive company of Erin, my future wife, whom I'd met when she came to Brunnenburg, I went back to the United States to help my grandparents on what would end up being their last year on their farm in the Sandhills region of North Carolina, a place famous for its peaches.

My grandfather was instrumental in building the peach industry and its reputation in the Sandhills. A plant pathologist at North Carolina State University, he had established the Sandhills Research Station with his colleagues, and they developed more than a dozen new varieties of peaches geared to the landscape and markets of the sandy-soiled South. They also tested a number of grape varieties in the hope of rebuilding the wine-grape industry that had been decimated during the Prohibition era and the subsequent monopolization of the grape juice industry. Their ultimate goal was to create disease-resistant varieties of fruits, but with the insect and disease pressures of the hot, humid climate, he and his colleagues were also charged with developing cultivation and pesticide programs that would create the best fruits possible.

A burgeoning fruit industry was a beacon of hope for economic opportunity in rural areas that could supply the growing urban areas in the South. While worker and consumer safety was a clear priority for my grandfather and his fellow researchers, the concept of safety was established within a paradigm of the necessity of pesticides, complete with the vocabulary of thresholds, maximum exposure, and parts per million. For someone who had seen the economic destruction wrought on his sharecropping family by the cotton boll weevil, in my grandfather's mind, pesticides made up for what plant breeding couldn't quite accomplish — or at least not quickly.

A Precautionary Tale

The pesticides we used at Brunnenburg were relatively low in toxicity. Many of the sprays consisted primarily of copper and sulfur, and we almost never used any insecticides, except for a few sprayings against the destructive *Rote Spinne*, the European red mite. However, the pesticides used on my grandparents' farm were much more dangerous. Methyl bromide fumigant was used to treat the soil in the nursery where peach trees were propagated, and a slurry of names only the agrochemical companies could market were mixed and blasted through the foliage of the orchards and vineyard. My grandfather didn't hesitate to use what he and other scientists had produced in order to give consumers the blemish-free and full-sized fruit that they clearly wanted.

One day selling fruit at our roadside peach stand was lesson enough in consumer disdain for any fruit with a harmless spot, catface, or discoloration. A carful of travel-weary vacationers would sort through bushel basket after bushel basket before deciding on a peck of edible peaches. While one or two customers might ask about the reason for an imperfection, virtually no one would ask about how those imperfections were avoided — and customers would almost always choose a large or particularly beautiful peach variety over a much tastier variety that was smaller or slightly blemished, regardless of our recommendations.

In the process of helping my grandparents that year, I had hoped to find some alternatives to the high chemical inputs used in the fruit industry. In the mid-1990s, however, the national organic movement was nascent, and I didn't find the local successful models of less toxic management approaches that I needed to convince myself, much less others, of viable alternatives for tree fruits. Nonetheless, no one could assure me — someone who had already spent too much time in pesticide-laden fields — that pesticides were definitely not going to impact my health, much less that of Erin and the potential offspring we might bring into the world.

As it turned out, I spent almost as much time that year caring for my grandparents as I did for the farm. My grandfather had been diagnosed with Parkinson's disease several decades prior, and he'd beaten the prediction of being wheelchair-bound by almost as many decades, in large part because he just never would quit farming. While I was living with him, though, the disease overtook his quiet obstinacy. Up until the end of his time on the farm, he would determinedly stumble around its sandy furrows, usually with a hoe or pruners in his hand, taking care of business. In a sense, the farm had saved him — at least we thought so. In subsequent years more and more studies strongly correlated on-farm pesticide exposure and Parkinson's disease.

It became clearer that Erin and I were going to have to search further for answers and try out some different kinds of agriculture — in a place with the mountains that we so desperately desired. With a reputation for organic farming, the Green Mountain State sounded perfect, and as luck would have it one of my former employers, Tom Benson, had headed to Vermont to transform a beautiful but dilapidated New England campus into an "environmental liberal arts college" in his role as college president, with a goal of creating one of the most sustainable colleges in the country.

I went to visit the campus and traipsed through the deep February snow, examining the barn and outbuildings that had once been the heart-beat of the college farm. Leased out to several local horse trainers, the old facility looked ideal for the testing ground of a big idea: What alternative models of agriculture could we develop on a college farm that would be truly sustainable and also educational for a new era of farmers, entrepreneurs, and food advocates?

By the time the winter's heavy snows had melted and the new leaves were unfurling on the campus sugar maples, Erin and I had moved to Vermont to begin answering that question, both at Green Mountain College and also on our own homestead and farm. Since then we've experimented with a number of crops and animals on a homestead scale while simultaneously building a grassfed cattle operation with American Milking Devon cattle, a breed with nearly four centuries of adaptation to the New England landscape. Farmers like Günther were models of sorts as we experimented with livestock and crops in our rugged, off-grid terrain, without electricity or running water for nearly eight years.

For the past two decades I have worked with an extraordinary cohort of students, staff, faculty, and growing numbers of alumni to build a certified-organic college farm operation that exemplifies pesticide-free methods, as well as high-quality animal welfare practices and low-input energy systems. Along the way we've found that producing vegetables and livestock without synthetic chemical inputs is not only practical and economical on our scale, but also much easier and more enjoyable than mixing and applying all sorts of pricey concoctions with hefty generational price tags.

A Precautionary Tale

After leaving my grandparents' farm, I stepped away from intensive fruit production. Growing and marketing organic perennial fruits at the farm scale seems the most challenging of all organic production sectors. Whereas you can rotate vegetables and livestock on a daily, weekly, monthly, and annual basis, rotation among tree crops is a long-term strategy at best. Rotation of crops and livestock helps break certain pest and disease cycles — a management tool seldom available to orchardists and viticulturalists.

In the process of building the college farm operation, my colleagues and I have created undergraduate and graduate curricula and programs. One key offering is an opportunity for our students to go to Brunnenburg Castle and learn from the museum and farm operation there as well as from other farms in the area. Ironically, it was when I led a recent study tour to Brunnenburg that I found my way back into the looming questions of fruit production and pesticide use. I also found myself having experienced life on both sides of the fence, or in the buffer zone, given my time working in both fruit and livestock farming.

In the late summer of 2014, I was sitting at Brigitte de Rachewiltz's castle kitchen table as we finalized the details of a South Tirol study tour that was to begin two days later. "Turning Traditions into Markets" is a graduate course I designed to explore the agricultural traditions and foodways of the South Tirol. It's also my way of keeping in touch with the farmers, chefs, and food entrepreneurs who bridge the region's deep agricultural history with modern markets. With Brunnenburg as our base, we explore the valleys and high pastures in search of ideas that might inspire students' professional or academic work in the United States.

Brigitte, a longtime mentor and friend, mentioned that an unusual referendum was about to take place in Mals, a place she knew I loved from an extended walking tour I would lead there every semester while working at Brunnenburg. Citizens in Mals had put forward a ballot measure for a "pesticide-free future," so she thought that it might be interesting for me and my students to learn more about this unusual intersection between democracy and agricultural practices.

I was floored: It was the first time the citizens of any town in the world had ever voted on whether to eliminate the use of all pesticides in their community.

On the surface, it sounded absurd. How could the citizens of any town ever get to that point, much less think that they might succeed? It was a story I wanted to learn about, and it seemed like an excellent opportunity for the students to explore what could be a global first. I shook my head in slight disbelief as Brigitte picked up her cell phone to call a new acquaintance in Mals who could introduce us to the referendum initiative. Was there really an international precedent happening in a place that I'd been studying for more than three decades?

I certainly didn't imagine that one field trip with my students, exactly twenty years after I thought I'd parted ways with my spray gun in the South Tirol, would vault me back not only into the complex questions of pesticide use but also into a dramatic David-and-Goliath story.

"Just drive toward the village of Plawenn and ask for Konrad," Brigitte had said.

She hadn't taken into account our bus driver's unfamiliarity with the area. About an hour and a half after leaving Brunnenburg, we'd finally gotten to the upper end of the Vinschgau Valley, and our driver saw a sign for PLA . . . She didn't bother to read any further before starting the steep and windy ascent to what would turn out to be the village of Planeil instead of Plawenn. Ordinarily, such a mistake wouldn't make much of a difference, but in this case the road was so narrow in spots that there was no room for another vehicle to pass our sixteen-seater bus. Mirrors at the hairpin curves did little more than provide an impending sense of doom coming from the opposite direction. Even our seasoned driver was nervous.

We got to Planeil, a stunningly compact village clutching to the mountainside at 5,249 feet (1,600 m), only to discover that there was no space to turn around at the tiny parking area just outside the village. Only pedestrians, residents, and authorized guests were to enter the village proper, with its tight, twisting streets. It was clear that the medieval mind was focused on shelter rather than passage, with houses and barns hugging every available thoroughfare through the village. The villagers had long ago tossed aside the notion that right angles are a prerequisite to construction. Planeil's buildings are constructed to fit the available space, and if that means sacrificing the sanctity of a rectangle, so be it. Tucked into the contours of the mountainside, they seem to melt into one another with the overlap of white plaster. In fact, they are so tightly knitted together that separate fires in 1985 and 1986 nearly destroyed the village's future. Both times, flames moved effortlessly from one structure to another. Despite having fewer than two hundred residents, the village rallied and rebuilt, maintaining its ancient character.

With no other option, our driver drove down the narrow village street and managed to find a convoluted turnaround into a guesthouse parking lot. With the smell of a burning clutch, she managed something resembling a 183-degree turn (no right angles) on a crazy upward incline, and we made our way back down to the main road in search of a sign for Plawenn.

The idea of asking total strangers for a guy named Konrad seemed just shy of absurd, but our driver slowed to stop as we neared a farmer raking the straggling strands of hay bunched up along the edge of the road. "We're looking for Konrad — Konrad Messner. Do you know him? Do you know where we can find him?" she asked the old farmer.

"Konrad? Messner Konrad?" he asked, putting the family name first, as is customary in a region where long family histories take precedence over the relatively short life span of individuals. He peered at her sharply with one eye squinted shut. "Up there. The pink castle," he said, and he turned back to the company of his wooden rake. It all seemed a bit surreal for our driver, so she asked me for the cell phone number that Brigitte had written on a scrap piece of paper. She called it and got an answer — "*Ja . . . ja . . .*" Yes . . . yes . . . — and nodded as she looked intently at the village's distant facade. She hung up, mumbled a veiled curse in dialect, and popped the bus into first gear, leaving the farmer to his solitude. He looked askance at our puff of diesel exhaust, shaking his head.

We could barely make out the unusual salmon-colored crenellations of a building — located at 5,577 feet (1,700 m) and set against a dramatic backdrop of craggy peaks — bounded by the more traditional wood-and-white-plaster farmhouses and barns. Bordered by hayfields and outlined by utility poles, the sinuous road took us up to the village edge.

Our American invasion surprised at least one villager: A topless sun worshipper grabbed her towel and scurried through an open balcony door. As we stepped down out of the bus, the village seemed hauntingly still, except for the distant *clink-clunk* of cowbells in outlying pastures and the occasional lowing from the shadows of the village barns. Given the activity we'd seen in the fields, it seemed that most of the roughly forty-six village residents were out helping with the midday hay harvest.

CLUB OF MULT — I had no idea what it meant, but the decorative sign was on the front of the unusual building, so I began to search for an entrance. I walked up the tiny street paralleling the courtyard wall toward what I guessed must be the entrance of Konrad's rather unusual guesthouse. Billed as a "culture club" rather than a restaurant, it was obviously a word-of-mouth affair. Still spooked by the almost total quiet of the village, I jumped when a barn cat shot out of the cracked doorway of a nearby farmhouse just as I was homing in on two doorbell buttons to the left of a low-lying gothic-arch doorway. Tipping up my sunglasses, I got to choose my own adventure: either FAMILIE MESSNER or CLUB OF MULT. Giving the trending uncertainty of the day, I pushed the latter.

With the thickness of the medieval walls, I couldn't tell whether the bell had actually rung inside, and I couldn't hear anyone coming. I went to push it again when the heavy wooden door flung open and out popped more energy in one human form than I had encountered in quite some time. "Konrad!" he said, sticking out his hand. "You must be Philip."

Before I could utter an answer, he flung his arms wide and greeted the group — who had just caught up with me — in German. "So do you all speak Chinese? If so, we can have a good conversation!" With that, he whisked us all in, signaling to everyone to duck so that no one would leave flesh and blood on the low-hanging stone lintel.

We swept back a heavy curtain shielding the entrance to the lower level of the house from cold air that would cascade in during winter months and made our way down the stone stairs into a vaulted gothic hallway, all plastered in white stucco that revealed only a hint of the stone texture underneath. Konrad flung open a rustic door to a wood-paneled *Stube*, the traditional gathering space in a Tirolean house, and ushered everyone inside, signing with a finger that he would be back in one minute. He disappeared like a fleet-footed sprite back out into the hallway and ducked into an adjacent doorway that turned out to be his kitchen. Once an ancient chapel, its ornate gothic arches were still intact, but the ceiling was now covered in soot from several centuries of smoke spilling out of what must have been a series of cookstoves.

Long wooden poles ran the length of the blackened ceiling, ready to hang the traditional cured meats at a moment's notice.

His facial features and his quick moves gave me the immediate impression that we'd just met the Tirolean version of Robin Williams. He danced back and forth between the kitchen and the Stube with glasses and pitchers, followed by baskets of bread and several cheese boards. With each delivery came a quip framed in English but sprinkled with German and Italian. Sporting a handsome tanned and ruddy complexion, Konrad had a smile that would erupt from a nearly expressionless facade a fraction of a second before any of us had fully grasped the intent of what was consistently a humorous poke. His eyes squinted each time he burst out in contagious laughter as he handed out glasses and teased us one by one. Whenever he would make room for a quiet pause, it was simply bait for a razor-sharp one-liner that would make its comical incision before the victim had any sense of what had just happened.

Before long, we all had a combination of glasses on the tables spread around the room, and students at different tables were trading tastes and impressions of the mix of breads and drinks that had appeared without a single order. The taste of homemade *Hollundersaft*, elderberry flower syrup and mineral water, blended with scents of fresh-cut hay pouring through the open windows, and the floral bouquet of several carafes of white wine only added to the sense that we were ingesting the best of a South Tirolean summer day. Once he was satisfied that he could shift from bartender to raconteur, Konrad moved a wooden chair beside the centerpiece of the room, a tall barrel-shaped masonry stove covered in white plaster. It was easy to imagine the yarns that would emanate from that spot in the winter when everyone would huddle next to the radiating warmth and pass the long days with stories steeped in bittersweet concoctions.

Just as comfortable in the role of a teller of tales as that of waiter, Konrad stretched out his legs, leaned back into his chair, and paused to gather his thoughts as he smoothed out the wrinkles of his charcoal-colored apron.

"*Ja, so . . .*" He looked at me. Then, with an air of contrived seriousness, he asked me in perfect English, "Where do we start? The beginning or the end?"

In professorial form, I answered smugly, "The beginning, of course." Little did I suspect that one story could have so many beginnings. But we started in the middle — the middle of the Vinschgau Valley, where one family was living the nightmare of pesticides without buffers and monoculture without limits.

CHAPTER 3

Bufferless

orced into a translucent bubble of their own making, the four generations of the Gluderer family were the unfortunate harbingers of what Günther and Uli most dreaded was coming their way. Just a few short years after they transformed their family farm into an organic herb operation, they found themselves directly in the path of Big Apple as it rolled up the Vinschgau Valley.

They could have uprooted everything that they had worked collectively to build and tried to find another farm, but they decided instead to cover their assets: They went from planting and harvesting their organic herbs out in the open to spending their entire year cultivating their crops under plastic. Soon all the crops on their 1.5-acre (0.6 ha) farm grew beneath enormous steel-framed high tunnels. The structures were the only way to protect their herbs, their consumers, and their organic certification from the pesticides that were infiltrating their farm from every direction. They also gave the youngest Gluderers a safe place to play. Toy tractors, backhoes, and garden implements are always strewn about underneath the high tunnels, clear evidence that the Gluderers are cultivating the newest generation with the same care they give the herbs and flowers.

Separated from Mals by 19 miles (30 km) in distance, 1,300 feet (400 m) in elevation, and a decade of change, the Gluderers are located farther down the Vinschgau Valley, and they had seen that wave of the future coming for several decades, although it was more like a slow-moving tsunami in the way it advanced upon them. A tsunami may be nearly indiscernible far out at sea, but when it comes closer to shore and meets the upward incline of the coastline, its immense energy is transformed into a wave of ever-increasing height and potential for destruction. The Gluderers had watched the growing power of the wave as more and more of the trellised orchards moved up the valley, and they began to wonder if they should rapidly gather everything that they'd worked so hard to build and run for higher ground. Their organic herb farm seemed likely to be swallowed up, rent asunder first in the intensifying power of the oncoming surge and then again in the devastation of any later retreat. With so many apples flooding the valley and the marketplace, a wholesale retreat seemed inevitable at some future point; it was just hard to say whether the collapse would be economic or ecological, or a combination of the two.

For now, though, it seemed like the tide of Big Apple had worked its way up the Vinschgau Valley and eventually reached its logical — albeit absurd — conclusion in their town, until they were adrift and seemingly alone in a sea of apples. To most of their neighbors, however, the inundation was just a fact of life in the village of Goldrain; there was nothing to be done about it. Besides, almost everyone seemed to see apples as the most lucrative option for the small plots of farmland so characteristic of the valley — even the Gluderers had had a small plot of apples before going into the organic herb business.

But for the Gluderers, the invasion of apples finally became too overwhelming. It wasn't the fog of war that pushed them to the extreme; rather, it was the war against fog: They had tried growing hedgerows to protect against the pesticide drift coming from their neighbors, but that hadn't been effective enough. Then they installed a 26-foot (8 m) high *Wassersprühnebelwand*, an enormous "water curtain" that sprayed upward from a series of water jets positioned around the perimeters of their property whenever the neighbors were spraying. However, the clouds of pesticides and their residues continued to make their way onto the Gluderers' farm, sometimes from farms much farther away. They decided that they had only two alternatives: wave a white flag of surrender from the top of their "castle of herbs" storefront or stubbornly duck and cover. They chose to cover.

Flanked on every side by apple orchards, with nothing but failed buffers between their organic herbs and the orchards, they felt the only way they could retain the family business was to shield their fields of crops with expansive greenhouses covered with plastic on the top and a breathable fabric on the sides. Despite the fact that it would cost them more than 150,000 euros (around $200,000 at the time), it seemed the only way to protect their organic crops from the onslaught of pesticides coming from all directions.

They had invested much more than euros into building a business that now supported four generations of their family — all without applying pesticides. But that didn't mean pesticide residues wouldn't be detected on their crops. With apples on three sides and surrounding them up and down the valley, it was only a matter of time.

For Urban Gluderer everything had happened so fast. Nothing in the valley resembled what he remembered from his youth. "Apples were only part of life here back then," he mused. "They were only one of many things that farm families raised, so the landscape was more open and diverse than it is now . . . now it's nothing but apples."

Like his herbal goods, Urban is clearly a product of mountain air and sunshine. Tan and muscular, he still leaps from delivery trucks and heaves cases of packaged herbal products with no sign of effort. You wouldn't guess that he is in his early fifties, much less a grandfather of five. Sporting a close-cropped salt-and-pepper goatee, he is a multicultural entrepreneur who can, at a moment's notice, switch from his high-velocity Tirolean dialect to a slower-cadenced but lilting version of Italian.

Urban long wished that his children and grandchildren could somehow inherit the vistas he'd taken for granted as a child. It was some consolation to have his parents, Karl and Rosa, still on the farm as a touchstone to a past that had been sliced and upended like the sod from a moldboard plow. Whatever might have been plowed under and replaced by apples and other fruits was still very much alive in Karl and Rosa's memories, and Karl's stories could stitch landscape and tradition back together with a fine thread and a deft needle, even if the events of a week before sometimes eluded him.

When asked about the changes he'd seen in the area during his lifetime, Karl reminisced about how much the topography of the valley floor had changed since the 1960s. Pointing outward with his gnarled mason's fingers, he fanned his arm from one end of the valley to the other in a series of undulations. "The valley wasn't flat when I was a child," he said. "It was filled with little hills, and if you were looking out from here on a winter day, you'd probably see kids playing on their sleds. But then in the 1960s they brought in the bulldozers to flatten it all out to make it easier to plant apples and other crops." That bucolic scene was a far cry from what was now an uninterrupted mosaic of interlocking orchards, with trellised apples, trained and true, holding their ground in every available niche.

Growing up, Urban could look across the Vinschgau Valley from his family's farm and see hay meadows, mixed livestock in their pastures, and a mix of grain and vegetable plots. He remembered chasing butterflies and grasshoppers and watching bats flit their way through the summer darkness in hot pursuit of tiny prey. Now, while tending his crops several decades later, he can't see past the opaque coverings of the greenhouses that protected all of his organic herbs and flowers from the tainted mists threatening to drift onto his farm from every direction. Since covering his herbs with the high tunnels, he is a bit relieved not to see apple trees every time he looks up from his work, but he misses bearing witness to the constant testing of wills between incoming weather and the defiant mountain ranges just to the north and south of the farm. "Our hope is that these high tunnels aren't the final solution. The real goal is to be able to remove these structures within ten years, presuming we can get people to farm in a different way, without pesticides. Besides," he said, wiping away the light beads of sweat on his forehead, "there's no way to enjoy working in these tunnels when it's 113°F (45°C)."

It isn't as if he didn't understand how it had happened: He'd once been an apple farmer himself. Like almost everyone else in the valley, he and his family had seen apples as a reliable means of making a good side income with an acre or two and even a reasonably lucrative living with around 10 acres (4 ha). Those economic possibilities contrasted sharply with the subsistence living that his father and mother had witnessed during the early portion of their lives, with the difficulties of Alpine life only exacerbated by World War II. Karl would not only hold court at the long family dinner table but also hold unwitting customers hostage, regaling everyone with stories of a world now relegated mostly to picture books and documentaries.

Urban had grown up in the village of Goldrain, the place where he and his wife, Annemarie, decided to raise their family. It was familiar terrain for Annemarie, too, as she had grown up only 6 miles (10 km) away in the village of Tschars. In 1990 Urban's parents gave them 0.9 acre (3,647 m²) that was planted with apples — a handsome gift in a region where every square foot of productive ground was coveted. Their family managed the orchard conventionally with pesticides, like most of the orchards scattered throughout the area at that time, and it yielded a nice side income.

Urban didn't have a farming background, but his interest in working with people recovering from psychological illnesses led him into organic agriculture. He and a colleague had decided to establish a local job training center designed to serve people coming out of hospitalization for psychological problems. Their clients needed to learn new workplace skills while also reacclimating to the rigor of regular working hours. Urban and his coworker opted to focus on teaching organic horticulture, providing their clients with a therapeutic environment and skills geared to a profession that would give them a positive sense of purpose. However, that meant inviting a nearby organic farmer, Peter Teppeiner, to train the instructors before they could set out on their new venture. Little did Urban realize that what he would teach his clients would eventually lead him and his family not only to a new business but also a new understanding of agriculture.

Given the medicinal qualities of herbal teas, Urban and his colleague decided that their clients would benefit not only from consuming herbal teas but also from learning how to develop a product from seed to tea bag. They would teach the students each part of the process from planting to market. Unfamiliar with growing herbs, much less organic growing methods, Urban and his coworker tapped their neighbor's wealth of organic agricultural knowledge to teach them the proper cultivation techniques so that they could pass on the skills to the participants in the program. In a sense what they were teaching was nothing new — the use and lore of medicinal herbs certainly dates back to the earliest human settlement in the region. The astounding range of soil types and microclimates in the southern Alps has long provided people living there with a living apothecary.

Urban found himself unexpectedly smitten by the beauty of growing herbs and flowers, not to mention the historical wisdom and lore associated with each of them. Pulling open drawer after drawer of different flower petals from his carefully regulated dryer and sifting through the intensely colored flowers, all separated by species, his fascination with the wonders of nature's bounty is clear: "The intensity of the colors and the smells reminds me all the time of the biodiversity that we have to protect here in this monocultural desert."

His mentor in the project also got him thinking about how he could manage his home orchard organically. However, Annemarie wasn't easily convinced. "I thought he was crazy," she said. She'd grown up on a farm with an orchard, and for decades her father had done the spraying in the traditional manner of running a pump from a concrete trough to the apple trees by way of a hose and sprayer. When tractors became more common and sprayers were mounted on them, her father bought a tractor and had her brother get his licenses to drive and spray. But after her brother left home for his required military service, Annemarie's father asked her to get her driver and spray licenses, too. She took the requisite pesticide applicator's test and adopted the techniques and mind-set associated with pesticides in those days.

Even after Urban returned from a biodynamic agricultural conference and described how they were going to convert their apples to organic management, Annemarie was skeptical, to say the least. "When everybody does the same thing in the same way all around you, you accept it," she explains. "Urban eventually convinced me, not with his words but by what he was able to do."

It wasn't long, however, before Urban realized that his interest in apples, even organic apples, was waning. His real passion was the cultivation and use of herbs and flowers. The colors, fragrances, and diversity had seduced him. He gradually began to think about ways of selling them, perhaps even turning his newfound passion into a business.

Urban delved deep into the principles and techniques of organic agriculture, and with the support of various associations and a small network of organic growers, he began investigating not just organic and biodynamic apple production but also different business models for his family's plot of land. He began to plant small experimental pockets of herbs and flowers between apple trees in his orchard and think out loud about his business ideas with Annemarie, who was slowly coming to appreciate Urban's evolving interests and business ideas.

In the end, turning forty was a watershed moment for Urban and the rest of the family: Either he and his family were going to find a way to tap into what seemed to be a viable business niche, or he would simply continue his job at the training center until retirement. When Urban announced that he wanted to quit his job and begin building the infra-structure necessary for an organic herb farm, Annemarie's first reaction nearly put an end to the dream. "This time, I didn't just think he was crazy — I actually got really mad at him." It took a lot of discussion among the entire family, but eventually they all decided to pool their talents and resources and pursue the dream. That dream was much more than just one family's entrepreneurial venture: If they were successful, it might also offer a new path forward for other organically oriented entrepreneurs.

With apples dominating the mind-set and the market, it looked like they could tap into a niche with minimal competition. Besides, an agricul-tural economy built almost exclusively on apples wasn't any healthier than a diet of nothing but apples. They began to chart a different way forward. They wanted to set an example for others. Before long, however, others would be determined to make an example out of them.

Next to the power of their combined skill sets, perseverance would prove to be the Gluderers' greatest asset. From the outset, nothing proved easy as they worked to build a business out of little more than ether and enthusiasm. Instead of waiting until they had the infrastructure in place to quit his job at the training center, Urban opted to quit earlier so that his organization could more easily find a replacement for the upcoming growing season. That gave him more time to begin setting up the meager beginnings of their business, but they still needed a building permit. "We didn't know how difficult that was going to be," noted Annemarie as she described the labyrinthine permit-ting process they encountered. Pioneering a new concept is never simple.

When they applied for a building permit, Urban and Annemarie had submitted their plans for their new facility to the town with little reason to doubt that local officials would share their excitement about this new kind of agricultural venture. However, despite the fact that herbs were the quintessential blending of Alpine and Mediterranean cultures, the idea of an herb processing, storage, and retail facility was completely foreign to their town officials, and they were perplexed by how such a small plot of land could possibly support a farming venture. Whenever most locals inherited a piece of property, they tended to put it into fruit production, not create a vertically integrated production facility that involved growing, processing, distribution, and sales all in one small location. The local officials were befuddled by the request simply because they hadn't seen a parallel business model. It didn't fit the norm, so they said no.

The family was surprised by that first rejection. They resubmitted a revised proposal in good faith, but the planning commission still didn't know whether the model fit the provincial standards, and they weren't inclined to go and research that for themselves. At that point, some local officials suggested that they ask the province for help in interpreting whether their business plan could fit within the intent of the development regulations. They had only one more chance to submit a permit for review, so Annemarie used her connections as a municipal employee to gain the support of several provincial officials who provided documentation that the Gluderers' request fit the necessary guidelines. At the same time, the Gluderers took the time to meet with the individual planning commission members and explain precisely how their project conformed with the law.

By the end of fall 2003, Urban had left his day job and turned his entire focus toward getting their plans approved. When 2004 came into full swing, they finally received the needed permits and began construction. As the year drew to a close, they had completed the building and passed the final inspection.

The three older generations of Gluderers — everyone who could safely wield a tool — went into overdrive in preparation for the culmination of so many years of preparation. Plans turned into plantings and painting projects, until success seemed imminent. In June 2005 they threw open the doors of their new business, the Kräuterschlößl, or "Castle of Herbs." Whimsically modeled after the architectural elements of the hundreds of castles and ruins in the region, their calendula-tinted castle outpost gradually rose above the adjacent orchards, creating a sharp contrast with the regimented greenery that covers the valley floor for miles in either direction.

Jutting up from the monotony of apple plantations, the eye-catching crenellations and bright gold facade of the business immediately garner the attention of anyone driving by. Little did the Gluderers suspect that their medieval motif would soon symbolize their strategic position as one last local bastion for an oncoming siege — and they were going to have to come up with the equivalent of a modern-day moat.

Building a family business requires more than a shared passion: It also takes a variety of talents and a division of labor that gratifies the individuals and propels everyone toward the common goal of success. Fortunately, the three adult generations of the Gluderers possessed a diverse suite of talents ideal for building a business from the ground up. "Everyone pitched in and did whatever they could," Annemarie remembers. "Karl's professional masonry skills were critical, and Manuel and Michael had construction experience, while Marion helped with building details. We only needed to hire in some help with plumbing and electrical work." Having so much in-house construction talent proved critical: Within a year they were already embarking on further expansion of the "castle."

They all continued to hone their production skills and expand areas under cultivation. In the fall of 2006 they uprooted all but one of the remaining apple trees on their parcel, with herbs and berries filling in the remaining available areas. "We left it there simply as reminder," Annemarie notes. However, it would soon become a symbol of how they had flipped the local business model.

But it was business as usual outside of their bubble, and Big Apple was on an uphill roll, with no sign of slowing down. Urban understood his neighbors' motives and inclinations, but his appreciation had its limits: "We've always valued fruit production in South Tirol, and all farmers should be able to farm in the way they want — but without disturbing others."

There's something about the history of farming. As soon as we start doing something well, we often start doing it so well that things turn out badly. The plow, the cow, and now the apple. Tool, animal, crop — when we capitalize too heavily on any one thing, we devalue other things that might be even more important to our communities than money.

Nonetheless, how apple came to be king in the South Tirol is a fascinating story rooted in the best intentions of the cooperative movement, plant breeding, agricultural technology, and regional marketing. From pip to power, the history of the modern apple is what one might call a Stark but Delicious rise toward Empire. In the South Tirol, it is a tale of unintended consequences. At least for the neighbors.

A Precautionary Tale

Although it's difficult to pinpoint the precise arrival of what we commonly think of as the domesticated apple in the South Tirol, its first documented appearance probably goes back several thousand years. Archaeological and genetic evidence points to the presence of wild crab apples in Europe as far back as the Neolithic (11,500 years ago) and Bronze (4,500 years ago) Ages. But our modern apple has its native roots in Central Asia and is a relative newcomer to Europe. The apples of Central Asia were a key species of the famous "fruit forests" of the region, an area in which many of our contemporary fruits had their origins. Scientists and archaeologists believe that the apple might have arrived in Europe by way of the great trade routes that ran from China to the Danube as early as the Neolithic era.[1]

Through a combination of natural and artificial selection, the domesticated apple quickly evolved, particularly as humans learned the art of grafting, allowing them to replicate genetic clones of their favorite fruits. Some Mesopotamian cuneiform from nearly four millennia ago featured the grafting of grapevines, and the techniques represented were easily transferable to apples and many other fruits.[2] As propagation techniques evolved, so did methods of efficient cultivation. Ancient methods of orcharding began to crop up, with Persians passing on their skills to the Greeks and Romans. It is likely that the Romans first introduced the domesticated form of the apple to the South Tirol, probably by way of their well-established westward thoroughfare through the Vinschgau Valley and their route northward through the Brenner Pass. The fertile soils and ideal climate of the Adige River basin created conditions well suited to the propagation of apples, grapes, and a host of other fruits, vegetables, and grains.

By the medieval era, the apple was relatively well established, with many farms in the region boasting one or more trees as a rare source of something sweet. Dried fruits became a staple of traditional breads, many of them reserved for holidays. Monasteries were often centers of propagation. Monks were reliant upon fruit propagation skills for growing the grapes that would become the wine so critical to serving the sacraments (not to mention other meals), and those transferable skills enabled them to control and care for apples over the course of generations within their cloistered walls. Their erudition also contributed to their breeding successes, and despite their vows of celibacy they found a way to pass on a genetic legacy.

Regardless of its challenges, apple production in the moderate climes of what is now referred to as the South Tirol offered market opportunities as far away as Austria and Russia, even in the 1500s. Peddlers moved apples from the southern flanks of the Alps to the less hospitable urban centers farther north, with most of the traffic moving through the renowned Brenner Pass, the most reliable of the north–south passages in that part of the Alps. The imperial courts of Vienna, Berlin, and even St. Petersburg were big fans of the South Tirolean apples, and they had the treasury to pay for them.[3]

Even in that era, the tyranny of the middleman dominated the commerce. Farmers not having the time or ability to travel to distant markets would often sell their perishable products to merchants at whatever price they could fetch, or, worse yet, they would sometimes sell to a peddler without setting a price. Price would then depend upon what condition the apples were in upon their arrival at their destination and, of course, the honesty of the broker who controlled the purse strings and was responsible for paying the farmer his earnings once the goods were sold. Needless to say, the farmer had little control of the individual sale, much less the marketplace.

In the early to mid-1800s, a call for fair markets and reasonable wages began to echo throughout Europe, spurred on by the inequities created through challenges such as industrialization, rural isolation, and concentration of wealth. There was a proliferation of cries for justice and possible solutions, but one experimental effort by twenty-eight weavers of scarce means would generate a response that would reverberate with miraculous resonance across decades and international borders.

Faced with atrocious labor conditions and meager pay, these twenty-eight brave weavers, about half of whom were from the town of Rochdale in Lancashire, England, decided to try to raise £1 each to contribute toward the purchase of goods that could fill a store. Calling themselves the Rochdale Society of Equitable Pioneers, they opened their leased storefront on December 21, 1844. They first offered a modest menu of basic goods, including butter, flour, sugar, oatmeal, and some candles, gradually adding tea and tobacco to their offerings. Those candles proved especially useful when the gas company refused to sell them gas to light their lamps. Despite deep distrust from other merchants and modest shop displays constructed of boards laid atop barrels, the Pioneers were successful in ways they had never imagined as they'd each scraped and saved to come up with that first £1. Within just ten years more than one thousand cooperatives had sprung up across Britain. The Rochdale Pioneers had wisely created an easily replicable system by putting forward their agreed-upon principles, emphasizing the need for the individual members to take business into their own hands through self-help and self-responsibility.[4]

Industrialization wasn't the primary impediment to equity everywhere in Europe, however. Rural poverty was a different beast, but the cooperative principles were versatile. Friedrich Raiffeisen was a mayor of three different towns in Germany who adapted the basic cooperative principles to help address the ills he saw in his rural region. He had witnessed the starvation wrought on rural areas by the severe snows and cold temperatures of 1846–47, and he wanted to provide safeguards against a repeat of that tragic scenario. He was also deeply disturbed by the plight of farmers who were suffering at the hands of ruthless lenders and business owners.[5]

Familiar with the cooperative principles that were cross-pollinating across Europe at the time, he felt that dependency had to be conquered before poverty could be alleviated. That thinking eventually led him to believe that the solution was to establish lending cooperatives, essentially rural credit unions, a tool to promote what he called the three-S formula: *Selbsthilfe*, *Selbstverwaltung*, and *Selbstverantwortung*. Self-help, self-governance, and self-responsibility became the foundational principles of many cooperative-based initiatives in German-speaking parts of Europe, and they played a key role in the growth of Big Apple in the South Tirol.

The cooperative concepts promoted by Raiffeisen and others began creeping southward into the deep valleys of the South Tirol while the first rail line through the Brenner Pass was completed in 1867, suddenly opening up new markets to the north.[6] Raiffeisen's rural credit banks, which remain a central cornerstone of the region's banking industry to this day, began to proliferate, and in 1893 the first apple cooperative in the South Tirol was founded in the Adige Valley. Fruit cooperatives began to blossom in the area, only to be nipped in the bud by the economic and cultural devastation of the First and Second World Wars.

In 1945 leaders of the various fruit cooperatives decided to use a collective approach to overcome some of their individual marketing challenges.

With the motto "Strength through Unity," they formed the Verband der Südtiroler Obstgenossenschaften (VOG), the Association of South Tirolean Fruit Growers' Cooperatives.[7] Still in existence, the VOG wields significant economic and political power, and its offshoot, VOG Products, is the largest fruit processor in all of Europe. Together with the other newer federation of cooperatives located in the Vinschgau Valley, the Association of Val Venosta Fruit Growers' Cooperatives (established in 1990), VOG helps the twenty-plus regional cooperatives to store, process, and market their products.[8]

Today the scale and intensity of apple production in the South Tirol is hard to fathom without looking down from the rocky peaks shooting skyward from the valley edges or using a time-lapse camera. The orchards in South Tirol, the largest contiguous region of apple production in Europe, produce 10 to 12 percent of the continent's apples — to the tune of 600 million to 700 million euros ($653–761 million) per year.[9] That's *one million tons of apples* — all from a province about half the size of the state of Connecticut with an average family orchard size of 6 to 7.5 acres (2.5–3 ha).[10]

In the short period since World War II, apples have been core to the transformation of the South Tirol from one of the poorest regions in Italy to its wealthiest province. The Rochdale Pioneers and Friedrich Raiffeisen shared the belief that geographic proximity and identity mattered in the formation and success of cooperatives. As a land and a people caught between competing nationalistic fervor to the north and the south in the first half of the twentieth century, the South Tiroleans used the second half of the century to bond together and transform their Alpine survival instincts into a cohesive brand built on quality and origin. They were so effective, in fact, that the FAO sent in a team of researchers to study their phenomenal success and then published a report in 2014 titled *Apple-Producing Family Farms in the South Tyrol: An Agricultural Innovation Case Study.*[11]

Just as Champagne, Parmesan cheese, and other foods have an official association and label with a given region, eleven varieties of South Tirolean apples have the protection of the EU's geographical origin program. This protected branding (PGI, protected geographical indication) has helped to put the shine on South Tirolean apples in the globalized marketplace. If there is any single clear sign of the region's effectiveness in tempting consumers to pay the price for taking a bite of a perfect South Tirolean apple, it is probably that the fact that an apple grower can generally support a family on the income from about 10 acres (4 ha) of production.

While the success of cooperatives and their federations has been critical to the growth of the apple industry, none of it would have been possible without creating a top-quality product as efficiently as possible. How the South Tiroleans found a way to produce more than twice as many apples with less than half the labor in a span of fifty years is one of the most extraordinary feats in twentieth-century agriculture — and it created one of the most vexing legal issues of the twenty-first century, one into which the Gluderers and Günther Wallnöfer had run headlong and unwittingly.

———————

Most agricultural leaps are a series of technological hops. So it was with the growth of the apple industry in the South Tirol. Apple production and sales began to expand with the draining of the swampy areas surrounding the Adige River in the late nineteenth century and the development of cooperatives' centralized warehouses for sorting, packing, and distribution. Despite the excellent growing conditions for apples in the mountainous regions — the crispness of autumn apples and fall mornings seemingly blended — the threat of frost during the sensitive stages of fruit development in the spring is always challenging in a land prone to dramatic shifts in weather.

In 1949 B. Holler, a fruit grower in the South Tirol, read about using overhead sprinklers to protect blossoms and fruits by coating the trees with water, encasing the burgeoning fruits with a protective layer of ice. Although not effective in extreme freezes, frost irrigation can mean the difference between a successful year and a total crop failure when the temperatures are within a few degrees of freezing.

Holler ordered and installed overhead sprinklers for his fruit operation and successfully employed them in 1950.[12] Within eight years South Tirolean farmers had installed overhead irrigation systems for watering and frost protection on nearly 10,000 acres (4,000 ha) in the region![13] It was one of first examples of how quickly apple and other fruit growers in the region could test and disseminate new production methods. One benefit of being caught in the middle of the nationalistic aims of the Italian fascists and the German Nazis was that the development of a tight regional cultural identity and mutual cooperation strategies were key survival mechanisms that could be transformed into farmers exchanging agricultural knowledge to the shared benefit of their beloved homeland.

Just as the South Tiroleans were finding ways to capitalize on their small size, they began to take a hard look at apple trees of a diminutive stature. No single development would more dramatically impact the region's apple production — or land-use patterns — than the adoption of what sounds like nothing more than tenure-protecting academic jargon: the slender spindle trellis system.

The apple trees that dominated the European and American landscapes up until the latter decades of the twentieth century were tall and broad, stretching their boughs to heights that seemed to taunt anyone intent on stripping their limbs of fruit. South Tiroleans had developed a unique system for harvesting apples that might be 20 or 30 feet (6–9 m) up. With the traditional *Loanen* — an amazingly lightweight single-pole ladder with a flexible cleated foot for dealing with steep slopes and wooden steps mortised through the pole's center ladder — harvesters would climb to the far reaches of a tree and carry their cache down in a *Tschaggel*, a cloth picking bag slung over their shoulders.[14]

While the locals had done what they always did best — innovate and climb — such a system didn't have the efficiency needed to compete in an increasingly globalized marketplace. Their response was to innovate once again — and have the apple trees do the climbing instead of the harvesters, with the help of a high-tensile trellis system that would within decades turn the region into a geometric mosaic of perfectly placed concrete posts punctuating the landscape, from valley floor to terraced hillsides. The South Tirol was about to become the equivalent of a leafy solar panel in which the perils of slope were offset by the power of captured sunlight. Photosynthesis had never seemed so profitable.

Some revolutions begin with Woodstock; others begin with rootstock. The South Tiroleans chose the latter. Once they discovered what the ever-innovative Dutch were doing with dwarf rootstock, they traded in their Loanen, their slender pole ladders, for a slender spindle trellis system.

Tired of getting advice from salespeople representing a host of agricultural products, a group of around fifty fruit growers had decided in 1957 to invest in yet another cooperative-style approach. They created their own independent research and extension service — formally known as the Beratungsring für Obst-und Weinbau but generally referred to by the locals as the Beratungsring. As part of their early work, the Beratungsring hosted a January conference in 1959 on developments in fruit tree cultivation, and one presenter introduced what was happening with dwarf apple production in the Netherlands. Within eight months a delegation from the South Tirol set off to visit apple producers in the Netherlands and returned with an idea that would transform the South Tirolean landscape more dramatically than any empire could ever replicate.[15]

The beauty of a bountiful, full-sized apple tree weeping with a cascade of fruit is magical, but harvesting those apples can be terrifying and sometimes crippling or even deadly. Plant those trees on a steep slope and the dangers magnify. It's no wonder that the smaller trees and trellis systems appealed to Alpine fruit growers, to the extent that it is now just as difficult to find a full-sized apple tree in the South Tirol as it is to find a mountaintop view of any valleys void of trellised orchards.

Dwarf apple trees have a long history, as they were first documented and collected by Alexander the Great in 300 BCE, but their use as rootstock for passing on that dwarfing tendency became widespread only in the latter half of the twentieth century.[16] Precisely how the dwarfing tendency is passed on from the rootstock to the scion wood — the wood taken from a tree of the desired fruit variety — remains a bit of a mystery. Nonetheless, the rootstock seems to influence the growth pattern for the rest of the tree through chemical signals in the form of plant hormones.

The Dutch orchardists grafted their penchants for agricultural innovation and economic efficiency to come up with the slender spindle trellis system — a means of training a dwarf apple tree to grow with the support of horizontal trellis wires and a thin upright pole of bamboo or metal. There are various methods of pruning and training dwarf apple trees to achieve different heights, outputs, and management intensity, but the common factor is the dwarf rootstock. For decades researchers have been developing different fruit tree rootstocks for cold hardiness, disease and pest resistance, and size. While the reliance upon smaller trees seems counterintuitive for maximizing fruit production, the key elements of enhanced production and payoff reside in the intensity of planting and the efficiency of management. If a farmer can maximize the number of trees per acre while reducing the labor and costs necessary for pruning, spraying, mowing, and harvest, then adopting a trellis system can make a lot of sense.

Within two decades the South Tirol went from an experimental plot of approximately 75 acres (30 ha) in 1969 to more than 39,500 acres (16,000 ha) of slender spindle plantings by 1990.[17] Today there are more than 45,467 acres (18,400 ha) in production.[18]

With an average of thirty pesticide sprayings per year in those orchards, it's not just the apples that are spreading. It's hard to picture what it looks like. Until you photograph it, that is.

In 2012 Urban decided that it was time to start documenting the spraying that he was observing not only from his own farm but also in the local area. He began making videos of farmers applying pesticides, in all seasons and during all sorts of different weather conditions. While pesticide drift is extremely difficult and expensive to document after the fact, it is not especially difficult to capture the spraying methods or timing of pesticide applications. It wasn't a strategy that he embraced immediately, but sometimes push comes to shove, even among neighbors.

The Gluderers are bounded on three sides by apples: One neighbor is an organic apple farmer, and another is a conventional farmer who is always respectful of the Gluderers' need for established buffers. Both farmers are careful not to spray when weather conditions pose significant risk for drifting of the chemicals they use, since the Gluderers don't even use copper or sulfur, substances allowed in organic fruit and vegetable production.

However, one adjoining neighbor consistently showed blatant disregard for their requests that he be more careful about the distance and timing of his sprayings. He continued to push the limits of the law, up to the point that the Gluderers finally decided to file a complaint with the local police in 2015. It turned out to be the first time in the South Tirol that a complaint against a neighbor for breaching required buffer distance resulted in a fine. The farmer had to pay a modest 500 euros (just over $500), but he was allowed to continue spraying.

Urban continued to make videos of farmers spraying pesticides in order to demonstrate how far pesticides were drifting and the intensity with which they were being applied. He documented some farmers applying them in windy conditions and others blasting their aerosols into the air — with spray reaching 30, 60, and even 90 feet (9, 18, and 27 m) high even though the trees themselves seldom exceed 13 feet (4 m) in height. In some cases, he captured a farmer parking his tractor in one spot for an extended period of time in an effort to push the pesticides into areas not accessible by the tractor, meanwhile allowing the wind carry the excessive applications high into the air and down the valley.

The videos didn't show anything locals didn't already see on an everyday basis in apple country, but they did document the carelessness of some farmers — and what some would begin to call an abuse of the public trust.

Urban and Annemarie couldn't help but worry about the health of their family. It wasn't uncommon for farmers to spray their orchards twenty or more times in a season. Surrounded by so many different pesticides, in cocktails known only to the farmers spraying them, the Gluderers couldn't possibly assess what might be the biggest threats to their health — or if the combination of certain chemicals warranted even greater concern. While their high tunnels protected their crops, their family couldn't spend their entire existence under the protection of their translucent bubbles, nor could they control the impacts of pesticide drift outside the high tunnels.

As they monitored the crops in the show gardens that surrounded their high tunnels, pesticide residue levels exceeded the rate at which those herbs and flowers could be sold even as conventional products. Furthermore, the water that was shed by the high tunnels was so contaminated with residues that it couldn't be captured and reused and instead was piped away.

The economic threat to their business was real. Everything that Urban had worked so hard to build was at risk — and not just at home. Some of the fields that his job training center had used for growing herbs were now off-limits to organic production due to pesticide drift from an orchard located 0.5 mile (800 m) away. After enduring several years of the herbs consistently testing positive for pesticides — resulting in the disposal of the entire crop each time — the center decided that only vegetable root crops could be planted in the fields: crops that wouldn't be immediately exposed to drifting pesticides. The absurdity seemed as widespread as the drift, and it was headed for Mals. Urban minced no words in his assessment of the threat crawling up the valley: "In Mals, they have no chance if our problems become their problems."

With the growth of Big Apple, so much was at stake. And it wasn't just the future.

CHAPTER 4

Frozen in Time

He was dead within two minutes. The subclavian artery just under his left shoulder blade was severed by a weapon that would go undetected for the first ten years of the forensic investigations, despite the fact that experts from all over the globe had probed every orifice and noted each scar, tattoo, and deformation that covered his perfectly preserved skin.

Virtually no cadaver had ever raised so much international interest among forensic experts, scientists, medical technicians, and anthropologists. Yet not only did they miss seeing the arrowhead buried deep in his shoulder during the first decade of initial research, but they also hadn't been able to find their way to his stomach with their endoscopic probe. It would be eighteen years before they finally discovered that the small, misshapen organ had mysteriously migrated up just underneath his lungs, hidden from researchers and their tech-heavy peering and prodding.[1] That freeze-dried pouch turned out to hold not only the secrets to his last hours but also much more. It was the Ice Man's stomach, and it contained an undigested meal that would make anthropologists around the world salivate in anticipation of the forthcoming analyses. They all wanted to know what the Ice Man ate and what secrets his shriveled stomach held about the southern flank of the Alps thousands of years ago. Few people, if any, knew at the time just how relevant those findings would be in thinking about the fate of agriculture in the twenty-first century.

As it turns out, the stories of ur-ganic and organic aren't that far apart in the South Tirol, at least not in distance. The Ice Man, dubbed Ötzi

45

(*ERT-zee*) by the locals, in honor of his resting spot 10,532 feet (3,210 m) high in the Ötztal Alps, was discovered only 17 miles (28 km) from Günther Wallnöfer's organic dairy in Mals and a mere 10 miles (16 km) from the Gluderers' organic herb farm in Goldrain.

The evolving discoveries of what Ötzi ate would bring to mind not just the carbonized remains of Copper Age offerings but also the twenty-first-century sacrifices made to the idols of agricultural "progress."

Like Günther, Ötzi came from a culture reliant upon domesticated dairy animals. Like the Gluderers, he and his contemporaries were familiar with the nutritional and healing powers of gathered and cultivated plants and fungi. The food and health traditions that had sustained this long lineage of mountain dwellers since Ötzi was first encased in ice were under siege in the beginning of the twenty-first century. The agricultural biodiversity, livestock traditions, and healthy soils that had been fundamental to human survival surrounding Ötzi's old stomping grounds risked being wiped out within a generation. All for the almighty apple.

The stories of the discovery of the Ice Man and the movement of Big Apple up the Vinschgau Valley intersect at a variety of points, but the most obvious nexus is geographic proximity. Ötzi's final days were spent in the Schnals Valley, a staggeringly steep-sided valley that drops in a southerly direction from Similaun — an 11,798-foot (3,596 m) peak — to where it connects with the eastward dip of the broad Vinschgau at an elevation of 1,837 feet (560 m), only about 5 miles (7.7 km) northeast of the Gluderers' organic herb farm.

But the stories of Ötzi and Big Apple share more than just geography. The two narrative threads also share a twisted conspiracy of climate change and wind. Just as the warming of the Vinschgau Valley has allowed apples to creep into ever-higher elevations and the winds of the region have exacerbated the problems of pesticide drift, it was the combination of receding glaciers and the blowing of fine Saharan sands across the Mediterranean and onto the already dwindling snowpack above the valley that hastened the emergence of the Ice Man.

Ötzi's icy sepulcher was slowly conceding to the precipitous climbing of temperatures in the latter decades of the twentieth century. Then a massive sandstorm in March 1991 blew yellow sand particles from Africa to Europe, amplifying the sun's intensity and opening the lid to Ötzi's crystallized tomb.

On September 19 of that year, two German hikers, Helmut and Erika Simon, were traversing the upper elevations of the Ötztal range just above and to the north of the Vinschgau Valley, along the ridge that separates the contemporary borders of Italy and Austria. As they picked their way across the landscape of stone and ice just above 10,000 feet (3,000 m), they stumbled upon an unnerving sight in a slight depression of rock that cradled the last remnants of a dying glacier: Facedown, the head and upper torso of a mummified cadaver was protruding from a dwindling basin of water and ice atop the craggy ridgeline.

At first, it wasn't clear whether the Simons had found the remains of a missing hiker or even a soldier from one of the world wars. In fact, it wasn't even obvious who should be contacted — the authorities from Italy or from Austria — since the cadaver was situated so close to the jagged border between the two countries, a borderline that had never been completely delineated because the site was covered with more than 60 feet (20 m) of snow when the border was established by treaty in 1919.[2]

Austrian officials presumed jurisdiction initially, and they attempted to extricate the corpse the day following the discovery, but they weren't able to pull it free from the ice. They did, however, find the ax with a copper head and a finely crafted yew handle that would become not only Ötzi's signature tool but also the tool that would later force anthropologists to reconsider their established starting point for the Copper Age, now categorized as the period between 3500 and 2200 BCE.[3]

However, Ötzi's origins and his modern destiny were very much in limbo during the first weeks following his discovery. On September 21, the father of the owner of the nearest mountain hut set out to try to free the corpse from the ice, but with no success. Coincidentally, two world-famous mountain climbers, Reinhold Messner and Hans Kammerlander, happened by the site, and Messner estimated that the body was at least five hundred years old, a guess made without the advantage of seeing the ax, which had been taken down the mountain by a police officer the day before. A day later, an Austrian team finally freed the cadaver from the ice and readied it for transport to Austria, but a sharp drop in temperatures allowed the ice to reclaim its prize for yet one more night, until the forensic specialists were finally able to extricate the Ice Man on September 23. They transported him and a portion of his increasingly interesting tools and clothing by helicopter to Vent, Austria, where he was then transported by hearse to the Institute for Forensic Medicine in Innsbruck.[4]

What followed was one of the most fascinating and complex forensic investigations ever undertaken. Ötzi had died a hauntingly lonely death, but his reemergence into a world of prehistorically inclined paparazzi and scientists armed with every kind of probe, scalpel, and scanning device imaginable was enough to make even the coolest of characters blush. Not only was Ötzi the best-preserved mummy of his time, but almost all of his clothing and tools were also frozen in time with him. However, it was what he ate in those last hours that would shed so much light on what was at stake more than five millennia later down below in the Vinschgau Valley, the place where scientists would determine that he had spent a good portion of his adulthood.

———————

High above where the Schnals and Vinschgau Valleys meet sits a rocky outcropping known as Juval. Situated just above the entrance of the Schnals Valley, overlooking the east–west expanse of the Vinschgau, Juval's strategic location and its southern exposure weren't missed by the people of Ötzi's time and even earlier. Recent archaeological excavations have revealed the remains of a Stone Age settlement at Juval. At approximately 3,280 feet (1,000 m), the site is actually the highest Neolithic settlement yet discovered in the region. It seems almost certain that Ötzi was well aware of the Juval site; in fact, some researchers use various forms of evidence to suggest that he may have inhabited the site in some fashion.

As is the case with so many of the Neolithic settlements and cultic sites in the South Tirol, a medieval castle now sits atop Juval. First appearing in written history in 1278, Juval Castle is perched atop a promontory that intimidates today's casual visitors, much less medieval invaders. The castle is now owned by Reinhold Messner, the mountain climber who happened by the discovery site and hazarded the first guess at Ötzi's age while the glacier mummy was still ensconced in ice. Messner's estimations carry a lot of weight in the South Tirol, given his status as the world's most renowned mountain climber. A native of the region, he was the first climber to scale Everest without oxygen, and the first person to conquer all of the world's peaks over 8,000 meters (26,000 feet).

Messner spent years restoring Juval Castle, eventually renovating a portion of it to be one of six locations housing different elements of his Messner Mountain Museum. Juval Castle was dedicated to the theme of the Myth of Mountain, focused on the spiritual aspects of mountains in different cultures. In addition to exhibits of cultures with deep spiritual affinities with mountains, Juval also features a farm, vineyard, distillery, and restaurant, all of which maintain a focus on local, traditional, and sustainable practices.

Perhaps, then, it should be no surprise — given their geographic proximity and their philosophical alignment — that Messner sells the Gluderer family's herbal products from his gift shop and has lent his name to the Gluderers for a line of ecofriendly body-care products. They not only share a vista of a landscape overrun by apples but also a view that there are better ways to farm, methods rooted deep in mountain traditions.

As it turns out, the exchange of resources between Messner and the Gluderers, between the inhabitants of Schnals and Vinschgau Valleys, was indicative of a back-and-forth movement of goods that stretched far back into history. Ötzi would turn out to be a case in point.

The question of where Ötzi belonged had two sides to it: the legal aspect and the scientific question. In the initial weeks surrounding the discovery of "the man in ice," it was thought that he was found on the Austrian side of the border, but by early October it was clear that the discovery site was within the Italian domain. Nonetheless, Ötzi would remain in Austria until 1998, at which point he was escorted under tight security and international fanfare to his newest home in Bozen (Bolzano), Italy.

Diplomacy aside, the burning scientific question wasn't where Ötzi was going to chill long-term but rather where he came from before he was murdered in cold blood atop a high mountain pass. The answer came in rather surprising form: toilet paper. Well, organic wipes, anyway.

As it turned out, one of the types of moss Ötzi was carrying was a dead giveaway as to which side of the mountains he had come from before meeting his violent end. It's not that the moss (*Neckera complanata*) he was carrying was special; it was actually quite mundane. This species of moss was a coveted toiletry item not only for Ötzi's contemporaries but also for the roving shepherds and high-altitude hunters of the twentieth century. Gathered below, somewhere in its habitat range from Juval down into the

Vinschgau Valley, it was commonly used for wiping, among other things.[5] The moss remnants were among the best early clues as to where Ötzi called home, at least for the latter part of his estimated forty years.

However, investigators wanted more specific answers about Ötzi's origins. Detectives are renowned for stomaching a lot of things, but it's not every day that they're called upon to retrace a cadaver's digestive tract and determine not only a victim's final meals but also his last travels — 5,300 years ago. Scientists estimate that the progression of food through the entire gastrointestinal tract follows a general time frame of about thirty-three hours. In general, it takes four to five hours for the stomach contents to reach the transverse colon — the middle part of the large intestine that crosses the body from right to left — and another nine to twelve hours for it to reach the end of the small intestine before beginning the fourteen- to fifty-five-hour passage between the beginning of the large intestine and the end of the colon before being excreted through the rectum.[6] Using those figures as a benchmark, scientists can deduce the approximate time between meals. But that doesn't tell them where those meals were eaten.

However, if a human is traveling between different altitudes — as is almost always the case in the Alps — scientists can examine the types of pollens that were ingested by eating, drinking, and swallowing at different elevations in order to determine where the person traveled in terms of altitude. The dramatic differences in elevation in the area where Ötzi was found yield vast differences in plant communities at each altitude, and today's plant communities are roughly parallel to those of Ötzi's era. As a result, scientists have been able to combine what they know about what they found in Ötzi's digestive tract, the pace at which food and other materials move through the digestive system, and the correspondence between pollen types and elevation to re-create his movements during his last two living days.

Given the different pollens that they found at targeted points in Ötzi's gut, scientists have re-created what must have been a tumultuous final few days for him. Clearly he was, by today's standards, a veritable athlete. According to an analysis of the different pollens that he had ingested in his final forays, he apparently covered a distance of approximately 37 miles (60 km) in the two to three days prior to his death.[7]

The pollen analysis of four points in his digestive tract provides a rough picture of his intense final journey between his final resting spot and the

Vinschgau Valley. Through gut research and perhaps even a little gut instinct, scientists have determined that the day before he died Ötzi for some reason went from a coniferous subalpine level down to the more deciduous valley bottoms, perhaps in search of mosses that grew only in that environment. However, nine to twelve hours before he died on that spring day, he rapidly made his way back up toward the subalpine environment, arriving some four to nine hours later. He then headed up above tree line and toward the treacherous snow and ice leading to the Tisen Pass, a potential crossing point toward modern-day Austria, near where he met his end.[8] Evidence indicates that he ate his last meal some 30 to 120 minutes before he was mortally wounded by an arrow and presumably finished off with a sharp blow to the back of his head that shattered his skull.[9]

During those final days, according to the high-tech scouring of his digestive tract, Ötzi consumed at least three meals, surviving primarily on meat, grains, and probably some vegetative matter including bracken. Scientists found that ibex meat was the mainstay of his diet in those last two days, although he also consumed some meat from a red deer. The ibex is a mountain goat still found in the South Tirol, and red deer are also common. Neither of the meats showed any signs of the molecular changes that would indicate they were cooked, so they were probably eaten raw or dried.[10]

Still coveted for their meat and organs, the ibex and the red deer are reminders of a culture that had a strong hunting and gathering component, but it is important to bear in mind that Ötzi and his local Copper Age contemporaries seem to have been, first and foremost, farmers. Ötzi carried other food remnants in his body and on his person that combine to tell a tale of an Alpine diet that has been in constant evolution since the Stone Age, sustaining not only the people but also the landscape. However, the gift of Ötzi's final days is jeopardized today by the *Gift* — German for "poison" — spreading its way through the valleys down below. Such is life in the Irony Age.

———————————

Given how transient our industrialized societies have become and the homogenization of our food supply, it's extremely rare for a culture to be able to retrace its foodways back to a story with as much intrigue as the discovery of Ötzi. This kind of evidence of ancient food resources and traditions provides a touchstone for the future — one that can be embraced or simply cast into the cold, heartless gears of industrialized "progress."

For the South Tirol, what Ötzi ate matters. It goes beyond just food or even nutrition and into questions of stewarding an inherited landscape in a way that will ensure a cornucopia for generations to come.

Ötzi is, of course, but one representative of a culture that inhabited the valleys and slopes of the region, but he is the embodiment of agriculture, nutrition, and land management in the millennia preceding the Age of Big Apple, an era in which a group of concerned citizens in one small town stood up and called the sacrifice of their inheritance what it is: a travesty, albeit a travesty that wouldn't be tolerated.

Ötzi's discovery site was a virtual inventory of Copper Age foodways. Not only were scientists able to study his gut for clues to his diet, but a number of items were also discovered on his clothes and in the icy pool surrounding him. Although the extraordinary array of tools found with him indicated that he was a masterful hunter, the entire spectrum of food-related items made it clear that he came from a farming community, and correlated tightly with the findings from other archaeological sites nearby.

However, Ötzi and his associated artifacts differed from other finds in the region. The research at many of the other sites involved sifting through buried strata in search of inorganic artifacts such as stone tools, ceramics, and metal, along with sundry carbonized organic materials like charred bones and seeds left in fire pits or ancient ovens. Other archaeological sites involved the complicated extraction of organic and inorganic materials from submerged lake dwellings preserved through anaerobic conditions, sometimes yielding a sound overview of basic village architecture and infrastructure, including clear insights into construction materials and techniques. The case of Ötzi was much different due to the extraordinary set of circumstances that led to nearly ideal preservation of the corpse and his diverse belongings.

Known as a wet mummy, Ötzi and the other artifacts found with him were freeze-dried during their long encasement in snow and ice. The fact that he had collapsed into a gully 9 feet (3 m) deep meant that Ötzi and his belongings were protected from the subsequent glacier that formed and scoured the landscape above him. Glaciers are known for ripping apart cadavers and strewing the body parts and belongings hither and yon. Ötzi, however, escaped the ravages of predators and ice and left us to put the puzzle pieces back together and frame them in a broader historical context.

At first, given his relatively pristine condition, researchers thought it most likely that Ötzi died in the autumn, at which point he would likely have been covered with snow before scavengers could ravage his body. That idea was reinforced by the discovery of a dried sloeberry at the site. The existence of this wild sour plum led researchers to believe that the time of death was probably during the autumnal ripening period for the sloe bush, but later pollen research of Ötzi's gut indicated a strong presence of pollen from the hop hornbeam, a tree that typically blooms in late spring.[11]

Scientists began to surmise that Ötzi's body might have lain on snow for a period of time before being submerged in water prior to the freeze-drying process that occurred when he was finally encased in snow and ice.[12] As evidence of a late-spring death mounted, researchers then began to suspect that the Ice Man was carrying sloeberries in dried form, probably more for their nutritional value than their taste — or perhaps because sour berries are appreciated by hikers for minimizing thirst by stimulating saliva production.[13]

Having lived right on the cusp of the Late Stone Age and the beginnings of the Copper Age, Ötzi was well equipped to traverse, hunt, and forage his way across the treacherous high elevations just north of the Vinschgau Valley. His bow, made of yew, was a powerful weapon, 7.9 inches (20 cm) taller than Ötzi himself, who stood 63 inches (1.6 m) tall.[14] Replicas of the bow indicate that it could be used to kill large game or humans at a distance of 90 to 150 feet (27–46 m). The fletching of his arrows with feathers demonstrates an understanding of aerodynamic stabilization that scientists thought too advanced for such an early era. Along with a quiver full of arrow shafts in various states of readiness, he was also carrying his flint knife — sharp and at the ready — and a knotted net made of grass string that was probably used for catching birds and other small game.[15]

And then there was the ax. The 2-foot (61 cm) yew handle features a straight main stem, with the head formed from a branch that creates a 90-degree sweep. Into this the 3.7-inch (9.3 cm) copper blade was fitted and secured with birch tar and leather cordage. Trapezoidal in shape and made of 99.7 percent pure copper, the metal for the ax blade originated from ore in South Tuscany.[16] Ötzi may have suffered a desolate death, but he and his contemporaries were not constrained in travel or commerce. Nonetheless, they were, as a culture, sedentary farmers who combined their agricultural savvy with their hunting prowess and an encyclopedic understanding of wild plants and their many uses. Their knowledge would be developed, refined, and passed on for generation after generation for the next five millennia. Survival in the treacherous tumult of the Alps has always involved an intimate understanding of the diverse ecosystems at multiple elevations and the unfolding subtleties of each season. Ötzi and his contemporaries were almost certainly much more intelligent than they are portrayed in our superficial discussions about ancient peoples. In fact, Ötzi might have been exceptional in that regard, since it seems he exceeded the average life expectancy of his time and survived four decades.

Stone Age, Copper Age, Bronze Age, Iron Age — they all connote "primitive" cultures. And yet when we note the mastery involved in transforming a concept into a functional product with nothing other than know-how and native materials, our culture of synthetic convenience suddenly seems less equipped to confront the bare essentials of survival. Understanding how these ancient cultures laid the groundwork for the highly nutritious foodways and sustainable agricultural practices of the Vinschgau region provides a window into the ecological wisdom carried forward by Günther Wallnöfer, the Gluderer family, and other farmers and artisans in the valley.

While Ötzi's tools and clothing proved to be of immediate interest to scientists and the general public, scientists began to digest the other cultural clues that he carried in more subtle form — in his gut, on his clothing, and among his other belongings. The analysis of the remains in his digestive tract and in his teeth indicated that he had chewed grains on a regular basis, probably in the form of bread, since some mica and charcoal were also found in his gut, likely residual from the milling of grains and baking of bread.[17] These findings were reinforced by the discovery of several grains on his garments, including emmer, einkorn, spelt, hulled barley, and broomcorn millet.

Bread made of these hearty ancient grains remains a staple of the South Tirolean diet, and all of these grains found with Ötzi appear in a variety of traditional dishes that fulfilled the high energy needs of mountain farmers and their communities for millennia. In addition, the extensive adaptation of these grains to the varied soils, microclimates, and vacillating weather of the region meant that human health and ecological health were tightly interwoven strands that stretched from the Stone Age to the present.

Ötzi emerged with two other surprises: the oldest oilseeds discovered in the eastern Alps. Both flax- and poppy seeds were found with Ötzi. Each is known for its tastiness and nutritional value, and poppy seeds were long coveted as one of the few sweeteners available in the South Tirol. Both seeds are still found in a number of traditional Tirolean recipes. Flax fibers were also transformed into linen on small looms, even in these ancient cultures.

Interestingly, those findings parallel much of what has been discovered at an archaeological excavation near the village of Latsch, located in the Vinschgau Valley between Juval (the entrance to the Schnals Valley from the Vinschgau) and Goldrain, about 10 miles (16 km) south of the Ice Man's discovery site. From the Stone Age forward, it is clear that inhabitants of the Vinschgau relied on a combination of farming, hunting, and gathering. The excavations in Latsch unearthed samples of barley, emmer, and einkorn from the Late Stone Age and the Copper Age, as well as naked wheat, a grain that wasn't found with the Ice Man. In addition, the Latsch discovery also yielded evidence of some cultivation of peas, which would have been an important source of protein in the Stone and Copper Ages, although evidence for pea cultivation is thus far stronger in northern reaches of the Alps than in southern areas.[18]

Ötzi was almost certainly part of the Remedello culture, the group that dominated the Vinschgau and other areas farther south during the Copper Age. Sedentary agriculturalists, they were nonetheless dependent upon trade for flint, copper, and other materials. It seems quite likely that Ötzi had some association with or at least knowledge of the Juval and Latsch settlements. The grains found in the Latsch site were probably cultivated in the fertile soils of the area surrounding the Adige River, which likely served as a primary or backup water source for some of the farming endeavors in Latsch.[19]

According to ethnobotanical researchers, it seems that land-use patterns shifted significantly after the Copper Age in the Vinschgau and Schnals Valleys, as they probably did in other places. Relying primarily upon the strata of pollens found in local lakebeds, scientists detected increases in pollens associated with grazing species of plants in the Bronze Age. Whereas there seemed to be minimal population pressures during the Stone and Copper Ages, with ample room for farming in the valley floor of the Vinschgau, population pressures in the Bronze Age seemed to have intensified the need to maximize the use of good tillable soil, setting the stage for . . . well, Heidi.

While that time leap may be overstated and the analogy a bit kitschy, there was a cultural leap that makes sense here. The postcard and Hollywood images of cattle, sheep, and goats grazing summer pastures high above tree line in the Alps are rooted in the Bronze Age demographic pressures that pushed livestock — with the help of shepherds — high up into the mountains during the peak of summer. It only makes sense: A growing population demanded increased production of grains, legumes, oilseeds, and other cultivated crops, so livestock were pushed upward to graze the coveted cool-season grasses that were hitting their nutritional peaks up on the slopes of the high mountains.

There were two other advantages to this practice, known as transhumance, the seasonal movement of people and animals up and down in elevation. First of all, taking the animals high into the mountains separated livestock from the tasty crops and thereby minimized the potential for fields being ruined by ruminants. Second, sending these animals up above tree line meant that land didn't have to be cleared for grasses to grow — Mother Nature had already taken care of that clearing, or at least most of it.

Transhumance became a central element of Alpine agriculture and the heart and soul of South Tirolean foodways. Taking animals to the alm, the high mountain pastures, became an ingrained tradition, exemplified by the vast array of mountain cheeses and cherished butters of the region. The stunning variety of microclimates, soils, and minerals of high-elevation valleys combined to yield distinctive plant communities that would, in turn, produce milk and meat of a distinctive character. Furthermore, since the milk couldn't be readily transported to lower elevations, it was turned into cultured products such as cheese, butter, and yogurt — nutritious and less perishable items that could be transported and turned into winter stores or even tradable commodities.

Goats, sheep, cattle — they were all part of the livestock mix from the Stone Age forward, and they are all represented in Ötzi's garments. Goat and sheep hides served as his coat and his leggings, while his underwear was made of sheepskin, and his belt was crafted from a calfskin. Animal sinews provided the necessary stitching material, and wild-animal skins were utilized as well, with bearskin used for his hat and the soles of his shoes and deerskin for the outer covering of the shoes.[20]

While Ötzi's fashion statement sheds minimal light on the specifics of livestock management in his home community, archaeological evidence from nearby settlements does paint a clearer picture of the typical agricultural practices surrounding him. In the Latsch excavations, researchers used bone fragments to determine that domestic livestock played a larger nutritional role than did wild game. They also compared the different percentages of bone fragments found to determine that between the Late Stone Age and the Copper Age, cattle played an increasingly important role in the community's diet. In the Late Stone Age, sheep and goats made up roughly 80 percent of the bone fragments, with cattle at 11 percent and pigs at 8 percent. In the Copper Age, cattle represented 26.4 percent of the findings, with sheep and goats declining to 62.1 percent and the domesticated pig going down to 5 percent.[21]

One important clue as to why cattle might have increased in importance comes from examination of bone fragments in another archaeological site about 62 miles (100 km) away from Ötzi's home territory. "Arbon Bleiche 3" is the site of a submerged village that is approximately contemporaneous with Ötzi. Twenty-seven houses made up the village, each measuring an average of 13.1 by 26.2 feet (4 × 8 m).[22] Located on the southern shore of Lake Constance (Bodensee) in Switzerland, this site provides a variety of insights as to how Ötzi probably lived. For example, dung remnants from cattle indicate that they were housed within the village confines during the winter. In contrast, scientists discovered a prevalence of insects that live in dung in the areas just outside the village, indicating that cattle were probably kept at a close proximity so that they could be used for milking and for pulling implements.[23]

As researchers at Arbon Bleiche 3 dug deeper for clues about the use of domesticated and wild animals in the village, they also discovered that many of the cattle bones showed signs of physical strain. Combining those findings with the discovery of a maple pole that was probably a yoke, they made a convincing argument that draft animals were beginning to play a key role in the development of agriculture in the region during the Copper Age.[24] Draft animals allowed for more intensive grain cultivation, improved fertility with the spreading of manure, and easier hauling of materials needed for farming.

As tools and technologies were further refined and developed in the subsequent eras, subsistence and survival in the land of Ötzi would become a little bit easier. Gains in efficiencies mattered, but it was the inherited wisdom and the conservation of resources that made the difference.

With around two hundred generations between Ötzi's disappearance and his reentry into a high-tech, chill world, what Ötzi ate is a powerful reminder that it's a problem when one farmer's choices negatively impact his neighbor's reality, but it's a travesty when those choices impact generations to come.

CHAPTER 5

Seeds

As Edith Bernhard unfolded the yellowed newspaper, her husband, Robert, pointed to the date, shaking his head: 1895. The mason who had brought it over to them was renovating a house attic several hundred feet up the village street from their house when he found the crumpled newspaper stuck in a dark corner. In a region where relics dating back several hundred years are nearly commonplace, he almost didn't think twice about the old newsprint, but something made him wipe his hands and pick it up. When he saw that it was much more than just an old sheet of newsprint, he headed to the Bernhards. At the time, he was one of the few people in the village who seemed to understand, much less appreciate, their obsession.

Two perfect heads of grain were carefully wrapped inside. Astounded by what appeared to be the find of a lifetime, Edith reverently picked up one of the two heads of grain, its seeds aligned in perfect alternating sequence along the tip of the stem. She delicately pulled out one of the pointed, reddish brown seeds and gently squeezed the outer hull to see if the grain inside still seemed intact. To her amazement, it felt solid. "*Na, na, na . . . unmöglich*," she muttered; impossible. Shaking her head in disbelief, she passed the kernel to Robert and began checking the other seeds on both heads, hardly able to fathom what a treasure they might have in hand. They looked at each other.

"*Dinkel?*" he asked. Spelt?

Edith nodded in silence, but it didn't stop a huge smile from creeping across her face, lifting her dimples beyond their usual points of prominence. If the seeds were viable, it was a chance to bring back not just a piece of history but also a missing nutritional link that had been casually cast aside in the region when, decades ago, grain imports and a taste for white bread had pushed out tradition in favor of ease and progress.

Spelt. One of the oldest cultivated grains in human history. Two spelt seeds were discovered in Ötzi's clothing, and it had remained a staple of the region's diet all the way up until the twentieth century when it began to fall out of favor, in part because of its tight protective hull — the very thing that now made the spelt seeds from 1895 look like they still might be able to grow. For thousands of years, that sturdy hull had been one of spelt's most cherished properties. It helped protect spelt from birds, insects, disease, and the vagaries of Alpine weather, making it a favorite of the pilgrims and Crusaders of the Middle Ages, who also valued the ancient grain's taste and ability to nourish. However, the hull also made spelt more difficult and costly to mill. Eventually, in a cost-benefit analysis like many in the modern food story that consider only economic costs and ignore environmental and nutritional ones, grains that lacked a tough outer shield eventually replaced spelt.

Edith and Robert were betting that, sooner or later, the negative consequences of simplistic calculations that didn't account for human and environmental health would become obvious and society would wake up to the fact that a more complex and therefore more accurate cost-benefit analysis was necessary. In the meantime, they had work to do.

In the fall they carefully planted the seeds in a protected plot where they could tend them with the utmost attention. They anxiously watched the seedbed every day until, finally, a few days later, they saw the miracle begin to unfold and push its way up above the tilled surface, in search of autumn's waning light. With the memory of millennia, each single stem emerged and quickly branched into two leaves, spread into tillers, and gradually created small, green clumps that would withstand winter's bite and hold fast until spring. When the weather finally began to warm and the days stretched into spring, the spelt stems began their skyward leap, transforming into hardy, thick stalks. By early summer, the spelt was about 3 feet (90 cm) high, with its tightly knitted seedheads beginning to arc ever so slightly with the weight of the ripening grains. Finally, as the thick stalks hardened, the seedheads began to shift from green to a light reddish brown color, and Edith and Robert prepared for the most exciting harvest of their lives.

Throughout the growing season, they began to see that the spelt was indeed an ideal match for the fields surrounding their village of Burgeis, high in the uppermost basin of the Vinschgau Valley, bounded within the township of Mals. Relatively short in comparison with many modern grain varieties, these rugged spelt stalks resist breaking or bending and are therefore well equipped for the Vinschgau's intense spring winds. As winter begins to ease its grip each year, cold air pours out of the surrounding mountains and converges to create days and even weeks of wind that sometimes arrives in intense gusts and other times in the monotonous form of a relentless gale that makes trees bend, animals cower, and humans stoop for days on end. Historically, grains growing there were left to their own evolutionary devices to adapt and hang tight until the seedheads ripened to the dry, golden hue that gave the signal — time to harvest.

As the harvest approached, Edith and Robert were ecstatic. Their century-old spelt had made the cut, and now it had a name: *Dinkel Burgeis*. "Burgeis spelt" would go down in history . . . again. Within a few years, Robert and Edith had a field full of Burgeis spelt and were beginning to provide seeds to interested local farmers. Fortunately, the rebirth of the Bernhards' heritage grain coincided perfectly with a renaissance of grain growing and traditional baking in Mals. Local farmers and bakers were just beginning to embark on an initiative to restore the region's historical reputation as "the Breadbasket of the Tirol."

Unfortunately, Big Apple and its covey of lobbyists and politicians were cooking up other plans for Mals and the rest of the Upper Vinschgau, and it was a recipe for disaster.

Wer der Saat hat, hat das Sagen. Whoever has the seed, has the say.

Edith and Robert took the old farmers' proverb to heart, even though they knew all too well that the forces they were up against — at a regional level, much less a global scale — had the bigger mouthpieces. It was bad enough that multinational corporations were scrambling to patent life and turn seedsavers and homegrown plant breeders into outlaws, but the lack of public knowledge about the basics of conserving agrobiodiversity made the corporate takeover of the home garden and the farmer's field all the easier.

However, the Bernhards were more concerned with action than words. What they created in two decades of retirement is more than what most people create in an entire career — and it would eventually win over the imaginations of farmers, bakers, chefs, historians, scientists, journalists, and tourists.

Originally from Austria, Edith began her professional career, somewhat ironically in hindsight, as a chemist. In her job with a pharmaceutical company, she worked in a lab testing and researching different drugs before the South Tirol — and Robert — lured her across the border with mountains and romance. She soon switched careers and became the "manager of their household" in 1970. They raised three sons together while living in the city of Bozen where Robert had his career, but they both felt the constant tug to return to Robert's childhood home in Burgeis, the village that he had to leave for his job when he was twenty-eight.

When they were finally able to "retire" to Burgeis in 1994, trading in what Edith notes was the benefit of a "regular vacation" for the constant demands of farming, Edith transformed her urban balcony exploits in tomato cultivation in the city into a full-blown trial garden that would eventually include more than three hundred heirloom tomato varieties. When I first met Robert, he teased that her tomatoes ranged in color from black to white and everything in between. Upon later visiting their gardens for the first time in the fall of 2015, I couldn't help but wonder if she actually didn't invent some colors on her own.

Edith was unwilling to stake her reputation solely on tomatoes, however. It wasn't long before she added 250 heirloom herb varieties to her collection, along with carrots, beets, beans, and salad greens of all colors, almost every kind of edible berry used in the region, and a number of antique fruit tree cultivars. The bulk of the plants were regional specialties, although any plant with an interesting history, nutritional quality, or medicinal trait was a candidate for their garden.

Complementary in personality, Edith and Robert approach conversation in ways as distinct as their roles in the garden, where Robert takes care of everything from the ground down, and Edith is in charge of everything from the topsoil up. Edith is the slightly reserved pragmatist who readily switches from the perfunctory laboratory supervisor in the seed room to a concise garden encyclopedia with an anecdote for every plant and a plant-based antidote for almost any ill. Robert, who is more effusive and philosophical, gesticulates so animatedly in his descriptions of compost that one becomes totally convinced that compost is a dynamic living organism of a higher spiritual order than we lowly humans.

Such a division of labor makes for a harmonious partnership. It also mirrors, in a sense, their mutual goal of advocating for farmers and gardeners to create a biological balance in which a healthy soil supports healthy plants, healthy animals, and healthy humans. Their approach must be working because the Bernhards now have six different sites that they manage, with a constant stream of international visitors. Their recent recognition is ironic, however, because they worked in quiet anonymity for many years.

Few locals paid much attention to what they were doing for the first two decades. In fact, they were virtually the only example of a substantial private seedsaving operation in the region, with few collaborators in the vicinity and no local network for the exchange of ideas and seeds. That all started to change, however, when the people of Mals began to see the transformation of the landscape that was working its way up the valley.

Sometimes it takes a crisis for a community to recognize the resources it might otherwise take for granted — and what it has to lose if no one takes action. Big Apple offered a stark contrast with the extraordinary show of biodiversity that Edith and Robert had created through their display garden — a vibrant counterpoint to the one-way dead-end monocultural highway heading their way.

The first time that I went to visit the Bernhards' display garden, I had the sensation that I was winding my way heavenward. The main highway going to the upper end of the Vinschgau Valley weaves its way through the agrarian villages of Schluderns, Tartsch, and Mals before opening up to a parceled patchwork of green fields that cover the tilted valley floor. Mesmerized by the dance of seedheads of grain and hayfields barely tickled by the cool air descending the valley, my fascination was interrupted by a sign for Burgeis, with the arrow indicating a sharp left that drops visitors into that village and back in time.

A Precautionary Tale

Like all eleven of the villages that make up the municipality of Mals, Burgeis has a character all its own, appreciated not only by its eight hundred residents but also by cyclists who seem to commandeer the village and its outskirts during the warmer months. Located about 500 feet (150 m) in elevation above the village of Mals, Burgeis commands a stunning view of the valley and its patchwork of villages, all set within a basin framed by some of the highest peaks of the South Tirol. Tucked into the western flank of the Vinschgau, the medieval village was constructed in an era when adapting to the landscape, rather than manipulating it, was the rule and natural building materials were the only option. As a result, Burgeis's architecture is a contoured mosaic of stucco, stone, crafted timbers, and cobbled streets, originally carved into the mountainside along waterways that would be harnessed for water and the power that it brought for grinding grains, sawing timber, making textiles, and powering blacksmith hammers.

Multistory houses built to hold multiple generations sit on thick, flared foundations, the omnipresent white stucco contrasting with the darkened woodwork of balconies, doorways, and roofs. Barn walls and roofs blend seamlessly into the architecture of the houses, and every square foot of earth in the village appears to have a designated use. Perfect right angles are a luxury in a village where storage is coveted — if there is an open space that can be covered, it will be co-opted. Such a mentality has led to what might best be called passageways that weave their way through the varied topography — *streets* or *thoroughfares* would be too generous a designation. Drivers need not abandon hope, but I did decide that it was a good idea to abandon my car on the outskirts of the village and enjoy the rest of my tour on foot. Flowers, fountains, crucifixes, and frescoes reward the slower traveler, as do the vistas.

It seems that any stunning vista in the South Tirol with strategic importance has been rewarded with a castle or a church. Burgeis got both, with an added bonus of gaining one of Europe's most famous monasteries. Marienberg Abbey was initially established as a Benedictine outpost in 1150 and is now a sprawling white enclave perched high above the village. While nine centuries may seem like a long time ago, it is likely that some elements of a settlement in Burgeis were already present, even at that time, since the name *Burgeis* probably stems from the Roman era, when a fortification was called a *burgus*.

Seeds

At an elevation of approximately 4,400 feet (1,340 m), Marienberg is the highest Benedictine monastery in Europe, but its real claim to fame is its stunning array of Romanesque frescoes, hidden for centuries in its ancient crypt. Constructed in 1160, the crypt is part of the original compound, but in 1643 it was renovated to provide a burial space for the monks, and the original twelfth-century frescoes that adorned the crypt were covered, only to be discovered again in 1980.[1] Protected from the elements for so many hundreds of years, the frescoes are not only intact but also extraordinarily vibrant in color, attracting tourists and scholars from around the world.

Although the monks of Marienberg have partitioned themselves from the world, the abbey itself still plays a vital role in the life of Mals. As it would turn out, having an abbot who is an organic gardener and a monastery that produces cheese can be a good thing when questions about the future of local agriculture begin to arise. Of course, the abbot and his fellow monks may also feel blessed that they can peer down from their windows and catch a glimpse of Edith and Robert working in their garden of botanical diversity, putting to good use the lessons of the world's most famous abbot, Gregor Mendel — another gardener whose interest in plant genetics wasn't fully understood or appreciated until decades after his death.

The Bernhards' display garden is less for show than for education and seedsaving, but its power certainly dwells in its appearance. A ten-minute walk from Robert and Edith's home in the village, the garden is just on the opposite side of Burgeis's other historic landmark, the castle of Fürstenburg. Built upon a rocky promontory between 1272 and 1282,[2] the primary feature of the original castle was its tower, constructed with walls nearly 10 feet (3 m) thick at the base. Its outer walls were added in the seventeenth century, during which time it became a getaway residence for the region's bishop.[3]

Ironically, the castle now serves as the South Tirolean province's School for Agriculture and Forestry. Separated by nothing more than a brook — across which there is a small bridge — there remains nonetheless a much larger, unseen gulf between what is taught in the predominantly conventional agriculture curriculum of Fürstenburg and what can be learned in the Bernhards' garden. A step across that bridge and through the Bernhard's arched metal garden gate is a step into both the past and the future.

A Precautionary Tale

As I walked across the bridge, Robert's long arm mirrored the gate's arch in its sweep as he waved me in with an enormous smile that seemed to keep the edges of his mustache pushed upward. He tipped his hat and appeared to make it to me in about half the strides it would take most mortals.

Edith wasn't far behind him. She made her way over, pushing a lock of salt-and-pepper hair off to the side of her damp forehead with the back of her dirty hand and extending her other callused hand with a dialect greeting of "*Grüßti*, Philip!" Getting an informal greeting usually reserved for locals made me feel welcome.

The Bernhards' 0.75 acre (0.3 ha) garden is a long, sloping strip that parallels the contour of the mountainside for about 300 feet (91 m). *Verdant* would be the wrong word to describe the first portion of the garden simply because there are so many hues of green that they seem to form their own spectrum. Herbs that creep, climb, and clump fill beds of various shapes and sizes, with inflorescences shooting up and using the backdrop to dramatize their fleeting appearances. I wondered for a second whether the garden would better supply a pharmacist or a chef — but then I realized that those are two professions we never should have delineated so distinctly.

Edith and Robert led me along the main garden path toward a small greenhouse where seedlings, some potted plants, a watering can, and a few tools were stored. All along the way Edith pointed out herb after herb, turning the landscape into a litany of recipes and prescriptions. I gave up on taking photos and notes of everything lest we not get from one end of the garden to the other before nightfall.

Suddenly herbs transitioned into fruit trees, and I was glad to see Robert pull out a knife and begin plucking different fruits for me to sample. Some were overripe stragglers from an earlier harvest and others weren't fully ripe, but we caught a few apples at their peak. All of them hinted at sunshine with their sweetness, cool nights with their crisp textures. None of them were the usual suspects — the standard varieties that you would find in a mainstream European or US market. Robert held up a perfect specimen: "*Keinen Pestiziden*," he noted with a twinkle. "No pesticides — not like most of them down there." He pointed farther down the valley where perfectly symmetrical rows of green and black hail netting covered row after row of apple trees.

"When the soil is healthy, then one doesn't need any pesticides whatsoever," he reminded me. "Look over here." I followed him to the center of his universe, his compost piles, contained in large wooden bins. He picked up a handful of compost from the pile that looked almost finished. He let it sift through his fingers — dark, fine, and slightly fluffy — before handing it to me. He signaled me to mimic his movements as he held another mounded batch in cupped hands, and it wasn't unlike tasting a special wine with a South Tirolean friend. As we let the compost flow through our fingers and back into the bin, it was clear we had a vintage year in our hands: earthy, with a slight hint of something close to a barrique character. "The earthworms have done this," said Robert. "Everything is worked up and is now so fine. There aren't any more earthworms in it. It's all completely worked by the earthworms."

Robert raised the remnants in his hand slightly skyward, toward the light, not unlike the way monks just up the mountain raise their sacraments, and then gave it one last smell before putting the rest back into the bin: "*Ah — super, herrlich, herrlich, herrlich. Exzellent, exzellent.*" He was a connoisseur. The superlatives flowed.

He then walked over to an upended log filled with hack marks on its face, a Tirolean hatchet left sticking in it. He pulled out the hatchet, picked up a handful of collected brush from the pile beside it, and started hacking. He then gathered the finely chopped pieces and tossed them into the newest batch of compost. "That's the secret," he said, "that and the stone meal." He explained that they had an excellent original soil in their garden plot but adding the stone meal provided needed minerals in faster form than would come from natural processes, given their constant planting and harvesting.

Edith waited patiently off to the side while Robert shared his craft, plucking a few weeds that had intruded in nearby beds. Once he was convinced that my fertile mind was fully saturated with his methods, he pointed over to Edith: "It's hot out here. Let's go over there and get a drink and a little something to eat." Edith nodded and ducked into a small wooden shed toward the far end of the garden, only to reappear with a large cutting board full of hearty bread slices covered with a variety of soft cheeses, herb pestos, edible flowers, berries, and nasturtium leaves. It was a culinary rainbow unlike anything I'd ever seen: biodiversity served up fresh, with herb-infused water to help take it all in.

A Precautionary Tale

Edith motioned for me to grab a few samples and walk with her through rows upon rows of raised beds chock-full of vegetables. The garden was somewhat different from an ordinary modern kitchen garden: Instead of being harvested, many of the crops were left to go to seed. Annuals, such as old varieties of lettuce, had gone from leafy bunches to stalky spires of seeds. Carrots, of which Edith had a rainbow of heirloom varieties, were biennials and had been left in place to go to seed in their second year. The complexity of placements, seed harvest, and rotations was mind boggling, but having Edith walk me through the rows was like having a parent read the lines of a well-worn book out loud, rote in content but delivered with fresh enthusiasm each time it was shared.

As we walked along, Edith would pluck samples for me to taste. At one point she bent over a bed of carrots and pulled three varieties for me. Using the top of a plastic barrel for a makeshift tabletop, she diced them up into bite-sized slices. Robert came over to join us in the taste test. I tasted each of the three, trying to see if my palate could detect any way in which the slightly different tastes somehow related to color. As we compared our impressions on the subtle differences in flavor, they followed my gaze out over the valley.

The garden location provided a perfect vantage point for capturing the topography of almost every village in the Mals township as well as a sweeping vista of almost the entire Upper Vinschgau. To the right lay towns just below Mals, filled or filling with new apple plantations, while the view to the left was much different, at least for the moment, with the broad, flat valley floor tilting sharply upward toward the Austrian border, tall mountains flanking either side. Robert pointed toward the unusual sloping of that end of the valley. "You know what it's called, that part of our valley, right . . . ?"

"*Der Malser Haide, meinst du?*" The Mals Heath, you mean? I asked.

"Yes, exactly. Our Mals Heath is something very special. It was famously known as the Breadbasket of the Tirol."

Robert went on to explain that the traditional grains of the Vinschgau were known as some of the finest in all of Europe. They were even a favorite of the Vatican in Rome and the royal family in England prior to the twentieth century. There was something special about the Mals Heath that produced exceptional grains, and as it turns out, it all goes back to geology.

Throughout my three decades of living in and returning to the Vin-schgau, I'd always admired the curious character of the Mals Heath. It seemed obvious that there was some unusual geological origin to it, but I couldn't interpret what it was, and I certainly had never linked it to the famed grains and breads of the region. However, in 2011, three geologists took a new look at the feature and came up with a new theory for its origin. It seemed unlikely to them that the 6.8-mile (11 km) long Malser Haide was formed simply from gradual alluvial deposits, as long assumed: It is simply too broad and long, and the deposition too deep, for such a scenario.

After looking at the topography and geological history of the surrounding area, they speculated that the Malser Haide and similar formations in the Vinschgau were created by the collapse of a mountain that was likely more than 10,000 feet (3,100 m) high — probably through seismic activity. As the mountain broke apart and tumbled downward, it deposited massive amounts of material all the way from the village of Plawenn (Konrad's home) to just below Burgeis. In essence, the agrarian heritage of the township of Mals was rooted in what these geologists dubbed a megafan.

The geologists weren't sure if this megafan formation, similar to a sprawling river delta formation but confined between mountains on each side, was the result of one enormous cataclysmic event or several such events spread out over time. Either way, the megafan theory helped make a lot more sense of the unusual geomorphology of the vista Robert and I were admiring. It also helped explain in part how the area had become the Breadbasket of the Tirol.

The unique soils and climate of the Vinschgau proved ideal for cultivating several historically important grains such as rye, spelt, emmer, einkorn, barley, and oats, as well as hay. The dry, steppelike conditions created by a combination of sun exposure, steady air currents throughout the year, and well-drained soils minimized disease, while the deep soils and broad valley made for good plowing, planting, and other cultivation practices. In addition, the megafan forced the two rivers in that part of the valley to its edges, on either side of the collapsed mountainside that now formed the Malser Haide. The Adige River and its tributary, the Puni River, would — in conjunction with other mountain streams — feed the ancient network of irrigation canals that crisscrossed the Malser Haide, supplying farmers with needed water for their grain, hay, pastures, and vegetable crops at critical times.

As we looked out over the valley, I remarked that I could remember seeing many more grain fields when I'd first come to the South Tirol in the early 1980s. In a valley where conditions were so optimal for them, their dramatic decline in recent decades didn't make sense to me. Where had they all gone? Grain production in the Vinschgau Valley went from a peak of 24,710 acres (10,000 ha) in 1906 to 366 acres (148 ha) in 2013.[4]

Robert said the answer could be summed up in one word: *Verarmung*. Impoverishment . . . of both landscape and culture. The irony in it all, he noted, was that the rising economic status of the valley's people created the impoverishment he was alluding to. In the decades following World War II, more and more people in the South Tirol finally began to move beyond subsistence lifestyles and have some disposable income. One of the first simple luxuries many took advantage of was the fresh bread available on a daily basis from the local bakeries. However, it wasn't just the frequency of fresh bread that they enjoyed but also the availability of white bread, that is to say, wheat bread.

It might be worth reading this twice: Until the latter half of the twentieth century, South Tirolean farmers traditionally baked bread only two or three times per year. Maybe four. The harder the times, the harder the bread. Making bread was hard work, and so was getting grain to the miller and back home again as flour, whether by cart or a wooden-framed backpack. To boot, farmers couldn't risk spoilage or loss of the flour — it was the lifeline that wove its way through the turning pages of the calendar. Turning the flour into bread sooner rather than later was some of the only insurance farmers had.

Rye and spelt were the most common and reliable grains in the Upper Vinschgau, although barley, emmer, einkorn, oats, buckwheat, millet, and some wheat could also be found. Some anthropologists surmise that rye probably came into the South Tirol as a weed seed when wheat was brought in for planting from Bavaria or elsewhere. As it turned out, rye was more reliable in the cool and wet mountainous areas than wheat, which performed much better north and south of the Alps. Although farmers continued to grow wheat in the South Tirol, rye became the dominant grain, followed by spelt. They relied on the tough-hulled spelt's hardiness in their Alpine conditions; it also grows well in poorer soils, as does rye. The very traits that help rye, spelt, and the region's other heritage grains thrive in the Alps also make them easier to grow without inputs. As Robert continually reminded me, grains like rye and spelt need neither synthetic fertilizers nor constant manuring — much less applications of *Gülle*, a liquefied combination of animal urine and manure. All of it is too strong, he says, and excessive nitrogen actually brings down the nutritional quality of the grain.

Grains beget breads beget traditions, and so it was in the Upper Vinschgau. In fact, the ur-bread tradition in the area came directly out of Marienberg Abbey, where monks purportedly abided by a bread recipe for several centuries before they finally shared it with the farmers. The *Ur-Paarl nach Klosterart*, the "ancient pair made in the monastic style," became the standard bread of the Vinschgau. It became so ubiquitous in the region that it is commonly referred to by its dialect name, the *Vinschgerpaarl*.

The traditional Vinschgerpaarl is a sourdough bread containing a small proportion of wheat flour but more rye flour, along with wildcrafted fennel, blue fenugreek, and caraway. Its distinctive flavor is matched by its unique form: The bread is typically about 1 inch (2.5 cm) thick, consisting of two connected circular loaves. Why this sourdough rye bread is made of a pair of joined loaves is left to conjecture, but there is no question about today's culturally embedded symbolism of a Vinschgerpaarl representing the sharing of bread and, taken a step further, a marriage.

Once baked in an enormous stone oven, typically on the outside of or even separated from the farmhouse, the bread was placed on edge in wooden racks that would be hung from the ceiling in a room with good air circulation to promote drying and to prevent mold formation. Of course, rodents also stood little chance of finding their way to the carefully located racks. Once dry, the bread was often too hard to bite, or at least without cracking a tooth. A special cutting board called a *Brotgroamml* was used, with a pivoting knife attached by a metal ring on its tip to the board for safe chopping and with vertical boards on three sides to catch the flying crumbs. Attaching the knife tip to the board prevented a slip of the knife as it hit the hard carapace of the dense bread.

The pieces of cracked bread would then be put into soup, milk, or even wine for softening. While it wasn't easy to eat, the bread was highly nutritious, and it was every family's best bet against starvation in an often unforgiving landscape. Plummeting temperatures, floods, blizzards, avalanches, landslides, and occasional droughts were all part of life for the mountain farmers, and bread could mean the difference between life and death in a landscape where one weather event could turn bounty into desperation.

The spelt bread laid out before us may have grown out of that cultural tendency toward nutrition-packed loaves, but its density was far more suited to modern times. I grabbed the last piece, topped it with cheese and a nasturtium flower from the cutting board, and asked Edith and Robert if I could see their seedsaving collection.

"*Natürlich, natürlich,*" Robert replied heartily, and he grabbed the empty board and waved us forward with another arc of his long arm. Edith and I picked up the glasses and our pace and hustled to try and keep pace with Robert's long gait. We rinsed the cutting board and glasses with a garden hose and tidied up a few tools before heading out the gate, over the bridge, and past the agricultural school on our way to the village.

The magnificent ruin had a long history as an agricultural and forestry school, but a recent earthquake had toppled part of the tower — and the classrooms and offices were impressively reconceived by the renowned architect Werner Tscholl. Did the students ever come to work with them in the garden? I asked. "*Nie genug,*" Robert replied. Never enough.

Edith laughed. "But when people like you from all over the world start coming here to see our display garden, then everyone at the school starts watching us a little more."

We walked through the curving, cobbled streets of Burgeis, dodging mountain bikers a good portion of the way, some of them solo while others followed the leader in weaving, serpentine chains. I decided that as long as there was a waft of cow manure in the middle of the village, the tourists still hadn't won. Agritourism is great, until the *agri-* prefix falls away like a shed reptilian skin.

We walked past several high-end restaurants tucked fairly discreetly into their stuccoed medieval carapaces but given away by ornate doorways crafted from tinted glass and fancy metalwork, then veered up a small side street. Edith pointed to the stairway of their house and pulled out her key. Their neighbors were bringing hay into their barn, located right in the center of the village. Hay chaff was thick in the air, and the sound of machinery drowned out any chance of conversation. A woman fit a large grapple hook around a load of loose hay on a hay wagon while a young boy operated the winch that would lift the load up on a cable and into the hayloft. Up above, an unseen character with a deep voice issued curt commands and pulled the load deep into the barn's loft, where he would release the hay from the grapple and send it swinging back above the hay wagon, at which point the lad would lower it to the woman waiting below. A faint hint of manure permeated the scene. There was still hope.

Robert waited for me at the top of the stairway and bid me inside, and by the time I entered Edith was waiting by the door of their seed room. Bundles of grain hung from above, all neatly tied and labeled. Below the sheaves of grain was a workstation, complete with a variety of storage containers, labels, and tools. The entire scene resembled a photo shoot for a harvest celebration, but Edith's previous skills in managing a lab were on display, too. She began pulling out container after container of different kinds of seeds, with everything carefully labeled, describing which ones needed to be replanted every year and which ones could be planted during alternate years or even a bit less frequently, since different kinds of seeds maintain their viability for varying amounts of time.

Then she took down a sheaf of her pride and joy, Burgeis spelt, explaining that spelt was coming back into favor among local farmers, bakers, and consumers. Some of them wanted to tap back into the disappearing agricultural traditions while others were interested in new market opportunities and more diversified farm operations. Consumers, on the other hand, were calling not just for local and organic products but also for more digestible grains, including gluten-free options. The gluten in spelt has a molecular composition more fragile and water-soluble than the gluten in modern wheat; it's broken down by heat and by mixing, and it also has a higher fiber content. This combination of factors makes spelt easier to digest than wheat.

Edith's smile waned as she continued, and she shook her head in dismay. Just when people were finally beginning to recognize the value of these old grains and how well they fit this landscape, culture, and even tourism opportunities, she lamented, monocultures and pesticides threatened it all.

Having started their seedsaving focused on vegetables, herbs, and fruits, Edith and Robert realized that there was a lack of focus in the area on collecting and saving heritage grains. So in 2000 they began trying to find sources for seeds of and information on varieties of grains once grown in the Vinschgau. They decided not to focus on rye varieties since rye pollen can travel such long distances, meaning that cross-pollination would be a constant challenge for them. The other grains proved a bit simpler. Local farmers could still remember the names of old spelt varieties and even had some seeds, whereas the Bernhards had very little luck in finding old barley varieties in the local area, even though barley is another grain that adapted very well to the Vinschgau's soil and climate. Barley was an important grain for soups and porridges; when roasted, it was even used as a coffee substitute — for the taste, that is, not the caffeine hit. Farmers also used it for chicken food, and it was known for its many healing capacities, including its help in treating digestive ailments.

Edith and Robert had assembled an extraordinary living library — seeds collected, cataloged, stored, and shared. As part of a small but growing network of seedsavers, they would travel to various seed swaps and conferences, where their display table was always inundated and their seeds tended to disappear almost as soon as the events began. In addition to their seed room, they had another storage facility next door, with pounds upon pounds of stored grains ready both for eating and planting. Robert took me to the adjacent storage area, where we cleared off the weighted-down lid of an intricately carved grain trunk and opened it up. Waist-high and approximately 3 feet wide and 10 feet long (1×3 m), it was full of different grains. Every farmhouse used to have at least one of those old grain trunks to sustain them between harvests.

"Do people know what a treasure you have here in your house?" I asked Robert.

"Not yet," he said, with a twinkle forming in his eye and an almost mischievous grin forming on his face. "But we have a surprise coming for the politicians and their lobbies." He carefully lowered the heavy wooden lid, its hinges creaking, and we put the weights back on top. He called Edith to bring some of her panels to the Stube.

I wasn't quite sure what he meant by "panels," but I followed Robert back through the simple foyer and through the door to their Stube. Every house in the South Tirol has its central room, the Stube, the center of the daily orbits of family and guests. Robert motioned for me to take a seat at the table, familiarly placed in the *Gottesecke*, God's corner, which was traditionally adorned with a crucifix and some token grains as appreciation for the previous year's harvest. Never had I been invited into a house in which the decorative assortment of grains hanging off the crucifix made so much sense.

Robert poured me a glass of Hollundersaft, a drink made with water and the sweetened syrup of elderberry blossoms, and a few minutes later Edith appeared with a large box containing about a dozen wood-framed panels. She set it beside the table and pulled out several of them to show me what she'd created. Each thick wooden frame contained several stems of grain with perfect seedheads, carefully aligned in artistic fashion, complemented by a description of the grain variety represented in the frame. The panels were stunning — the simplicity of the frames offset the natural beauty of each plant. I could see the sturdiness of the stems, the geometric alignment of the seeds along the grain head, the distinctive character of the seeds and their hulls — every variety suddenly had its own artistic grace and beauty.

"How many of these panels do you have?" I asked.

A smile swept across her face. "One hundred," she replied. She explained that the panels would all be part of a traveling exhibit of the history of grain cultivation in the Vinschgau and beyond. It would be an educational tool for helping people not only to understand their local history but also to see what was at risk in the South Tirol with the influx of monocultures, pesticides, and the patenting of life.

Edith and Robert had financed it all on their own. The politicians and lobbyists weren't interested in financing a project that would lead to questions about where Big Apple and its cronies were headed — and the Malser Haide was their ultimate goal.

Robert shook his head in frustration. "The environmental groups, like ours, we're fighting for a healthy landscape, and we're the unreliable voters, the ones the politicians can't count on, so they try to starve us out financially."

Robert and Edith were about to put that old saying to the test. They had the seed. Now they were going to have their say.

CHAPTER 6

Seduction

*L*and grabbing. At first I thought that he'd uttered a word in German, but then I realized just how universal both the word and the reality had become: It was happening in Mals. And nobody knows the nitty-gritty of a town's business better than a veterinarian with four wheels and a ticket to step onto the land and into the lives of the people who steward the bulk of a town's landscape.

The rest of Peter Gasser's point was in cadenced, regimented high German — an echo of the march that he saw coming up the valley: "*Das Landschaftsbild wird zerstört*" — the landscape is going to be destroyed — he said, "through concrete posts, plastic nets, chain-link fence. Trees have to be removed because trees make shade. Everything is unproductive. Everything has to go. Then a big fence has to be made so that the deer can't get in. And then come the concrete posts and plastic nets — and then comes the poison."

He shook his head and leaned over from the couch with a bottle tipped toward my glass, and he filled the silence for a moment with the quick gurgle and splash of the wine. Then he picked up his half-empty glass and peered into it before looking up with what should have been an expression of melancholy to go with the deep red wine. Instead I saw a face that had turned resolute, with a glint of mischief.

"There are two possibilities," he continued. "Either we just watch how the land is sold, how the land is destroyed, and how the poison is sprayed everywhere . . . or we somehow set ourselves in motion to do something."

The wineglass almost looked out of place in his thick fingers until he cradled its basin in his callused palm and gave his wine a quick swirl.

A Precautionary Tale

"If we just watch and don't do anything, then in twenty years we will no longer be the lords of our own village. We'll be bought out."

In a town that straddles the borders of three countries, the influx of people and ideas is likely to create a people who are comfortable thinking outside of their cultural norms. And so it is with the Malsers, who have a reputation for being, as Peter describes it, *relativ eigenartig*, or "somewhat idiosyncratic." Were they not eigenartig, the Malsers never would have begun to question what most other South Tiroleans had accepted — the influx of apples and everything else that came with them: money, power, influence, and a constant nod to the status quo.

However, not only did the Malsers question what was happening, but they also took it one step further: They decided to do something about it, in unusually creative ways.

As it turned out, Mals had a collection of people like Peter Gasser. Ordinary citizens, not practiced in politics or particularly polished in activism, they were nonetheless *Querdenkers*, a term that translates into "diagonal thinkers" or "cross thinkers" — people who think in a different direction, outside of the box. Where they come together is where an uprising starts, although sometimes even a beginning has a long history.

For thirty years Peter had been a member of the Umweltschutzgruppe Vinschgau (USGV), the Environmental Protection Group of the Vinschgau. The USGV had focused on issues such as biodiversity research and education, renewable energy, green transportation, and development pressures in sensitive ecosystems. All the while, Peter felt like something bigger was brewing, something that threatened the town in which he'd spent his entire life: the looming looting of his town's past and its future, all in one swift monocultural heist. He knew that his clients — mountain farmers who were scraping by in a peak-and-valley economy that mirrored their tended terrain — would be the first to throw their hands up, first in disgust but then, if they were ground down enough, later in surrender.

Peter didn't know what to do about it, but he had mentioned his concerns to Ulrich Veith soon after he was elected mayor in 2009, hoping the young new mayor might have a fresh perspective on what could be done to thwart the takeover. They were in sync on their concerns, but neither had an immediate strategy. And back then they were dealing with creep rather than crisis. Perceived threats are much harder to confront in the policy world than are dire realities.

The clarion call came soon thereafter, however, when Günther Wallnöfer called them both with the news that his first cutting of hay in 2010 had tested positive for pesticide residues, and he was going to have to dispose of it and have the summer's next two cuttings tested.

It was time to act. Peter, Ulrich, Günther, and any other allies they could muster would have to develop a strategy as they went. There were no real models. As far as they could tell, they were in unprecedented legal terrain, without a map. But at least they were on home turf.

Few people within a farming community get such a clear cross section of the daily realities of their town as the local veterinarian. Out on every kind of thoroughfare at all hours of day and night and invited into the shadowed crannies of a farm in some of the farmer's darkest hours, a large-animal vet brokers the covenant between human and beast. In the process the vet takes a constant pulse of farmer well-being and gathers a more complete picture of the local landscape than almost anyone else in the community. And the best way to get a taste of that life is to ride shotgun with him and see him in action with his clients — both the four-legged and the two-legged types.

I first met Peter in 2015 when Douglas Gayeton, Michael de Rachewiltz, and I were working our way through the Mals directory of Querdenkers, speeding from place to place, meeting the cast of characters who'd put Mals on the global map as a hot spot for ordinary citizens taking on giants in order to control their own destiny and pass on a better world to their children and grandchildren. The story was a perfect fit for Douglas, a multimedia artist and cofounder of the Lexicon of Sustainability who is always in search of David-and-Goliath stories. Michael de Rachewiltz, a friend of three decades from Brunnenburg Castle and Agricultural Museum, was intrigued by this history in the making and was kind enough to be our local networker, translator, and driver.

We were in pursuit of Peter while he was on his morning rounds, trying to catch up with him between appointments. As we got closer to Mals and tried to pinpoint a meeting time and location, it became a game of cat and mouse, but with cell phones. We'd get a time and location estimate and then a return call. He would be delayed. Call back in ten minutes. But by that time, he was in a barn or technologically incapacitated with an arm inside a cow, unable to answer. Finally we ended up at a café in Burgeis, the wrong one at first, it turned out, but we walked up in the direction of Edith and Robert's house and saw our destination. As soon as we entered, we could identify the man whose voice at the bar matched the deep dialect we'd heard on the phone.

Tall and broad-shouldered, Peter Gasser is virtually ubiquitous in the town of Mals, darting in and out of cafés for quick shots of caffeine between visiting the barns and fields of the surrounding villages in his jeep. We'd finally caught up with him in one of his favorite cappuccino stations not far from one of his usual regular stops — the barn that housed the herd owned by the Marienberg Abbey.

Peter's physical presence commands attention even without the green scrubs and big rubber boots that he dons for each farm visit. His thick mountain dialect, delivered in a gravelly baritone voice, blends seamlessly into the earthiness of stone, timbers, and muck found in hillside barns, while it has to be softened inside the cafés, where he catches snippets of the local news and checks his phone for emergencies and appointment changes.

His days are full, and the nights hold no guarantee of rest. No matter the venue, he keeps a close eye on the time, his day segmented by next stops. An engaging conversationalist, Peter is given to intense analysis more than relaxed contemplation. When considering a question, he tends to lower his head slightly and knit his brows for a fraction of a second before offering what is certain to be a pragmatic and unembellished diagnosis. If the topic is particularly complex, he is likely to lift up his sunglasses a bit and nestle them more securely in his tussled wavy hair before firing off a series of concise points in response.

Born and raised in Mals, he has come to know the region's landmarks, characters, animals, and stories in ways that stretch far beyond his five decades. He understands how they all fit together like interlocking puzzle pieces. Caring for livestock involves multiple forms of listening: While a stethoscope is a window into a cow's health, the farmer's observations are just as important to the diagnosis. By the time it's all over, the cow's story is often but a subplot within a much larger narrative. If anyone in Mals has a solid grasp of what's ailing farmers as well as their animals, it's Peter, so his diagnosis of land grabbing carries weight.

It wasn't just the insights gleaned from his daily treks from farm to farm, village to village, that kept Peter informed. Through USGV, he had long tracked issues related to land use, wildlife, and biodiversity throughout the valley. His combined understanding of animal and environmental health would prove critical to addressing not just Günther's dilemma but also a much bigger concern: who controlled the destiny of Mals.

Peter recounted the "monocultural wave" that rose up through the valley. For about two decades there had been several orchards in Mals, but they never created any issues or tensions in the community. The town felt pristine in comparison with the towns farther down the valley. In fact, his wife, Margit, had grown up in Schlanders, a town about 14 miles (23 km) away in the lower Vinschgau that is inundated in apples. When they married in 1993, she kept remarking how liberating and healthy it was to live in Mals where she could savor a varied landscape and not be surrounded by the constant spraying of pesticides.

However, something changed and those few orchards in Mals shifted from an anomaly to a harbinger. With the dawning of the twenty-first century, the mythical temptation of the apple conspired with the sweet taste of wealth — and seemingly overnight several more orchards appeared. While climate change played a role, Peter described how a heated apple economy accelerated the influx of orchards. Some local farmers were tempted by the fact that they could make four or five times as much money by growing apples as they could raising livestock and some other crops; however, it was the farmers in the lower reaches of the valley and elsewhere in the South Tirol who created a situation ripe for land grabbing.

Farmers in the lower Vinschgau and all the way to Bozen had filled virtually every available hillside and hollow with apples and other fruits, to the point that there was almost no additional land for planting or purchase. If a farmer could find an available parcel in those other areas, it would cost about 1 million euros (over $1 million) for a hectare (2.47 acres) in comparison with 70,000 to 80,000 euros in Mals and surrounding towns. Suddenly the buying spree was on, and within a few short years land prices in the town jumped to about five times their previous level, bumping up the value of a hectare in Mals to 300,000 to 400,000 euros.

While those prices seem astronomical and utterly unaffordable to anyone running a farm, the apple farmers down below were netting 30,000 to 40,000 euros per year on a single hectare — sometimes more, depending on varieties, quality, and the international markets. With such high net earnings and no obligation among farmers to pay any income tax — only a minimal parcel fee — apple farmers from outside were able to come into Mals and buy land at what was, for them, a bargain. The fast and furious land speculation drove prices up quickly.

Apple farmers seemed to have every advantage available over the traditional farmers in Mals. Not only were their incomes four or five times greater than the livestock farmers', but they didn't have to milk twice a day, 365 days a year. They even had several months in which there was little to no work to do in the orchards. One other key factor did not escape Peter's keen reckoning: The apple industry was just that. Farms become factories, and tasks became perfunctory. The apple industry was ripe for less skilled laborers, most of whom were being hired on the cheap to come in for a three- or four-week harvest period, whereas livestock farms required more sophisticated laborers for longer periods of time. However, with meager earnings, livestock farmers continued to function as they had for millennia — with the support of extended family and neighbors who would pitch in at critical times. "They continue to think that they are powerful and strong," Peter noted, "but they're weak when they have to survive in these international markets.

"Still," he added, perking up, "the young farmers in our town amaze me. They say they want to be livestock farmers — they don't want to grow apples. They want to continue to milk cows and send their animals up to the high pastures in summer, growing grains and other crops on a small scale."

That those young farmers and their parents remain so committed to the traditional farming of the region would strike any outsider as almost masochistic, but it makes sense to Peter. "Think about it," he said. "Farmers and animals have existed so closely together in this region for four or five thousand years, there's a bond there that isn't easily broken. For thousands of years, people lived in close proximity with goats, sheep, pigs, and cattle — at times in their houses but mostly underneath or directly beside their houses. That was the traditional architecture, the traditional way of life."

It's not all hopeless, though, he insisted, and he offered the Querdenker perspective. "Despite what you hear from the politicians and lobbyists in Bozen, agriculture itself doesn't play that big of a role in our economy. Fruit, wine, livestock, and wood products — combined, they are only about 4 percent of the South Tirolean economy. Tourism is 25 percent, and it depends upon a healthy, beautiful, and open landscape. Tourism doesn't benefit from having tourists sit at their hotel breakfast table beside the window, only to have pesticides drifting in." It wouldn't be long before those same politicians and lobbyists wished that there wasn't a veterinarian who was just as attentive to economic realities as he was to what was happening to livestock and their landscape.

At first Peter, Ulrich, and Günther all hoped for some common ground between fruit growers and the organic and livestock farmers in town. That common ground had a name: buffer zones. Everyone hoped that there might be a way to establish specified safe distances between orchards and other agricultural parcels, along with clear protocols of when and how orchardists should spray. With the prevailing Vinschgerwind showing its force by sculpting trees and forcing heavy-laden grain crops to bow prostrate, farmers had to agree on ways that spraying could be limited to still periods when the risk of drift would be minimized.

The USGV worked with organic farmers, organic farming associations, the South Tirolean Farmers' Association (Südtiroler Bauernbund, or SBB), the Laimburg Research Center, politicians, and others to convene and discuss different options through a series of meetings in the summer and fall of 2010. All three of Günther's hay cuttings that summer had tested positive for multiple pesticides, and the USGV decided to sample other areas for pesticide residues to gather data on the degree to which drift was already impacting the town.

While the level of alarm was high among organic farmers, livestock farmers, and grain growers, everyone also recognized that the issue could quickly lead to intense polarization among neighbors, not a pleasant scenario in a town of 5,300 inhabitants. It didn't make sense to create a toxic social atmosphere that would distract from dealing with the real toxins under discussion.

In general, almost everyone agreed, at least in public discourse, that farmers could manage their land in whatever ways they saw fit — as long as other neighboring farmers weren't negatively impacted. However, as discussions progressed, it became harder and harder for some participants to see how side-by-side coexistence could ever really work in a town with such frequent winds and small parcel sizes. And many Malsers began to wonder whether compromise was, in the long run, the same as surrender.

The chill of late-summer nights began to seep into daylight hours as the sun's arc fell lower, stretching the shadows of surrounding mountains farther and farther across the valley floor. Each village in Mals threw its last summer fling on different weekend days in September, celebrating the return of the cattle back to their home farms for the winter. Coaxed on by their respective farm families, rowdy cows trundled down stony paths from their designated *Almen*, or high pastures, finally bursting into the narrow village streets with a mix of certainty and fear. Most of them knew exactly where to go, but a few bovines always decide that it's their last chance to assert their independence before giving up long summer days of free-spirited grazing for winter stalls and tight barnyards. So they do, and neighbors pitch in as necessary with woots and calls, amplified at times by the beverages being poured from kegs and bottles in the makeshift concession areas.

The smell of manure-splattered streets mingles with wafts of sausage, french fries, and cigarette smoke. South Tiroleans begin to get serious about the party when the cows come home. Once the four-legged critters are all in their respective barns, the real party begins and continues well into the night while the animals settle back into their on-farm routines.

It was a seasonal pattern that stretched back for millennia, ingrained into humans and livestock alike. When the cows come home, so do the cheeses, butter, and other cured items crafted in the mountains over the course of the summer. The bright yellow butters and creamy, aromatic cheeses produced high in the mountains are all distinctive — every alm has different grasses, legumes, herbs, and molds. Even the mineral content of the waters varies, and of course each person crafting the various dairy products has different methods, cultures, and tastes. Some of the milk is transported down to central creameries for processing, with mountain milk bringing a premium price for the farmers, but the pride of the region isn't in the commodities as much as it is in the individual character of the products made in each different location.

Turn any direction in Mals and look up, and somewhere above you is likely to be a summer Alpine pasture tucked up between tree line and the shifting snow line, a place inhabited by people and animals reliant upon each other to fulfill a covenant established thousands of years ago. It's an unspoken promise but one that is nonetheless silently renewed and codified into culture and calendar. To give up that covenant would be to cast aside culture, but the economic pressures continued to escalate, while the work and long hours never got easier. The question of whether livestock agriculture stood any chance of surviving the encroachment of Big Apple was a question that would simmer in the background that winter, rattling quietly like a cast-iron pot capped confidently with a heavy lid — with an occasional splatter and hiss signaling when things got too hot.

Farming in Mals is an annual redaction — reflecting on what the past season brought and transforming those lessons into what will work best for the coming year — and winter is the peak season of that redaction. Families spend their time huddled around their masonry stoves, and friends meet in bars and cafés to while away dark hours and usher in brightly lit holidays. People trade stories, compare notes, and hash out differences of opinion. Throughout it all, farmers glance back, albeit with an eye toward the future.

If 2010 was the initial wake-up call in town, 2011 would be the year of collective awakening, spurred on by a few early risers. And the ringleader of these "woke" Querdenkers was Alexander Agethle. A dairy farmer and cheesemaker, Alexander's motto is a phrase borrowed from a friend: *Ohne Kultur kein Käse.* Without culture, no cheese!

Of course, the opposite might also be true if Big Apple got the upper hand in Mals.

A Precautionary Tale

Alexander Agethle grew up in the tiny village of Schleis, a puzzled assemblage of house and barns clustered around the village church, all tucked tightly into a mountainside halfway between Burgeis and Laatsch. Situated alongside a fast-flowing mountain brook that surges down a cleft in the mountainside, lending its gurgle-and-roar oscillation to the aural backdrop of village life, Schleis sits almost out of eyesight from the main road through the Vinschgau. Barely more than a blink of the eye in the age of fast-moving autos, the village quietly harbors what was and what matters still, at least to the Malsers.

About half a mile west of the main two-lane highway through the Vinschgau, Schleis is denoted only by a single blue-and-white arrow that directs drivers to bear sharply to the left. Most drivers don't take notice of the village, its tile roofs barely visible from the road, unless they are somehow compelled by curiosity to see what others might have missed. Halfway to the village, the rounded end of a World War II pillbox nudges out of the angled turf just below the road. With tufts of grass commandeering the turf on its bombproof roof and mosses and lichens gradually camouflaging its sloping sides, the bunker recedes further and further into the past. As if to add insult to its modern-day irrelevance, one of the newest orchards in the town took control of its commanding view, tauntingly surrounding it in militia-like formation.

The view from the pillbox tells the story: What had been a patchwork of square fields with hay, grains, cabbages, and root crops had turned into a chessboard. Smallholders were about to become pawns, unless they found a way to promote their interests and hold fast to their positions.

For Alexander, holding ground in what was looking to be a fast-paced game of winners and losers meant carrying on more than two centuries of tradition for his family. Nestled in the heart of the small village of just over one thousand inhabitants, his family's farm is typical of the smallholders in the village. While their fields are scattered around the outskirts of the village proper, all of the farm infrastructure, including the farmhouse, is packed into the already tight confines of the village. Alexander's barn, outbuildings, and house all seem to blend together with the smooth flow of plastered walls and interlocking timbers.

The cheese facility and the hay barn both abut the village's meandering main thoroughfare, their earth-tone plaster walls offset by decorative white trim and the dark brown of weatherworn doors and windows. A steep driveway bisects the two buildings with a zig and a zag that offer a semblance of visual privacy. However, privacy doesn't pay the bills — visitors do, and it doesn't matter if they speak German, Italian, or anything else. Cheese is spoken there, and it's universal.

Whether informed or unsuspecting, visitors are lured by the farm's modern logo, a nearly abstract *H* transformed into a cow with the addition of a simple dot for a head: *Hofkäserei Englhorn* — or, if you're more Mediterranean-inclined, *Caseificio Englhorn*. Either way, the point of the name is that Englhorn is a farmstead creamery, and the Agethle family has turned a tradition into a market.

Once you zig, then zag, the tight-knit beauty of Englhorn opens up. Customers to the left; cows to the right. That is to say, if you hang around long enough, you'll see customers ducking into the cheese shop on the left and cows entering and exiting the dairy barn on the right, likely being led (on a really good day) or prodded (on an ordinary day) by Alexander's children. His parents offer backup, as needed, stepping out of the medieval-era house or the surrounding gardens to remind the cows that the kids have reinforcements if any bovine thinks there's an opportunity for mischief.

Englhorn is a tightly managed operation, even amid the vagaries of weather, animal health, and tricky markets. A welcoming air of levity permeates the farm operation, with Alexander's wife, Sonja, and his mother handling most of the direct sales while Alexander manages the bigger sales and operates the farm machinery. Sonja has a presence all her own. Her tousled curls impart a sense of a person on the move, with a moment here and there to sweep her hair back before taking on the next task, and, indeed, she runs between children, the cheese shop, and her job as a whole foods cook in her family's hotel in Mals, carrying her broad smile all the while. Her lilting greeting whenever anyone comes for a visit or a purchase sets the tone for high-spirited banter that is slowed only when the cheese samples appear and customers' replies turn into guttural affirmations, inevitably punctuated by a string of superlatives from across the European continent.

Alexander matches Sonja's charm with a boyish smile embedded into sharp-cut facial features that are often mellowed with a 24/7 five-o'clock shadow (that's what happens when you're on the clock at five on both ends of the day) that seasonally morphs into a beard or goatee. His piercing eyes are alert to every movement happening in the busy courtyard of their farm complex. Children dart in and out, mixing chores and play, while customers duck in even as cows are being herded out. All of the hubbub swirls around the one place where chaos is banned, the cheesemaking facility. Inside, Maximilian, the cheesemaker, controls everything he can: time, temperature, pH, microorganisms, and casual visitors.

No culture, no cheese is true enough, but financing such an operation matters, too. A diversified farm the size of Englhorn is doomed in today's globalized markets unless it can produce what gets lost in those markets. Like Günther, who opted to tap into the premiums offered by the organic dairy markets, Alexander and Sonja had to find a way to capitalize upon their small herd of traditional cattle. Instead of finding a niche, they built one . . . paid for by a currency they created themselves. First, however, they had to build a financial model that others would trust.

With 12 milk cows, 25 acres (10 ha) of fields, and the vestiges of a medieval farm complex that had been in Alexander's family for more than 200 years, the Agethles knew that economic survival depended upon a blend of creativity and community support. They decided that their best option was to build a cheesemaking facility and turn their 132,000 pounds (60,000 kg) of milk into a high-quality cheese. In the face of daunting construction costs, they combined their own funds with a loan from an ethical lender and then sought out the additional balance needed – 180,000 euros (over $200,000 at the time) – from supporters.

After vetting their idea through some of the most feared bureaucrats in the country, the Italian tax authorities, they got the go-ahead to create a ten-year "Englhorn currency," complete with cow-cameos on the so-called *Englhörner*, the bills that they offered in several denominations. One Englhörner was valued at a kilogram of cheese, priced at about 23 euros per kilogram. The idea was to presell a certain percentage of their cheese for the first ten years of production, offering a minimum investment of 500 euros and then different levels above that amount. By the time all was said and done, they raised the entire 180,000 euros from 167 investors. Each January the investors are given their Englhörner Gutscheine, or Englhorn bills, along with an update of news from the farm, and they can swap their fancy notes for cheese not only at the farm but also at two organic food stores in the nearby cities of Meran and Bozen.

The Agethle family encountered one unexpected issue in the investment phase of the project. Several people wanted to invest more than 1,000 euros in the project but felt sure that they could never eat that much cheese. Alexander and Sonja pondered the dilemma and then came up with an intriguing solution that they also had to run by the tax authorities. Sonja's family runs the Hotel Greif in Mals, a small hotel in the middle of town renowned for its superb and health-oriented fare. They set up a deal in which Englhorn investors could use their currency to pay for their vacations and meals at Hotel Greif; the hotel would, in turn, purchase its cheeses from Englhorn using the currency given to them by the investors.

They replicated that model with a high-end restaurant in Munich, five hours away, where investors can either pick up or eat their Englhorn cheese at the restaurant. Most of the investors were from the Vinschgau and South Tirol, while others came from German-speaking areas of the Alps and even as far away as France. Alexander and Sonja had transformed not only culture into cheese but also money into relationships, relationships that would grow with their business and put them on the map throughout Europe.

But with the accelerated march of Big Apple in their direction, they risked being wiped off the map in fewer years than it had taken to claim their position. When they heard of Günther's predicament, worry turned to fear. Ninety-eight percent of their cattle feed was hay and grass; the other 2 percent was supplemental grain to keep the milkers in good condition. If their fields were to be surrounded by apples, their whole system would collapse — their landscape, herd, customers, and financial model were all doomed. Once again, the coming turf battle was all too literal: It was about hay.

"*Heu hat für mich, für diesem Betrieb ein absolut grundlagen Bedeutung,*" Alexander explained: Hay has for me, for this business, an absolutely fundamental meaning. Healthy humans depend upon healthy animals for milk and meat, and those animals are reliant upon the keystone of Mals's agriculture, healthy hay.

Alexander could summarize the dilemma in one sentence: "The cow is the filter between humans and their environment." Of course, there was a caveat: The cow has limits, not only as to how much it can filter when it comes to toxins, but also as to how much it can withstand before its own health is compromised. Alexander believed that a healthy local economy was dependent upon a healthy landscape, and Big Apple threatened all of it. His goal had long been to leave the land in at least as good a state as it was when he inherited it, but he and many of his fellow farmers in Mals were clear on the legacy left by a conventional apple grower: They would leave behind an *Apfelwüste*, an apple desert, filled with toxins and shortsighted dreams.

Big Apple even posed an existential question for Alexander: Was the fruit it produced actually food, or was it just an industrial product? The question mattered because of Italian tax policy. When the goal of farming is to export a product for the highest financial return, with minimal concern for human or environmental health, much less the future of farming in an area — should it still be rewarded with tax breaks?

Alexander appreciated the intent of the Italian tax policy to support the production of food at a reasonable cost by not requiring farmers to pay income tax on their food sales. However, like Peter Gasser, he questioned the wisdom of creating a virtually tax-free economic model that wreaked havoc on soil, plants, and the landscape — leaving the rest of society to pick up the costs of overseeing pesticide production, distribution, and use and addressing its impacts. Not only did that tax system give the chemical-intensive farmers the economic capacity to push out farmers like Alexander and Günther, but the near-certainty of pesticide drift meant that organic farmers, livestock producers, and grain growers were in peril. Paradise was under siege.

Beware the moment when Querdenkers begin to align. They are masters of parody, and parody would soon be Paradise's closest ally.

Today, temptation by apple is nearly as common a theme in regional tourist brochures as it is in South Tirolean churches. The allure is much the same — there are just more clothes involved in the modern version. In the areas of the South Tirol where the seduction has played out in full and orchards dominate, tourists are enticed to visit during blossom and harvesttimes. When apples are all that's left, farmers and the tourist industry both bank on what they've got to sell.

Alexander and a group of friends had long discussed the intensification of monocultures in the Vinschgau, and they realized in 2011 that it was time to turn their concerns into action. Josef Thurner, a farmer and town spokesperson; Jürgen Wallnöfer, an architect; Armin Bernhart, an educational scientist; and Konrad Messner, the cultural provocateur and guesthouse owner from Plawenn, joined forces with Alexander to jumpstart the dialogue.

An inventive lot, with a self-described penchant for cheekiness, they decided to launch an initiative called Adam & Epfl – *Epfl* being the dialect word for "apple," with a certain similarity in pronunciation to *Eva*, the German version of Eve. They chose a painting by the famous German artist Lucas Cranach from the 1500s to represent the predicament in the Upper Vinschgau: A serpent in a tree coaxes unwitting victims to partake of the tempting fruit in a quest for promises of a better life. It was the motif for what was to become a movement.

As far as Alexander and his friends were concerned, taking the apple wasn't predestined. It warranted discussion and perhaps even a bit of mischief in the long run. But the first task was to get people to *mitreden*, to talk with one another, and spring was the time to do it, before farmers got busy and temptations and the sound of yet more concrete posts being driven into the ground echoed throughout the valley.

On March 19, 2011, Adam & Epfl convened an information session for citizens to discuss a single question: "To what end is intensive fruit production seducing the Upper Vinschgau?" It was a question that had been discussed among families and friends, but it was the first time that a public forum had been organized to consider the creeping seduction. Held in the Mals Kulturhaus, a spacious cultural center located in the middle of town, the event drew a full house, surprising even Alexander and his fellow organizers.

The provocateurs knew that the topic could quickly polarize their community, so they invited a moderator, Heidi Kessler, to help foster some balance in the presentation. In the end, not everyone was satisfied with the success of how the session was moderated. Representatives of the fruit industry made it clear that apples were a profitable crop that could be produced in ways that didn't negatively impact the environment, and they reinforced the idea that apple farmers could be good neighbors. Apples offered an economic opportunity whose time had come.

The audience, however, seemed to be especially appreciative of the perspective offered by Alexander, who eloquently advanced the position against further expansion into the Upper Vinschgau. He spoke of the trade-offs Mals was facing in yielding to the temptations of Big Apple, and he made it clear that the apple farmers from the lower reaches of the valley were laying the groundwork for moving in by setting up sprinkler irrigation networks in the coveted Malser Haide and elsewhere. The concrete posts, trellised trees, and hail nets were not far behind.

But it was Alexander's expression of a vision for a town that wholeheartedly embraced and supported sustainability that won the audience over: It was a positive vision of cultivating Paradise, in lieu of succumbing to the seduction of easily won wealth, with long-term consequences. Any return on investment in Big Apple meant no possibility of return to the riches already in hand. Alexander articulated the fact that Mals had something different to offer its inhabitants and tourists, something already lost by much of the rest of the region: a diverse and beautiful landscape, filled with traditional farms as well as a growing organic sector and burgeoning farm-to-plate initiatives. The local enterprises like his were still small in number and size, but he asserted that the opportunities were there to be seized.

Some citizens of Mals believed that if they caved to the temptation of Big Apple, they would give up their collective birthright, with no chance of reclaiming it. Others felt that it was entirely up to farmers to determine what to do on their land, and it was no one else's business what they chose to produce or how they produced it. With winners and losers becoming all the more apparent, it was a question of public trust and whom to trust in protecting it. Nonetheless, Alexander and his compatriots left feeling like a door had been opened. In Alexander's view, "The goal of the discussion was to make the topic public, and we definitely succeeded. The discussion showed us that there is certainly room for different opinions."[1] Just as some farmers didn't want their organic operations jeopardized by pesticide drift, other farmers felt that they had the right to pursue the lucrative path of conventional apple production that thousands of other farmers were already benefiting from in other parts of the South Tirol. Different ecological approaches yielded different economic perspectives.

Over the coming weeks, Adam & Epfl's fecundity became apparent. A diverse array of citizens began to gather around the idea of *Paradies*

Obervinschgau, the Paradise of the Upper Vinschgau: from mayor to forester to biology teacher to university student to veterinarian to seedsaver and organic farmer, an alliance of Querdenkers was beginning to form. It was yet to be seen if Mals itself might be a town of Querdenkers — perhaps even a bastion of independence with the creativity and fortitude to take on powers much bigger than their covey of just over five thousand people. Even though hay was the impetus for a fomenting rebellion, pitchforks weren't the first line of defense. Creative education and advocacy would have to suffice.

Following the March meeting, the growing alliance of eclectic activists met half a dozen more times. They identified four key points of common interest: *Gesundheit, Vielfalt, Regionales Wirtschaften*, and *Existenzsicherung*. Health, diversity, a regional economy, and a secure future. It was a positive vision, one that contrasted dramatically with the hidden costs of biting into Big Apple, with its taste for toxins, monocultures, and vacillating international markets. Now that they had brought the issues out into the daylight, it was time to bring the discussion into the streets. The group organized an Action Day in June, filling the centuries-old streets of Mals with a five different conversation stations around the edges of the town center.

The first station, set up at a popular café in the heart of the old village, featured the motif of *Paradeis Obervinschgau*. Adam & Epfl came into its own that day as a *Bürgerinitiative*, a citizens' initiative. The gathering captured passersby who might never have attended a meeting featuring either an assemblage of eclectic personalities or politicians, and innocent queries turned into spontaneous opportunities to mitreden, to talk, with one another about everyone's vision for the future of the town. In the courtyard behind the library, representatives from health and environmental organizations teamed together with organic farmers to discuss the health impact of different forms of agriculture at the second station. Organizers set up the third station focused on diversity amid the bustle of the town hall, featuring an exhibit of grain varieties from the Bernhards' collection, information from regional seedsavers, a photo exhibition, and samples of international foods, as well as agricultural resources provided by the township. Participants then moved on to yet a historic weaving mill where a fourth station was dedicated to supporting local economies. At the last station, they encountered the looming question of how farmers might secure their existence and pass on the age-old farming traditions that had formed the fabric of Paradeis Obervinschgau. Hosted by farmers who represented the spectrum of possible philosophies and methods — ranging between organic and conventional — the gathering spot offered a sampling of not just food but also possibilities, and a spirit of hope.

Adam & Epfl had found a way to avoid doomsday scenarios and polarizing rhetoric. Opting to promote a vision rather than denigrate viewpoints different from their own, they set the stage for dialogue instead of diatribe. That foundational approach would matter — and it would soon be tested. A lot of testing was about to happen.

CHAPTER 7

Organic Uprising

"*Teilweise gehört das Futter auf den Sondermüll.*" In part, this feed belongs with the hazardous waste.

With yet another full house packed into the Mals Kulturhaus, it was as if an electric shock jumped from one person to another in the elbow-to-elbow audience the night of November 3, 2011. Had the statement come from any local layperson weighing in on the supposed dangers of pesticides, it would have seemed mere conjecture, and heads would have shaken amid muffled murmurs and a few louder curses eking out in hard-hewn dialect.

But the environmental group USGV had played their hand carefully. During the summer they'd sent the grass samples that they had collected from ten hay fields adjacent to orchards in the Upper Vinschgau to be tested and reviewed by Irene Witte, an internationally renowned toxicologist from the University of Oldenburg in Germany.

They had Günther's back. They had noticed the orchards that had appeared the year before, flanking his hayfields, along with others cropping up in and around Mals. With approximately 150 acres (60 ha) shifting to intensive fruit production in the Upper Vinschgau each year, Peter Gasser and his USGV colleagues knew precisely what was coming their way, and the only way to take a stand was to begin collecting and presenting empirical data.

Deciding who should review and present that data was paramount, so they selected Witte, a researcher who had helped transform the field of toxicology in ways that paralleled the paradigm-bending work of

Rachel Carson. In fact, Witte was awarded the Rachel Carson Medal for her pioneering research into the problematic effects of combined doses of chemicals, including even small doses of pesticides, and their relationship not only to traditional understandings of disease but also to the emerging field of genotoxicity, which explores how chemicals can mutate genes in cancer-causing ways.[1]

Together with two of the regional organic associations, Bioland and the Bund Alternativer Anbauer (BAA), the USGV billed the forum in a way that reminded Malsers of how fragile Paradise can be: *Wie belastet sind unsere Wiesen? Analyseergebnisse von Heuproben im Vinschgau* — How Polluted Are Our Meadows? Analysis Results from Hay Testing in the Vinschgau. Although every citizen in Mals wouldn't agree on the future of agriculture in Mals, virtually everyone recognized hay meadows to be the keystone of the valley's traditional agriculture. Any threat to the health and viability of those meadows was a threat to their way of life and their economic well-being, particularly as it related to tourism.

The results were chilling. Of the ten samples taken, all had pesticide residues and most contained five or more substances, including some samples of chlorpyriphos, a particularly toxic pesticide that is under serious scrutiny worldwide. Fungicides and insecticides such as copper, captan, and dithiocarbamates were detected, often at levels several times higher than allowed by law. Yet tests measuring levels of each pesticide only tell you if residues are present, Witte reminded the audience, and whether the substances have been applied within legal limits, not whether they are actually safe. Furthermore, she reiterated a central theme of her research over the years: "Some substances react chemically; the mixture is more poisonous than the sum of the individual effects."[2]

In an interview following the presentation, Witte and Peter Gasser both expressed their astonishment not only at the high concentration of pesticides found — well above legally acceptable levels — but also at the fact that some samples were contaminated with as many as ten different pesticides. It was the cocktails of multiple pesticides that worried Witte the most — and that focus had defined her career and, ultimately, her prestige, but not without earning her a fair share of detractors.[3] Whereas most scientists earned their degrees, promotions, and reputations by singling out and studying particular toxins, Witte had taken a more challenging but critical approach: She focused her work on the complexities of chemical cocktails and their impacts. Not only do these chemical combinations appear to contribute to diseases such as cancer, Parkinson's, and Alzheimer's, but they can also alter cells and even the human genome in ways that scientists are just beginning to unravel. Hence, the emerging discipline of genotoxicity — the study of the way chemicals damage genetic information within cells, causing them to die or mutate.

In Peter's view, the purpose of the conversations and the confrontations was to ensure that "the next twenty years don't continue just the same way that the previous twenty years had."[4] While the science of the health impacts was far from complete, the dashboard indicators were perfectly clear: Continued velocity in the same direction would result in both anticipated and unexpected impacts.

Sensing the growing discontent in Mals and its surroundings, the director of the Vinschgau apple growers' cooperative, Josef Wielander, showed up for the presentation and offered his conciliatory perspective on behalf of his apple farmers that everyone would prefer to have food products with no signs of pesticide residues. He also made the point that some farmers were the "black sheep" in the apple industry who created problems for others, and those few bad actors shouldn't be considered the norm. Apple farmers wanted to be good neighbors, and there was nothing to fear as they made their way into the upper reaches of the valley. In the end, he said, he believed that "every farmer must behave in such a way that the neighbors aren't harmed."[5]

While most of the audience seemed to appreciate Wielander's conciliatory approach, two distinct paths forward were nonetheless beginning to emerge among apple growers and apple opponents. Wielander and other conventional apple farmers thought the solution was to rethink and regulate buffers and spraying methods based on existing and forthcoming research.

For Peter and many of his colleagues, however, the experiences and data from 2011 led them to a much different conclusion: Coexistence might not be possible, and an outright ban of pesticides might be the only way to protect organic and traditional farmers, not to mention the health of the citizens and tourists who valued Mals for what it was . . . and for what it could be.

With each growing season for the past decade or so, the valley floor had begun to look more and more like a chessboard, and it was time to treat it as such. The Malsers decided to seize the advantage of making the first moves. Casual banter and commiserating would no longer suffice — it was time to get political.

Outranked, outnumbered, and with all resources coming out of their own pockets, the Malsers could barely even be classified as underdogs. Generally more averse to regional politics than well versed in such games, they nonetheless had two advantages: The match would be played out on their home turf, and it would be a long time before the opposition would take them seriously. And, of course, if you're new to a game, you just might play it a bit differently than anyone else.

***

About the only thing of less interest to Günther than making the traffic-filled three-hour drive to and from Bozen was getting into politics. However, after conferring with Uli — someone else who had never envisioned registering as a member of a political party, much less running for mayor — he decided to do what any rugged mountain farmer can do: find a path straight to the top.

Günther put in a call to the office of the governor of the province, Luis Durnwalder, and asked for an appointment to discuss his predicament. A gutsy move, it was nonetheless in keeping with a long-standing tradition in the Tirol. Tirolean mountain farmers had long had a direct line to their political sovereigns.

Mountain farmers, the Bergbauern, had been the fierce defenders of Tirolean culture and independence even before the Hapsburgs first took control of the area in the late fourteenth century. By no means submissive peasants, the Bergbauern gained even more notoriety and appreciation among the Hapsburg elite when they took on Napoleon's forces in the early 1800s. Given their allegiance and the imperial imperative of controlling the resources and passages of the Alps, the Tirolean mountain farmers earned a special relationship with the Hapsburg emperor, addressing him by the informal *Du* form for "you," in lieu of the formal *Sie* greeting.

Wearing that mantle, Günther and other farmers in modern-day South Tirol are quite comfortable speaking to authority. In fact, as the primary landholders and the keepers of the region's famous pastoral landscape, they often feel compelled to speak "truth" to power — although determining who holds the truth can also create problems of its own.

Günther and his fellow citizens would discover soon enough that truth and power can be awkward bedfellows in a democracy.

———

Günther set up an appointment with the governor for March 28, 2012. When the day finally came, he scrambled through his morning milking and jumped in his car to head eastward through the length of the Vinschgau Valley to the province capital of Bozen. As he sped down the valley, he was keenly attuned to the paradox of his drive. The dominance of apple production intensified with virtually every mile he drove, until orchards seemed to cover every square foot — not just of the valley floor but also of the lower slopes on either side of the valley. Indeed, sprawling apple storage facilities several stories in height were strategically placed at key production centers all along the 50-mile (80 km) stretch, many of them ultramodern in design and colorfully decorated with logos suggesting a harmony of culture and landscape.

Günther couldn't help but notice the occasional white mists that erupted out of the spring foliage of orchards and vineyards along the route. What had once seemed like everyone else's issue with the upward march of apples now felt very personal. The clouds of pesticides that *came with* the territory at lower elevations now appeared to be *coming after* the territory in the Upper Vinschgau. Günther and his fellow Malsers were the last holdout for diversified agriculture in the valley, much less the only remaining location where organic could really take root and bear fruit, fruit of a much different sort.

The provincial capital of Bozen, known as Bolzano by the Italians who make up the bulk of the city's population, was the seat of economic as well as political power in the South Tirol. It was a place where farmers like Günther were praised in public and given front-page prominence on tourist brochures, while the real cash cows were being tended behind the scenes.

Finding your way from the industrial outskirts of Bozen to the old part of the city requires some careful negotiation of the modern maze surrounding it. Günther was driving headlong into a bureaucratic labyrinth he could barely have fathomed. He was hardly alone, though — the rest of the people in Mals were unsuspecting passengers in what would become a long journey.

Not a frequent visitor to the provincial government offices, Günther negotiated the labyrinth of exit ramps and one-way streets until he found a parking garage near the governor's office and began to make his way through the city's moderate bustle. With about one hundred thousand inhabitants, Bozen seldom feels overwhelmingly busy, and clear-weather days slow everyone's pace, as they take in sunshine and majestic views of terraced vineyards and even an occasional glimpse of the oldest inhabitants, the Dolomite Mountains that spire upward on the city's eastern flank.

The heaviness of Bozen's mix of medieval and Fascist-era buildings is offset with cobbled sidewalks, brightly colored walls, and flowers tumbling from window boxes. Shaded sidewalks and the coolness of the gothic arches line the historic main shopping district and shelter an international mix of tourists and locals. As Günther passed, they were all savoring the local delights with the clink of porcelain and silverware and soaking up the sun's spring rays.

At last he made his way to Governor Durnwalder's office. Before entering, he checked his clothing to make sure that he hadn't brought along any unwanted souvenirs from the barn and gave his shirt one last pass of the hand to remove any wrinkles. He was dressed to offer the governor a modicum of respect but also a clear reminder that he was, first and foremost, a mountain farmer. The governor's assistant stood up to greet him with a handshake, commending him for his timely arrival before knocking lightly on the governor's door and, upon hearing a reply, gestured for Günther to enter.

Out of his element but confident in his mission, Günther thanked the assistant and stepped inside. Durnwalder was just coming out from behind his long wooden desk, filled with sheaves of papers and notebooks and a small stand holding a miniature red-and-white banner imprinted with the red South Tirolean eagle. With the slightly fatigued eyes of a shrewd deal maker and an aggressive handshake that put to rest any question of who was in charge of the proceedings, the governor welcomed Günther and worked through the customary greetings and questions about life in the Upper Vinschgau, a place he loved to visit anytime he could.

They both knew, however, that there was a reason for the meeting, and neither had time to waste. Günther had cows to milk; Durnwalder had hands to pump and deals to seal.

Günther put it all on the table. He had no issues with his neighbors, and even though he was an organic farmer, he didn't feel any different from his neighbors: They were all trying to find a way to make a living in a challenging world market on relatively small holdings. He wasn't about to tell someone else how to farm any more than he wanted someone else dictating what practices he used on his own farm . . . but when a farmer's practices started to impact a neighbor's ability to farm and make a living, then something had to be done.

Günther explained that it wasn't just him and his fellow organic farmers who were facing the dilemma of being surrounded by conventional apple farmers spraying pesticides — even conventional livestock farmers were threatened if pesticide residues began to taint their crops. And what was to become of the burgeoning efforts to reclaim the Upper Vinschgau's reputation as the Breadbasket of the Tirol?

A consummate politician, Durnwalder expressed his concern for Günther's situation. Similar scenarios would only become more likely as more fruit growers sought out the Vinschgau's last opportunities for expansion, he agreed. And like any good politician he was quick to seize upon the two best tools for appeasement: compromise and research.

As Günther had expected, the governor suggested a solution: The province's premiere agricultural research institute, the Laimburg Research Center, would construct a new experimental orchard in the Upper Vinschgau to study pesticide drift and determine what different orchard orientations, spray techniques, and buffer zone policies might be most effective. In fact, Durnwalder indicated that the new orchard would be ideal for determining precisely what approaches would be best suited to Günther's situation, since the research site would be established on the outskirts of Günther's village of Laatsch!

Prepared for Durnwalder's suggestion, Günther had opted to support the research proposal, even though he was worried that it would only lead to a stronger foothold for Big Apple and company. As a compromise, Günther proposed that the research site be established with the condition that no more orchards would be allowed until the results of the research were available and reviewed. Once it was clear how far pesticides were drifting, then any new orchards could be designed in ways that would be less likely to impact their neighbors' land and health.

Günther was no fool, but he was relatively new to such political machinations. He wanted to believe that the primary purpose of the Laimburg research site really was to study pesticide drift, and he could only hope that the governor had his concerns and the long-term interests of other Upper Vinschgau farmers in mind. Even though he was skeptical, he held out hope that definitive research on the impact of drift and new policies to protect adjacent landowners from drift might help resolve the growing issues. Within twenty minutes they had shaken hands, and Durnwalder welcomed him to return anytime if he needed anything.

Günther couldn't get out of Bozen fast enough. Little did he realize that there were actually already plans in play for not one but two research sites outside his village — and the researchers were particularly interested in testing out apple, cherry, and apricot varieties that would thrive in the high altitudes of the last frontier for fruit growing in the South Tirol. The "experimental orchard" was, in reality, a Trojan horse sent in by Big Apple, courtesy of the governor.

Unfortunately, it would be only a matter of days before Günther would come to regret his conciliatory response to Durnwalder's suggestion. The governor had made his first move, and Big Apple was about to assert control of two more coveted agricultural parcels, all in the blink of an eye. It's better to play chess at home than in the halls of power.

Bozen was a city of compromises. But to hold on to the organic certification that kept his farm afloat, Günther wasn't allowed any compromises. He would have to find more allies among his community if his farm was going to survive.

A natural nexus point, the city of Bozen owes its existence to the scouring powers of ice and water. Since the Ice Age gouged its way through the

Alps, the Eisack River has continued to tear away at the precipitous valley that runs southward from the heights of the Brenner Pass, the historic passageway between what are now the countries of Italy and Austria. Completely channelized by the time it reaches Bozen, the Eisack River dumps into the Adige, and the combined power of two rivers surges toward Verona and the Adriatic Sea.

Bozen/Bolzano is also a point of cultural confluence. A vibrant point of fusion for Mediterranean and Tirolean cultures, it is the meeting place for white bread and dark bread, wine and beer, pasta and dumplings, Italian frivolity and Teutonic precision. In its role as the capital city for the autonomous province of Südtirol — known by Italians as the Alto-Adige, or "Upper Adige" — the city bridges the historic divide between its Tirolean heritage and its contemporary Italian realities.

The idea of "Italy" originated in the early nineteenth century, but it never really transpired until Rome was designated as the capital of the collective city-states that ultimately combined and gave it the approximate boot shape that we now consider to be Italy. However, the boot would have been more of a low-cut version had it not been for a geography professor from Florence, Ettore Tolomei, who was tinkering with what a modern nation-state might look like in two dimensions.

Intrigued by the concept of watersheds as political delineations, he drew a line, not so much in the sand as in the mountains, and he proposed, by way of maps and even invented Italian location names, a northern national boundary that would bring the Alto-Adige into the new Italian fold. Few bothered to ask the inhabitants of what would eventually become the South Tirol about their opinion in this matter, but sometimes maps transform backroom imagination and topographic logic into political reality, leaving democratic inquiry behind.

In the end, the concept of the Alto-Adige became a hot topic among Italian nationalists who promoted the idea of an "unredeemed" (*irredenta*) Italy — a country that wouldn't be complete until it extended to its "natural" borders. That's why Tolomei's concept of the watershed delineation became so important — and it's a nutshell version of how the Tirol became divided into North and South. Simple enough in theory, but enter World War I from stage left and World War II from stage right, and the drama and complexity heightened.

The so-called Alto-Adige territory was part of the bait used by the emerging Allied Powers to entice Italy to join their cause. The 1915 Treaty of London dictated that the Alto-Adige would be ceded to Italy following a victory of the Allies, if Italy agreed to join the alliance. Once the Great War was over, the Treaty of St. Germain in 1919 broke up the Habsburg Empire and granted the territory to Italy. The Italian Fascists began moving in shortly thereafter, taking over rail, mail, water, electrical, and school systems. Bozen was the nucleus for the takeover, and the goal was clear: Italianize the region. Not only did the Italians take over civil authority, but they also tried to outlaw the native German dialect, even in the local schools and churches. "Catacomb schools" and underground resistance groups grew in proportion to the intensity of the territorial and cultural takeover.

The Second World War only complicated the situation. Straddling the embattled zone between the European Axis Powers, the inhabitants of what the international community was increasingly recognizing as the Alto-Adige were caught between the grinding cogs of Mussolini's and Hitler's war machines. Faced with unsavory biddings for allegiance by each of two terrible choices, they had no good options and no real say in the outcome. By the end of the Second World War, they found themselves still part of Italy.

The Italian government was able to exert most of its power in the cities and valleys, the places where the regional infrastructure was concentrated. The higher and more remotely you lived, the easier it was to maintain a rebellious spirit and a semblance of independence. The embers of the old Tirolean identity were carefully tended until finally, in 1972, Italy granted the South Tirol a unique form of political autonomy, allowing the region a governance system that would allow it to protect its cultural heritage and determine the best allocation of the bulk of its tax base.

In the end the South Tirol solution became an international model for cultural coexistence amid challenging political boundaries. With autonomy secured, more wealth shifted to the seat of provincial government in Bozen. Tourism and industrial development began to help fill the coffers of the autonomous province, gradually transforming it into one of the wealthiest regions of Italy.

With wealth comes power, and a call for conformity. But Malsers, people who lived at the outer reaches of provincial power and on the edges of

Swiss and Austrian cultures, had a reputation for doing things a little differently. Famous for growing grain, they also knew how to go against the grain.

On the long drive back from Bozen, flanked on either side of the road by fruit trees for almost the entire 50-mile (80 km) distance, Günther wondered how successful a group of Querdenkers might be in finding common ground, much less standing their ground in the face of such political and economic power. Watching for the telltale black with red and white trim that signified a police car, he was driving as fast as he could up the valley, back toward his cows, but he could see Bozen closing in fast from behind.

About 15 miles (23 km) from Mals, the valley floor of the Vinschgau rose up quickly, albeit with the geological vestiges of a heavy list down toward the southern left side. Perched on the upper side of the valley sat Schlanders, a rustic jewel of a village overlooking a mosaic of fruit production. The highway horseshoed its way around the village and then immediately twisted its way around the adjacent smaller village of Kortsch before shooting straight out into yet another gauntlet of orchards. From the road, the apple plantations and their fettered minions all looked the same. But there was one clear exception amid all the rest, farther down and hidden from the roadside.

As he passed the exit for Kortsch, Günther pushed down on the gas pedal a bit more, peering out the driver's-side window and into what was fast becoming a sea of white blossoms, wondering how Ägidius Wellenzohn's trees and vines were faring with the spring weather.

If other fruit farmers followed Ägidius's lead, there wouldn't be a need to test for pesticide drift — much less worry about coexistence.

The first time I met Ägidius, he was waiting for our media team at the edge of his orchard, casually leaning on the empty end of a bladeless scythe. We'd come to document how he had managed an organic orchard for thirty years, just down the valley from his home in Mals.

As someone who loves to mow with a scythe, I was perplexed. Not only was Ägidius's red metal scythe missing a blade, but he also had it turned upside down, with the rubber-coated handle looking more like a well-worn tool than a grip. Indeed, when I pointed to his scythe and noted that it seemed to be missing an important part, Ägidius smiled ever so slightly, and without a word he picked it up, walked over to a patch of weeds several feet tall, and swung the bladeless instrument in one broad, sweeping gesture, breaking and bending the stems of the weeds but leaving them in place. It was our first lesson in how Ägidius turns the whole idea of fruit production upside down in almost everything he does. For three decades, he has been blazing a new path forward, in his own quiet way.

That path, as it turns out, isn't particularly well mown. Excessive mowing would only interrupt nature's processes and diminish the natural biodiversity that provides the ecological balance he is looking for in his orchard. "I actually don't want to do anything, but rather be a human in the Garden of Eden as it is envisaged by God — just live without having to work so that nature does the work for me. I only want to intervene in the natural processes to regulate things a bit and to steer a little, but nature does the rest. Nature is perfect — she doesn't need humans; humans need nature."

Despite his parents and his neighbors suggesting that he was getting lazy when he began to forgo conventional orcharding techniques and shift to organic methods, Ägidius let the weeds grow — and the hedges, the insects, and the dwarfed fruit trees. Farming in nature's image is a messy business, particularly in the eyes of a Tirolean culture steeped in an appreciation for order and control.

Not that Ägidius doesn't own a tractor. He does. He simply prefers not to use it any more than he has to. He mows the tractor paths between the rows of trees once per year, usually in late July. After mowing the paths, he takes his bladeless scythe, turns it on its head — along with most other conventions in modern agriculture — and knocks down the weeds between the trees with its rubber handle. Breaking the stems slows the growth of weeds while retaining the necessary habitat for the beneficial insects residing in his 7.5 acres (3 ha) of chemical-free Paradise. As the weeds become senescent, they drop their seed, leaving more of the nutrients for the surrounding fruit trees and the table and wine grapes trellised amid the rows of apples, pears, and apricots.

Most surprisingly, Ägidius doesn't own a spray machine. He doesn't even spray copper and sulfur solutions on his fruit trees and vines, as do most other organic orchardists. Copper helps prevent fungal diseases in cooler weather, while sulfur is particularly effective against those worrisome threats in hotter temperatures. While neither of these organically derived chemicals poses serious threat to humans or the environment, copper is a heavy metal that can interfere with a plant's ability to absorb nutrients from the soil once it reaches high levels. In fact, one critique of organic fruit growing — both by insiders and by conventional farmers — is that many organic fruit growers rely too heavily on copper and thereby overload the soil in their orchards and vineyards.

But Ägidius takes a different approach — perhaps even a radical approach — from most organic farmers. If his strategy could be summarized in a word, it would be the one written in bright yellow on the brown T-shirt he was wearing when we first met him: G'MIATLICH. A beloved term in the South Tirol dialect, *g'miatlich* derives from the high German *gemütlich*, meaning "easygoing, mellow, chill, or going with the flow." The more I learned about Ägidius's methods, the more I began to think of that T-shirt as his farm uniform. As he explains it, his low-key approach fosters biodiversity, the linchpin to his success: "For me, biodiversity is essential, a basic requirement, and it is important that many different plants, insects, and creatures exist to complement one another. That's all very important, that there is a big diversity so that the system can take care of itself without humans having to intervene."

Querdenker extraordinaire, Ägidius is a pedestrian observer, not a distracted tractor driver. As he walked us through his orchard, pointing out a stunning array of fruits that would rival those of any conventionally managed orchard in appearance, he was constantly scanning the vertical layers of his orchard — from soil to trunk to branches to uppermost tip — regularly pushing his wire-rimmed glasses back up the bridge of his nose as they slipped with the rise and fall of his head. Tall and trim, he had farmer's hands that seemed perfectly formed to the size of the robust fruits he picked for us to sample, occasionally cutting one open with a pocketknife. With long forearms and muscular legs, Ägidius possesses the perfect build for pruning and picking. In his fifties, he climbs a tree ladder like most schoolkids bound up steps. Only the gray in his day-or-two-old beard hints at his age as he darts through his fruit trees and vines with the agility of a free-ranging pollinator.

Ägidius plants his fruit trees at half the density of his conventional colleagues and he prunes less aggressively, both of which cut his yields and seem at first to be an unreasonable economic compromise. When I asked how that low density can ever pay off, his tightly maintained smile melted into a full grin, and he tipped the apple cart: He essentially has no inputs. Virtually zero. Not even compost or manure. His low-key approach to managing the vegetation in his orchard maintains a self-perpetuating cycle of fertility. And he needs only enough diesel fuel to mow his tractor paths once a year between the rows of fruits and then to haul the harvest back to his home in the village of Glurns, one of the smallest walled villages in Europe and the architectural gem of Mals. When costs are down, profits are up, and Ägidius is completely content with a modest income and a table never wanting for superb food and drink.

By the time we had made the full round of Ägidius's fruit trees and vines, I'd consumed enough dietary fiber for the better part of a week. The fruits were worthy of a study by the Dutch masters — and certainly eye candy for any tourist brochure. I marveled at the lack of disease and insect damage, not to mention the heavy fruit-set on the trees and vines.

"*PIWI Sorten*," he said, handing us yet another apple to try — this time a Topaz, a variety he'd grown successfully not long after it was first created in 1984 in what is now the Czech Republic. "You know about PIWI varieties — fungus-resistant fruits?" he asked us.

Indeed, I had learned about PIWI fruits several years earlier from my friends at Brunnenburg Castle, who were experimenting with them. *PIWI* is an abbreviation for *pilzwiderstandsfähig*, or "fungal-resistant." Bred by crossing fruit varieties demonstrating resistance to one or more fungal diseases, PIWI fruits can be grown not only without synthetic pesticides but also without any organically approved pesticides. PIWI varieties are slowly gaining popularity among apple and grape growers not only in the South Tirol but also in other regions of the world. As a viable alternative to fruit varieties that require pesticides when planted in moderate to high densities, PIWI varieties are beginning to catch on among farmers and consumers, although some PIWI varieties represent a new a taste that requires buy-in from both parties.

Ägidius was an early adopter of PIWI varieties, and his PIWI fruits sell themselves on appearance alone. He has no problem selling out of all of his fruit, and the demand is higher than what he can produce on his acreage. Plus, his first priority is to feed his family; he sells whatever is left over. The balance of product for sale is no small measure, however — he typically produces about 3 wagonloads, or approximately 4 tons, of apples per acre (10 tons per ha). By having no significant input costs and commanding a 30 percent premium for organic, he is able to meet a significant portion of his family's nutritional and financial needs, while also producing vegetables and grains on some additional land closer to his house.

Maintaining that organic certification isn't a given, however, when one is surrounded on all sides by farmers spraying pesticides. The beauty of Ägidius's piece of Paradise seemed constrained more by what we couldn't see than by what was visible. Surrounded by conventional orchardists, his Eden seemed predicated on the good behavior of his neighbors — and even on the beneficence of the wind on any given day. I struggled to understand how Ägidius could have maintained his organic certification for more than three decades in such an environment, so I pushed him to explain how it could be possible to be an organic farmer surrounded by toxic mists.

The answer: hedges. They are central to his success in avoiding pesticide drift — and also maintaining biodiversity. And Ägidius has planted them around his entire fruit operation. He selects tree and shrub species that can grow tall enough to block most direct drift in three to five years. These hedges also offer habitat to insects and wildlife, as well as protection from wind damage. Of course even tall, thick hedges can't block all pesticide penetration, and that is where coexistence between conventional and organic fruit farmers is easier than between conventional fruit farmers and livestock, grain, herb, and vegetable farmers, regardless of whether they are organic or not.

Since Ägidius's fruits ripen at approximately the same time as those of his neighbors, he benefits from the fact that they are legally required *not* to spray their fruits three weeks before harvest. Therefore, he is protected in part from harvesting any fruits with detectable pesticide residues. To ensure that he is in compliance with his organic certification, his fruit is tested regularly for residues, and he has experienced only a few minor issues during all of the time that he has farmed organically.

Livestock, grain, herb, and vegetable farmers who suddenly find themselves bounded by conventional fruit growers aren't so lucky, however.

Pesticides are often sprayed during or near the time when those other farmers are harvesting their crops. With no buffer of the calendar or hedgerows, these other farmers risk having their crops coated with pesticides just as the products need to come in from the field. Those farmers don't have the luxury of a no-spray period that might minimize the risk, and few of them want to feed their livestock, families, or customers crops that were recently doused with unknown mixtures of pesticides. When harvest and spraying coincide, "coexistence" becomes a one-sided affair . . . and it disappears like an aerosol mist.

Another old proverb was proving true, both in its literal and its figurative senses: "It's an ill wind that blows nobody any good."

CHAPTER 8

Rallying Cry

*U*prisings. They tend to be about bread — and the revolution in Mals was one more uprising in a long lineage of bread-inspired citizen revolts.

Few can provide clearer testimonials as to why it makes little sense to trade in a backbone food tradition in the Upper Vinschgau than brothers Franz and Pius Schuster, the fourth generation of their family to carry forward the bread traditions of the Mals and its surroundings.

You could say the brothers inherited their mother's business savvy and their father's mother. That is to say, it takes a steady hand at the helm to run a successful bakery — exemplified by their mother, Paula — as well as a recipe for success, which in their case was the sourdough starter, also known as the "mother," that was older than either of them and was handed down by way of their father.

Situated beside the engineered mountain stream that cascades a stone-lined channel through the center of Laatsch, Bäckerei Schuster — the Schuster Bakery — sits just across the street from a restored mill saved from ruin by Angela Latsch and her family. The juxtaposition of mill and bakery are a reminder of the vital role that millers and bakers played in the economy and survival of farmers in the area. It was one thing to raise grain and a large family, but without the efficiency of a water-powered mill, doing both was a serious challenge. That said, farmers in previous times were also wary of millers and bakers, since both had the opportunity to take more than their agreed upon cut of the farmers' grain or flour during the business transactions. Today, however, bakers like the Schusters can be a guarantor of a farmer's economic well-being.

The Schuster Bakery is a state-of-the-art facility housed within a medieval shell. With the warm welcome of Paula and the waft of breads and confections coursing up from the basement ovens, to step into the bakery is to inhale traditions amid displays of everything from the most rustic of breads to fruit- and chocolate-filled confections that help offset the array of healthy options. Rye dominates as the primary ingredient among the diverse bread selection, but spelt, wheat, oats, barley, einkorn, and other grains are added as flour and whole grains.

The members of the Schuster family blend business and daily life under a single roof, hurriedly navigating between the labyrinthine multistoried bakery and their home, which connects seamlessly to the bakery complex. The swish of rubber-soled shoes and loose-fitting aprons mingles with the calls between the sales area, office, and baking rooms. A midsized business with a broad reputation throughout the province and beyond, Bäckerei Schuster has found a way to maintain tradition without sacrificing quality or ingredients, at a scale that supports the family and its employees.

Although the bakery has been in the Schuster family for four generations, they are passing along a culture — a microbial one, in this case — that goes all the way back to those same Bavarian monks of Marienberg Abbey. When the monks first came to the region, they brought a lactic acid bacterial culture that lives on in lore, if not in some strange microbial lineage that was passed on by a people utterly dependent on their living bread — the now famous sourdough, *Ur-Paarl nach Klosterart*, "the ancient pair in the monastic style." Today the abbey's sprawling white facade is visible on the mountainside just up the valley from Laatsch, where the Schusters and their bakery use the age-old culture to replicate the monk's marriage of two small and relatively flat, round loaves connected in a figure-eight shape. The bread remains a staple for locals and a culinary mainstay for tourists.

Having grown up in the family business, Franz and Pius — in their thirties — are now serious masters. In their case, youth should be equated with vivacity, not lack of experience or foolhardiness. They wear their baker's whites and chef's caps fully aware of the weight they carry on their shoulders. Like a Bergbauer carrying an enormous sack of freshly ground flour up to a farmhouse clinging to a steep slope in years gone by, they carry on traditions that have shaped their region, albeit with the support of much finer coffee and the plague of an array of constantly available confections — delicacies that might rouse even Ötzi from his 5,300-year sleep.

Long a fan of the bakery's delicacies but unaware of its story, I visited one day with our media team only to discover that unraveling that story is all a matter of going to the left of the display-case cash register and heading downstairs to the storerooms, the milling area, and the inferno, squeezing past and waving to family members and employees along the way. So, following Franz's lead, we headed down the brightly lit stairs and bumbled and banged our way toward the bakery.

A pungent aroma with a hint of citrusy pear became increasingly intense as we made our way downstairs. We turned a corner and found the hallway filled with crates of oddly shaped, yellowing fruits. They looked like pears that just couldn't quite achieve the quintessential pear shape. There was no elongated end near the stem. At least in comparison with the traditional image of a pear, they were slightly misshapen — more spherical and also bumpy. *Palabirnen*.

Other than its breads, perhaps nothing is more a testament to the uniqueness of the Vinschgau's culinary traditions than the Palabirne, a fruit whose particularly tall trees once played a leading role in the staging of spring and summer in the area but are now relegated to a minor part, serving as a contrast with the dwarf apple trees taking over coveted field fields and meadows. Nonetheless, the Palabirne is still revered and sought after by everyone attuned to its aromatic sweetness. Some still call it the *Apothekerbirne*, the "pharmacist's pear," because of its high levels of vitamin C and other nutrients previously coveted in more meager times. In fact, an old saying in the region spoke to the Palabirne's revered nutritional status: *Wenn die Palabirnen reif sind, hat der Doktor keine Arbeit.* When the Palabirnen are ripe, the doctor has no work.

It is believed that the Palabirne originally came from the Near East in the 1600s. Frost-hardy, fairly resistant to a number of fruit diseases, and prolific in its yields, it was much beloved. But with the influx of other fruits and sweets and sweeteners of all kinds, the Palabirne fell somewhat out of favor in the late twentieth century — or perhaps too many people feared falling from the skyward reach of its heavy-laden boughs.

At one point in time, the reach was worth the risk. The Palabirne was one of the few products in the area that could be used as a year-round sweetener. Families would cut the Palabirne into thin slices, thread them on a string, and hang them from the ceiling in order to dry. The fruit was then used in breads and other recipes to add a hint of sweetness. While the Palabirnen ripen quickly and don't fare well in storage, they are excellent for drying. And that is just what Peter Schuster, Franz and Pius's father, did several decades ago in a move that not only gave them a surprising new market opportunity but also helped save the Palabirne from disappearing.

Franz explained that the crates of Palabirne were only a small portion of the Palabirnen that they were buying in during the latter weeks of August. By the time the harvest was done, they would purchase about fourteen tons of the fruits, all of which they would cut up by hand, with the help of extra workers. When the ovens were turned off from baking bread at the end of each day, they would use the cooling ovens to dry the pears. Over the course of the following year, they would bake a continual supply of *Palabirnebrot*, Palabirne bread, and also feature the tasty fruits in special Christmas and Easter breads.

Thanks to the Schuster family, and to several local distillers and vinegar makers, the Palabirne now has a week of proclaimed fame in which the village of Glurns, a quick walk from Laatsch, hosts seven days of celebration around the dishes and lore of the special fruit.

Further down in the basement level of the bakery, we came across another tradition the Schuster family is helping to conserve. There, kept alive by regular feedings and the warmth of the "Riders of the Apocalypse" — the nickname for their big ovens, complete with a nameplate situated above them — is the secret to the bulk of their enterprise. Heaving and frothing in a giant vat in the bakery, the "mother" of all breads (or at least nine of them) demands constant care and daily feeding lest she expire. Thirty years old, she has been around as long as both of the sons and is a veritable part of the family. To lose her would be to start over — losing valuable time and money, if not a bit of character.

When we got to the bakery, Franz washed his hands and forearms with vigorous strokes up and down each arm. He was preparing to dive deep into the sourdough starter vat and bring up a sufficiently sized *Dampfl*, the rye-based pre-dough starter. With his long arms disappearing into the vat, he pulled out a huge blob that tried to escape in every direction at once, as if it were an octopus. Once on the table, the Dampfl resigned itself to nothing more than an unlikely creeping escape.

Franz, meanwhile, folded in the ingredients for one of their classic breads, *Schüttelbrot*, literally meaning "shaken bread." Rye flour, one-third wheat flour, water, a little yeast, salt, one part fennel, and one part fenugreek for the spices — Franz kneaded it all together in rapid fashion with his lean but powerful hands and arms, then quickly divided the mound of mollified dough into small, hand-sized loaves. At that point, the etymology of the word *Schüttelbrot* became clear. He placed one of the loaves, still in a slightly wetter form than most traditional doughs, on a thin wooden board. He then surprised us all by holding the board with two hands and flipping the dough up into the air, only to have it come back down on the board with a gentle splat. Before the dough had a chance to stick, Franz had it flipping up and landing again, continuing every few seconds, with the dough becoming flatter and more spread out each time. Once his artisan eye determined that the dough had reached the correct size and thickness, he deftly slipped it onto a larger rising board, which would be placed in a ceiling rack alongside a whole host of other bread-filled boards, until the bread had risen sufficiently and was placed under the hot-tempered supervision of the Riders of the Apocalypse.

When the bread came out of the oven, it would be one of the most quintessential culinary treats of the South Tirol — a light, crispy bread that depends more on molars than incisors, with the tastes of fennel and fenugreek waiting for the company of an Alpine cheese or a wash of local wine. The difference in physiques between Americans and South Tiroleans might be attributed simply to the preferences for highly processed corn chips rather than Schüttelbrot.

Franz and Pius make nine different sourdough breads every day, all from the same starter. The staple product is the one most tightly tied to their family history and the traditions of the area, the Vinschgerpaarl, typically referred to by the locals as *Paarlbrot*. Other than using a machine to mix the dough, they do everything just as their grandfather did, although he was able to work primarily with rye that he got directly from local farmers. In the old days, the farmer took the rye to the miller, and the miller then took it to the baker. The miller would keep a portion of the grain, and the baker would keep a portion of the bread, with the farmer picking up the balance of the bread from the baker. Wheat didn't grow well in the region, so it wasn't until large amounts were available in the 1930s that the bread recipes and local preferences began to shift.

The Schusters are hoping that the current grain renaissance in the Vinschgau continues to expand. They use their purchasing power to invest in regional and local grains, and they educate their consumers about area grains as well. The supply is limited, however, and they are only able to meet about 20 percent of their needs through these purchases. When asked about the quality of the local products, Franz had a pragmatic response: "Since there isn't so much regional flour, we have to take almost any quality we can get . . . the flour that grows here in our region isn't so perfect, but it gives the bread a better taste — it is more active as flour because the flour isn't dead, like the flour that is brought in from outside. It has more life inside it, and one observes it first with the sourdough, and then one notices it with the bread."

He then paused and straightened up, looking out the window as if he could see the checkered landscape of fields just outside of the village center. "It's always nice in late fall when I see how the grain is sprouting up, such as the rye, and then the snow falls on top of it and then I almost forget that in the spring it will grow further again. Yes — it's always beautiful when one can see where a product comes from, when we can simply drive over to the next fields and look. I can also watch the weather, and I can imagine approximately what the quality will be and what I can then bake with it. Naturally, it puts me at ease when I know the farmer personally and know how the grain was produced, and of course it's also an advantage to know the miller, and I can be assured that this flour I get is the grain I observed growing."

With that, he picked up his board and formed the final loaf with four tosses before sliding it onto the long rising board and heaving board and bread artfully up into the ceiling rack for its final rise. As he scraped the remnants of dough off his hands, he confessed that his affinity for locally grown rye was rooted in more than just taste. "Rye doesn't need to be fertilized, it doesn't need pesticides, it requires nothing. It's sowed, it has to be watered on occasion because it doesn't rain much here, but otherwise it doesn't need anything."

Washing his hands in the sink, with flecks of dough swirling toward the drain, he turned his head and wrapped up the lesson: "If you lose bread, you lose a piece of culture."

In spring 2012 the cold air from the high peaks around Mals began to mix with the warming air down in the valley, and the intensity of the wind in the Upper Vinschgau began to build and blow as it did every other year that the locals could remember. But something was different. Like the contrasting air masses, opposing forces appeared to be building in strength. It was if the famous Vinschgerwind were somehow fanning the smoldering discontent among the Malsers.

With the grain renaissance under way, researchers at the Laimburg center had teamed up with Kornkammer (literally, "the granary") — a group of farmers, bakers, and others who wanted to bring back the grain-growing varieties and traditions of the area — to test fifteen new varieties of rye that could grow at an elevation of about 5,000 feet (1,500 m). The goal was to assess how the varieties performed agriculturally and their potential for solid economic return, but they also tested the baking qualities of the yields. It was one thing to grow the grains successfully, but if the resulting breads didn't meet traditional culinary expectations, the likelihood of using the new rye varieties to help restore the Upper Vinschgau's status as the breadbasket of the region was slim to none.

Just as the "rye data" were released and excitement was building about several promising varieties that met the needs of farmers and bakers alike, Günther returned with news of his meeting with the governor on March 28. Distraught by the news of the proposed research orchard — and still unaware that there would actually be two research orchards — the Malsers saw their excitement turn to discontent. Despite the fact that Laimburg was responsible for overseeing both the grain research and the new experimental orchard, the locals didn't see the two visions of the future as compatible.

It was clear that the politicians and lobbyists had aligned, and they were sending a well-heeled vanguard up the valley to be the first boots on the ground. It was less about research than it was about putting a stake in the ground — concrete posts, actually, followed by an army of fruit trees.

In Minuteman fashion, as soon as it became clear to the Malsers that Big Apple was moving in, they activated their own troops — of activists. Ägidius, Peter, Alexander, Günther, Konrad, and others began to rally their colleagues from Adam & Epfl, the USGV, Kornkammer, the Association for Alternative Agriculture (Bund Alternativer Anbauer, or BAA), the Working Association of Biodynamic Agriculture, and organic farming organizations. Appreciative of the specialized points of focus and the tactics of each group, some of the Malsers belonged to more than one group. It was clear that in order to take on the larger forces making their way into their community, they needed to band together and use their home-turf advantage, along with guerrilla tactics that might somehow undermine the conventional power plays born out of Bozen. It was a long shot, though, with politicians, the apple cooperatives, and the South Tirolean Farmers' Association (SBB) all eager to see Big Apple grow in every direction it could.

Still, one person's frontier tends to be another person's heritage.

By March 31, three days after Günther's visit with the governor, the activists had organized a public *Lokalaugenschein*, or inspection, of the proposed research site. They met at a local pizzeria in Laatsch in the early afternoon, just below Günther's dairy farm, and walked up the paved hiking and biking path that runs between the villages of Laatsch and Schleis — right in between Günther's and Alexander's farms and amid a patchwork assortment of fields: a mix of hay meadows, grain fields, and small pastures. Positioned beside the recreational path and a small but fast-flowing river, the site offered the perfect opportunity to research the impacts of drift on nearby farms, recreational areas, and waterways. It was hard to imagine a better spot to ruin in order to learn what was already obvious to the locals.

Not far above the research orchard site sit several dozen small farms in the tiny village of Schleis. One of those farms is located on one of several side spurs off the main drag in the village, a side street that seems busiest at dawn, when all the farmers along the street pull their large milk cans on wheels up to the main road for the daily milk pickup. There's barely enough room at the intersection for the farmers to line up their shiny metal containers along the stone walls of the adjacent houses, and the ritual is a reminder that small-scale, diversified agriculture continues even as fancier facades don the village's barns and houses. Just as important, the early-morning banter of farmers waiting by their milk cans for the milk truck driver and whatever news he brings with him is core to the village's tightly woven social fabric.

Migihof, the Migi Farm, is similar to cheesemaker Alexander Agethle's farm just across the stream in that they both feature a courtyard created by a tight cluster of house, big barn, and an assortment of storage buildings. The blend of darkened wood, tasteful stonework, and white plaster offers protection from the worst of winds and a harbor for the sun's lingering warmth, as evidenced by the flowers, herbs, and trees that bring it all to life. On the far end of the courtyard from the street entrance, a path follows the left edge of the barn to the barnyard gate, where the vista opens up and mountains take over the bottom third of the sky. The view from the barnyard drops toward Laatsch, in the direction of the research orchard.

It was at that barnyard's gate that Eduard Marth put one boot up onto the lower rail, leaned in, sprawled his long arms over the edge, and invited me to step up and do the same. Spry and fit, thanks to his twin passions of farming and cycling, he sported a full head of wavy white hair set off by salt-and-pepper sideburns. With his lean frame and long stride, he looked like he could easily vault the gate if he had the mind to do so. Tight on time but not on energy, he'd given up part of his chore-filled Sunday afternoon to show us his farm and introduce us to his family, even though he wasn't quite sure what to make of three Americans and an Italian so intrigued by his grain fields.

When he learned that I raised a rare breed of cattle back in the States, the uncertainty faded and any issues of communication melted away. The two of us had slipped to the back of the farm where his favorite cow was in the picturesque barnyard, milling about and nibbling at various treats an hour or so before it was time to step into the milking parlor for the day's second milking. There's a certain communion between humans that can happen only amid the utter contentment of satisfied ruminants, and it's intensified when both people appreciate just what it takes for nature and humans to create such a magnificent animal.

A Precautionary Tale

As she soaked in the sun, we basked in the delight of the sheen of her coat and the perfection of her straight back, broad hips, and sound legs. Sensing our admiration — or maybe it was my accent — she meandered over to let Eduard rub her cool black muzzle while I scratched her right above her tailhead, the universal point of cattle appreciation the world over. The Marth family kept a few cows on their diverse 12.5 acres (5 ha) and shipped the organic milk their family didn't consume to a local processor. Much like his ancestors who had run the farm before him, Eduard and his wife, Helga, also had draft horses and grew grains, potatoes, cucurbits (members of the squash family), and an assortment of vegetables. And they grew a number of old varieties of fruits in a traditional *Streuobstwiese*, a mixed orchard consisting of apples, plums, pears, apricots, and berries.

Eduard and Helga had inherited more than a farm when they married in 1977; they had also inherited a traditional approach to agriculture. But it wasn't until their first daughter encountered health problems at a young age that they really began to consider just how important traditionally raised and prepared food was to their family's health — and the degree to which it contrasted with the highly processed and chemical-infused foods that were beginning to stream in by way of grocery stores.

Helga recalls the moment she realized that they had to make a conscious choice about how they wanted to grow their food. Eduard's father was an avid rose gardener, and one day he was preparing to spray his roses with pesticides, covering all the rest of the garden with cardboard to prevent any contamination of their food. The thought of using something potentially toxic to their family near their food and the children's play area didn't settle well with Helga. The risk didn't seem necessary, and at that point, Helga decided that all of their food would be organic, and they would do all that they could to produce most of it themselves. The goal was to feed themselves first; anything extra would be sold to support their family.

For more than thirty years, they have been growing their own grain, processing it, and baking their own bread. Now a certified "farm teacher," Helga offers classes to school groups and others interested in understanding farm-to-table, soil-to-mouth, historical traditions, and future health. With the village kindergarten on the same street, in full view of the agricultural cycles as they unfolded in the valley below, Migihof was in the perfect location for helping the next generation to savor their heritage and perhaps decide to stay on and preserve it — or at least come back after finding out how rich the traditions were in a world already stripped of so much.

Of course, Helga and Eduard had long known that theirs was an uphill cultural battle in an era when tools were traded in for devices and nutrition was sacrificed for convenience, but they had never thought that farmers would be the biggest threat to a sane and healthy agriculture. Looking down the valley from their farm, however, they could see the grim realities.

Earlier in the afternoon, while out in his grain field, I'd asked Eduard about the future of livestock agriculture and growing grains. He waved his hand across the vista to point out the checkered landscape in the broad valley below us, field sizes ranging from a partial acre to several acres. "We have very many small parcels. You can't grow hedges there, and, well, . . . why should I protect myself from pesticides? The polluters have to protect their neighbor so that their pesticides don't get to their neighbors' property. The perpetrator has to protect the neighbor, and I as a farmer shouldn't have to protect myself from my neighbor's pesticides. That's a completely wrong attitude, don't you think?"

When we went to his farm afterward, he pulled out a beautiful sheaf of spelt, still on the stalk. Eighteen sheaves were tied together to make the shock, which was as tall as Eduard himself. He pulled off a few grains and showed me the hull that makes spelt less appealing to some farmers and consumers — it's not easy to remove — and hard for birds to eat. It also protects the grain from pesticides. "But the neighboring farmer should be protecting me against pesticides," he said, "not the grain itself."

At that point Helga chimed in. "Good bread is very important for my family. We've baked our own bread for over thirty years. Bread can only be good if the grain is good, and the grain is only good when there are no pesticides in it."

What appeared perfectly logical to a farmer didn't seem to concern others, however, who apparently had no qualms about replacing the fundamental sustenance of grains with an international commodity.

A walk can bring things into focus sometimes, and the informal group inspection of the proposed research orchard at the end of March did just that. The chatter of the folks walking up the bike path melded with the gurgle of the spring-fed waters in the river paralleling their short promenade. Once they arrived, the chatter turned to dialogue, with the organizers explaining what they knew of the proposal and fielding questions and comments from the group.

As they discussed their options, it seemed clear that they had little opportunity to influence the governor or his covey of bureaucrats, but there was still a possibility of getting the mayors of surrounding towns to weigh in on the misguided idea. Representatives from the different organizations that had helped to organize the site inspection took note of the various responses from the participants and decided that their best course of action was to write a public letter to the mayors laying out their concerns.

Within days, they had all agreed upon the wording of the letter, and they sent it to the public officials and the local media in early April. It was their first collective political move, and the carefully crafted letter laid out what would become the fundamental principles of a grassroots political campaign that no one could have predicted, least of all the provincial powers and one of their most esteemed cronies, Big Apple.

The letter, addressed to the mayors of Mals and four surrounding municipalities, came from five organizations committed to sustainable development in the Upper Vinschgau — Kornkammer, USGV, BAA, Working Association of Biodynamic Agriculture, and the citizens' initiative of Adam & Epfl. "The future of this valuable cultural landscape lies in the direction of local resources and the biological and natural health of humans and nature, rather than the furthering of intensive fruit production," they wrote. They rattled off their reasons for concern: the dusting and drift from pesticides, exacerbated by regional winds; the high levels of pesticide residue found in grass and hay samples; the threat to organic growers and food producers, not to mention tourists on open bike paths and walking trails and children on playgrounds. Every one of their watercourses, the letter writers noted, was impacted. All this, together with the fact that there were "increasingly alarming investigations into the effects of pesticides on humans and animals, especially when the active substances work in combination," made the people of the region "increasingly concerned about their habitat and their health."

Since concerns like these prompted the Laimburg Research Center to set up an experimental research site to study drift and spread near Laatsch, they wrote, authorities should heed the precautionary principle. In other words, potentially harmful activity should cease until those doing it can prove it is safe.

A sleeping giant isn't easily roused, but it will occasionally twitch and swat when it senses a pesky presence swirling about its head. Such was the case when the Südtiroler Bauernbund (SBB), the powerful farmers' association in the region, got wind of the letter, especially this part:

> Despite the fact that we reject the experiment, we find it important that the gathered data should be established in another location and especially that the possible dangers to public health be taken seriously. On these grounds, we hope and expect that you, as the responsible parties for public health in our communities, stop any pesticide applications until the results of the research are presented. The right of the local citizens and the vacationing guests should be understood as urgent. The potential health risks from drift and spreading, which leads to the research, requires that further use of pesticides stop until the data is received and the dangers can be ruled out.

Irritated by any suggestion that its member farmers or its allies were somehow out of line and emboldened by their friends in high places, they mounted enough energy for a mild swat at what they were sure was a passing pest, not a future fly in the ointment.

The SBB put out a statement in favor of the research project, with their regional chair, Andreas Tappeiner, noting,

> We need scientific data to answer the outstanding questions and then to discuss them in a substantive and scientifically sound manner. . . . Our goal must be to manage our fruit in a manner that is as environmentally friendly as possible. We must be clear that the further development of agriculture and the establishment of new cultural methods in the Upper Vinschgau must go hand in hand. The Laimburg trials can be of help.[1]

The statement also noted that it would be interesting to explore pesticide drift issues related to spraying stone fruits such as apricots and cherries — possible new crops in the Upper Vinschgau. Those words would prove prescient, or at least politically informed. Local residents would soon learn that not one but two different experimental orchards were to be established, one for apples and one for stone fruits. Goliath got a twofer without exerting any significant effort. It was barely worth celebrating. After all, when there's no perceived threat, there's no real victory.

Little did Big Apple know that as the petals were falling that spring, so were the gloves. Savvy local officials in Mals had quietly made a change in the town's municipal code: *Successful referendums would now be binding.* Chapter 4, Article 40, Point 5 in the Mals municipal code was a quiet but decisive step toward direct democracy: "The affirmation of a referendum serves as a decision that the municipal council or the municipal committee should again take up and reconsider the issue on a broad basis."

David had quietly put a stone in his sling, and Goliath hadn't noticed.

CHAPTER 9

A Precautionary Tale

The telltale black car with the red trim and blue lights reappeared and parked by the Mals pharmacy several times a day for months and months. The Carabinieri, the Italian national police, had made it quite clear that they were ready to protect the town's eclectic pharmacist from anyone who might decide to turn threats into an actual physical assault. They pulled up every so often while he was at work in the pharmacy or when he was opening and closing its doors and metal security gate.

Johannes Unterpertinger had spent months lending his scientific expertise and his rhetorical savvy to the Mals activists. As a result, he was harassed repeatedly with abusive phone calls and disconcerting death threats. While those threats to the normally jovial pharmacist's life and limb were deterred, the perpetrators directed their aggression elsewhere. Johannes's family grave site was desecrated, his organic garden destroyed. And then there are the lawsuits that continue to dog him and have already cost him thousands upon thousands of euros, simply for being the point person in a legitimate democratic process. Goliath had been roused, and his minions lunged first for the person at the tip of the spear.

Johannes is a striking figure whether he is cloaked in his white lab coat in the Mals Apotheke or out walking his dog, Bono, through the streets of Mals and up the peaceful paths along the gurgling irrigation canals above the village. Standing tall amid most crowds, he is easy to spot in town or at his daily litany of appointments and meetings. His clean-shaven head may give him away — or it may be hidden underneath a whimsical cap. He's a druggist by day and author by night (pen name Hans Perting) who somehow finds time in between to run his own publishing company. Such a combination isn't such a challenge for someone who suffers from insomnia and seems to recognize no bounds in his intellectual and artistic pursuits.

Johannes's round wire-rimmed spectacles fit tightly on his head, and his broad grin lifts his cheeks repeatedly throughout the course of a conversation. That conversation, by the way, will be rapid-fire, whether in Tirolean dialect, high German, or Italian. And bystander beware: Give him a few feet of extra space, since he is armed with a blended lexicon of Teutonic and Mediterranean gesticulations that will animate any conversation.

The only child in his family, Johannes was, by his own reckoning, the *Erbprinz*, the destined inheritor, so he was "programmed from the beginning to be a pharmacist—there was never any choice." The pharmacy in Mals formed a strong part of his family's identity, but it had also played a central role in the town ever since its establishment in 1807. Its location beside the town's main square and a stone's throw from the town hall and the main church add to the pharmacy's central role in the town's commerce and communications, and Johannes was generally happy to be fully in the mix of things.

However, he had always found joy in getting away from the shiny, sterile environment of his father's pharmacy for a healthy reprieve on his mother's family farm. He worked there every summer prior to his required military service, even spending five seasons in a hut on the high pastures. He'd milked ten cows, brought in hay, and harvested rye and wheat to supplement the cattle feed. As he put it, "I've gotten my hands dirty and my feet have been in the manure."

Although he eventually had to focus on the demands of managing the business after he completed his doctorate in pharmacy in Florence, Johannes continued to cultivate his connections with the local landscape by working a Streuobstwiese that he had inherited from his mother just above the town of Mals, at an elevation of 3,281 feet (1,000 m). He grows his own grain there, planting spelt for three years and then rotating to rye for one year before leaving it fallow for the fifth year. He also grows potatoes, carrots, berries, apricots, plums, and apples. Those activities keep him attuned to the cycles of nature, as well as the deep agricultural traditions of the region.

Being a village chemist in an isolated rural area is by nature a much different occupation than that of a pharmacist in a city or a drugstore chain. A pharmacist has to be everything, he explains: "A pharmacist is, in a way, a doctor, a veterinarian, a therapist, a counselor, a first-responder . . ."

And sometimes a spokesperson, as it would turn out.

There was an irony in Johannes's new position as spokesperson for the activists in Mals. While a pharmacist is well prepared to dispense chemicals in minute doses that will help people find their way to comfort and overall health, a pharmacist isn't necessarily prepared to address the prescribed doses in parts per million or parts per billion related to pesticides — or, as they are known in the industry, "crop protection." Nonetheless, as it turns out, a pharmacist is one of the best-equipped members of a community for understanding the unknowns and the potential hazards of such unprescribed and unrequested dosages.

Johannes's pharmaceutical training included various courses in toxicology, and knowing what he knew, he couldn't remain silent, particularly given the excessive levels of pesticides used in the South Tirol. While the usage rates vary from farm to farm, statistics indicate the average application of pesticides in the area to be approximately 31 pounds per acre (35 kg/ha),[1] while according to Johannes some fruit farmers use as much as 44 to 53 pounds per acre (50–60 kg/hectare) on an annual basis.

Despite these stark statistics, the apple lobby and its cronies were masters at adopting, or co-opting, language and motifs that were meant to mollify concerns about the poisoning of air, water, land, and — at the top of the food chain — humans. *Pestizide* (pesticides) became *Pflanzenschutzmittel* (plant protection products), *Konventionelobstbau* (conventional fruit production) turned into *Integrierteobstbau* (integrated fruit production), and the nearly decimated *Marienkaifer* (ladybug) somehow found its way on the labels and logos of almost all things apple in the South Tirol.

Johannes's training meant he had to challenge the conventional viewpoint:

> As a pharmacist, you will prescribe medicine to people that can obviously also have side effects, interactions,

contraindications — and here the expert academic says "the dosage makes the difference." However, as a patient you go to the physician voluntarily, and the doctor will, to the best of their knowledge and belief, decide what medicine you alone require and at what dosage, and you are then still free to decide if you want the medicine or not. If, however, entire areas of healthy people are sprayed with pesticides, with poison, against their will, then there is no comparison.

Although he is adamant about his views on the necessity to protect human health whenever possible, Johannes is also a political realist. He describes the Upper Vinschgau as a place long defined by boundaries of all kinds. Not only is Mals at the junction of Switzerland, Austria, and Italy, but it is also a place where Italian, Tirolean dialect, high German, and Romansch (an ancient language used in isolated communities in the Alps, it is suspected to be a relic of Roman legions left in the area) are intermingled. And it's a place where the Catholic Church and the Calvinists collided and established boundaries of influence during the Reformation.

Therefore, he understands that boundaries are porous, whether they are cultural, linguistic, nationalistic, religious, or ecological; and he understands that apple cultivation isn't likely to be stopped altogether. But he and others were unwilling to accept the poisoning of the environment that came with chemical-intensive orchards.

By the end of 2012, it was clear to the concerned citizens of Mals that things weren't going to change if they didn't up their game. Plans for the two research orchards in Laatsch continued to move ahead. They were to be placed in contrasting locations and with opposite orientations to determine whether orchard rows should be aligned with or counter to the prevailing Vinschgerwind in order to mitigate drift. As plans evolved, it turned out that one of the orchards would also be dedicated to testing out apple varieties best suited to the upper elevations and the other to stone fruit varieties that could be grown in the area. It was a classic case of the fox guarding the henhouse — from the inside. If it wasn't clear before, it was now: The research had everything to do with testing how to advance "modern" agriculture in the Upper Vinschgau, and little if anything to do with testing pesticide impacts.

In an effort to address the growing tensions, the South Tirolean government and other interested (and invested) parties began to develop new spraying guidelines and buffer requirements in December of that year. Perhaps it was a lack of imagination, but by the time the recommendations were developed, 3 meters — less than 10 feet — from the trunk of outermost trees was determined to be a sufficient buffer between an orchard and another agricultural enterprise. Three meters wasn't going to do much on days with any wind and on parcels with no protective hedges or solid fencing. It was too little, too late. But it also spoke to the near-impossibility of developing suitable buffers in an area where land parcels are tiny and agricultural holdings spread out over many individual plots of land. Where one orchard or farm ended, another began.

When trying to dissect a movement, who better to ask about cause and effect than a pharmacist? I asked Johannes if he could clarify for me when he thought the movement for a pesticide-free Mals really gained traction, so he invited me to join him at his home for lunch one day. I met him in the pharmacy at noon, and he slipped off his white lab coat and went to lock the door for the long lunch pause. We made our way up an inner stairway to the door of his living quarters, guarded on the other side by an enormous dog with a tail that seemed to flog more than wag. Bono was ready for a walk, but Johannes gestured for me to take a seat in his Stube while he gathered the basics on a big cutting board: homemade bread made with spelt he had grown himself, along with *Speck*, cheeses, and olives.

He convinced Bono to relax for a few minutes while he explained how he and his compatriots hit a final tipping point in the whole process. Taking a moment to secure his glasses on his nose prior to his verbal sprint, he launched full-speed into a retrospective on the factors that would transform 2013 into such a dramatic year in Mals: "It started ten years ago when people from the lower and middle Vinschgau came and, for little money, bought what was, at the time, our very inexpensive land. Of course we couldn't prevent anyone from growing fruit or vegetables — we just wanted them to do it organically so that no one would be harmed by the pesticides." Some townspeople expressed concern and began to dialogue with the new apple growers. "But the discussions didn't help much, and then also the municipality of Mals produced a leaflet in which they said that we'll have to find a *modus vivendi* — a way of coexisting," he went on. "In fact, it featured a picture of a cow with fruit orchards in the background."

It would have been one thing, he explained, if those who wanted to spray grew high hedges around their plots, contained their spray within those hedges, and used spray guns instead of spray machines so that they didn't create spray drift. "Then everyone could do whatever they wanted," said Johannes. "But nobody complied with that. We took over three hundred samples, every one of which we found pesticides in — captan, chlorpyrifos, mancozeb, and so on. And at that point, we decided that it's not helping — all the good and reasonable talk, all the pleading, all the meetings — nothing helped. It just kept going on and on and on."

Some of the conventional apple farmers were doing their best to work with their neighbors, but the overall mind-set among the leaders of the apple industry didn't seem to be shifting. The strategy of gathering constituents of different perspectives together to discuss the growing encroachment of conventional apple plantations and the consequences of their pesticide use hadn't changed the status quo. One farmer's "crop protection" was fast becoming another farmer's death knell. And Mals had only so many farmers to lose before the takeover by Big Apple was a fait accompli.

Something had to change. On February 25, 2013, forty-seven residents of Mals, with the support of twenty-five others who couldn't attend the meeting, gathered together to form *Promotorenkomitees für eine pestizidfreie Gemeinde Mals*, Advocacy Committee for a Pesticide-Free Mals, to advance the collective agendas of Adam & Epfl, Umweltschutzgruppe Vinschgau (USGV), Bioland, the organic farmers of Mals, Kornkammer, and other looser affiliations. Big Apple had joined hands with lobbyists and politicians, so it became increasingly critical for these less powerful groups to begin to develop a united front. It was time to demonstrate that they weren't, in the words of Peter Gasser, "a bunch of green crazies."

At that meeting they elected Johannes to be their spokesperson. It was a vote of confidence that would put him and his colleagues directly in the path of some of the most powerful interests in the region — and it would forever change their lives, not to mention the way that the world thought of this virtually unknown Alpine town of just over five thousand citizens. In fact, the work of the Advocacy Committee would transform Mals into an international model of grassroots activism and direct democracy within less than two years. The miracle of Mals was about to unfold, but not without some serious hurdles and painful attacks from outside interest groups.

The new committee couldn't have selected a better spokesperson, and they would gradually learn that the townspeople also could not have elected a better mayor for pulling off what would be a series of coups, thanks to the highly organized guerrilla tactics of the townspeople. The group's extended efforts to promote civil discourse would be put to the test time and again, and Johannes would suffer the bruising effects of being the point person for what Big Apple and its allies felt might be but the first municipality in the province to begin to protest the extraordinarily high use of pesticides in the South Tirol — by conscientious farmers as well as the inevitable black sheep. After all, it was only a matter of time before enough concerned citizens realized they weren't isolated in their opinions and began to speak out. Even if they weren't particularly concerned about pesticides, many people were lamenting the destruction of the region's traditional agriculture.

Knowing that they would lose even more ground in the coming year, the Advocacy Committee began to discuss their next steps. Thanks to the strategic change to the municipal code in May of the previous year, if the citizens of Mals approved a referendum supporting a pesticide ban in their town, then the municipal council was required to take up the issue. However, drafting a version of such a referendum that would be legally acceptable was beginning to look complicated, and it was hard to tell how popular it might be among the majority of citizens in Mals.

There tends to be a certain caution about expressing one's political opinions in public in South Tirolean culture, so it was difficult for the group to ascertain whether they were in a minority regarding their concerns about Big Apple's advances and the dangers of more chemical-intensive agriculture in the Upper Vinschgau. They dared to hope that a slim majority of citizens might share their concerns, but even a slim majority felt optimistic. Nonetheless, to develop a strategy forward, they needed to have some sense of what others were thinking.

A Precautionary Tale

"Nichts besorgt ein Politiker mehr als Nummern im Schwartz und Weis." Nothing worries a politician more than numbers in black and white. That was the advice a politician had given Peter Gasser at one point, and it became a guiding star for the next big move of the gathering constellation of activists. In March the USGV decided that they would hire a polling firm to gather data from a solid sampling of Mals citizens regarding their views on the changing face of agriculture in the Vinschgau. What they discovered startled everyone: 84 percent of the Malsers polled viewed intensive fruit production to be detrimental to their future, and 70 percent of the respondents supported the exclusive use of organic resources in local agriculture.[2]

Suddenly, the future seemed much brighter — or at least the vision of the future embraced by the local citizens. It remained to be seen whether they were in charge of their own destiny or not. They were working within a complex environment. The power players in the South Tirol had no interest in their pesticide-free vision, but they were all beholden to the Italian national law, as well as European Union (EU) regulations. They were advocating for local control within three concentric legal circles: the South Tirol, Italy, and the European Union. It was a challenge to know who the ultimate allies would be — those close to home or farther away.

Fortunately, in that same month a court order in the nearby Italian province of Trentino overturned a previous court decision between the Trentino farmers' association and the township of Malosco. In the court's reversal of the judgment, Malosco was granted the authority to forbid the use of the two most toxic categories of pesticides in the EU (T = Toxic, and T+ = Very Toxic) and to push forward enhanced buffer zones in the town.

The Advocacy Committee was beginning to sense that there was not only hope but also some national precedent for using the legal system to protect human and environmental health from rampant use of pesticides. Trentino was the only province in Italy with a higher overall pesticide use than the South Tirol. It used more than twice the amount of fungicide but, on average, slightly less insecticides and acaricides (arachnid poisons). In fact, the two provinces' excessive uses of pesticides made the rest of Italy look like amateurs in "crop protection"; South Tirol and Trentino used between two and five times the amounts applied by farmers in the other provinces.[3]

The Advocacy Committee in Mals and the leading activists from Malosco began to share and compare knowledge and strategies. Suddenly the Malsers didn't feel quite so isolated. What they were doing made sense, despite messages to the contrary from farther down the valley.

Connecting with the Malosco initiative was one of several strategies that the Advocacy Committee would follow to advance their cause. Networking to build a web of people and organizations they could call on would prove crucial, as would tapping outside expertise, and consistent messaging through a single spokesperson. Johannes published a weekly email newsletter to supporters that went out first thing every Friday morning, with updates on the initiative, related news from near and far, new scientific research, and announcements of upcoming meetings. On the community-education front, the Advocacy Committee held more than twenty public meetings in less than two years, often featuring leading international experts not just on pesticide science and policy but also on organic agriculture, sustainable economic development, and methods of direct democracy.

Johannes described the overall strategy for garnering and galvanizing local support for a pesticide-free Mals: "To reach the goal you need objective, hard facts, facts that are hard as nails; it just has to be consistent and true, the whole thing. You need the best experts — so the best judicial experts, the best lawyers, as well as the best toxicologists, environmental physicians, pharmacists, physicians, biologists." Bringing in those experts also offered an opportunity to capture media interest and tell the Mals story to anyone who would listen. Sometimes that meant going outside the South Tirol. Not everyone wanted the story told inside the province, so the Malsers went to a neutral party . . . known in that part of the world as Switzerland. One of the committee's first official events was to bring in Hermann Kruse, a toxicologist from the University of Kiel, who tackled the question of how dangerous pesticides in fruit production really were. His presentation was scheduled for the evening of April 26 in the Mals Cultural House, and it proved a rousing success, but for more than the turnout and the information shared.

That morning an article appeared in the *Südostschweiz Zeitung*, a respected newspaper in Switzerland. The headlines in the paper version were enough to give the entire tourist sector in the South Tirol heart palpitations: *Giftige Gefahr in Südtirol: Spritzmittel verseuchen Ferienregion Vinschgau*, Toxic Danger in the South Tirol: Pesticides Spoil the Vacation Region of the Vinschgau. The headlines in the online version simply added a further sensation of cardiac arrhythmia, translating to "South Tiroleans defend themselves against the poisoning of their homeland: The Upper Vinschgau in South Tirol is considered an idyllic holiday region — Now the massive use of pesticides in orchards threatens to destroy paradise."[4]

Perhaps not coincidentally, it was one of the cheeky activists from Adam & Epfl, Konrad Messner, the innkeeper in Plawenn, who was interviewed (it probably pays to have connections in neutral places). In reference to the selling of land at high prices to incoming apple farmers and the subsequent spreading of trellising infrastructure and pesticides, Konrad summed up the reasons the Malsers were beginning to take a stand: "The question is, ultimately, do we want to watch, or do we want to do something about it?"

Governor Durnwalder caught wind of the article in short order; it was a downdraft of the Vinschgerwind. His response, captured in the local news magazine, was appropriately agricultural, although not altogether diplomatic: "That is simply unheard of . . . I find the reporting simply hogwash."[5] He went on to note that the article cast agriculture in a bad light, as damaging to the environment, when in fact the provincial guidelines for pesticides were set at less than half the allowable thresholds.

Of course, everyone knew that the timing of the article was auspicious: The apple blossom season is touted as one of the premier times to visit the region, and the article coincided with that influx of tourists. Ironically, spraying for certain diseases is considered optimal during the blossom period. The juxtaposition of an ocean of petals and plumes of pesticides can be a hard sell, especially to tourists savoring the beauty of hiking or biking through an otherwise romantic agricultural landscape.

While the story rattled the regional tourism sector and infuriated the South Tirolean Farmers' Association and the apple lobby, it also alerted Durnwalder and Big Apple to what was coming. The cat was out of the bag. Not only did the article report the shocking results of the USGV poll of Malsers on their support for a pesticide-free future, but it also noted a new development: "On the previous Monday, a request was submitted to the

Mals Municipal Council for a public referendum calling for a 'pesticide-free Mals.' Now it is being reviewed as to whether the request is allowable."

Indeed, on April 22, 2013, Johannes had filed an official request from the first forty-seven "advocates" to begin the required collection of signatures that would call for a referendum on the banning of pesticides in Mals. First, however, town officials were required to verify the legitimacy of all of the signatures and the residency of each of the forty-seven advocates who had signed the request. Three weeks later, at the meeting of the municipal commission on May 16, the request was rejected due to formal mistakes made by both the commission and the signatories.

Big Apple and the bureaucrats were getting nervous. The Advocacy Committee was asking a local question that would rattle the region. The provincial power brokers knew that if they could derail the question, they would never have to deal with the answer.

Local control or the control of local? It was an odd conundrum for a province that had fought valiantly for its autonomy for decades.

After the Swiss newspaper had identified Big Apple's cosmetic defects, Hermann Kruse's presentation was all the more pertinent, given not only the rumblings in the international media but also the recent use of herbicides to "burn down" fields in three of Mals's villages. Glyphosate, a widely used herbicide, was under much more scrutiny in Europe than in the United States, and recent scientific findings about the risks associated with glyphosate had raised red flags all across the continent. Concerns about the influx of herbicide use in Mals were particularly peaked at the time due to the recent sprayings, but Kruse wasn't there to allay concerns. Rather, his task was to lay out his views, as a toxicologist, on the dangers of the pesticides used in fruit production.

He offered several key themes for the evening, one of the most important being that all synthetically manufactured pesticides are slow to break down and therefore leave residues in the food chain. The results are weakened immune systems for people, animals, and bee colonies. He cited research on 6,022 conventionally produced fruit and vegetable samples in which 43 percent showed "very high" residues and 56.2 percent were in the "high" residue level category. Although they did not exceed legally prescribed maximums, his concern was the mix of different pesticide residues and their potential impact on human and environmental health. With up to eight substances on some of the products, the concept of acceptable limits begins to break down. These limits don't account for the effects of the mixtures, which can create unexpected problems for people with certain chemical sensitivities. In the worst cases, they even can be fatal. According to Kruse, "The structures of the substances are becoming more and more complicated today, making the analyses by the toxicologists increasingly difficult."[6]

Despite the unsettling statistics and the complexities of the issue, Kruse did have a reassuring conclusion to his presentation: Organic agriculture demonstrates no known human toxicological concerns.

Apparently, though, organic agriculture did create concerns for the health of the status quo in the South Tirol. But the status quo is seldom an aspiration. It is usually a default, and the Malsers had a different future in mind. Seizing on the now public question of whether Paradise was about to cave to the power of apple, they turned a sacred motif into political theater in a matter of weeks.

On the morning of May 19, starting with birdsong and biologists at 6 AM on the Mals Heath, Adam & Epfl organized a dawn-to-dark series of events around the theme of seduction. They had everything to lose — and they were going to make what could be lost obvious, with guerrilla art and a showcase of local food and drink. It was nothing short of collective genius, in one of the most magnificent settings in the world. It was, in fact, Paradise.

Residents of the Upper Vinschgau awoke to a jolting surprise that May morning. In every town and in unexpected places across the landscape, they saw serpents. Not terrifying serpents but colorful snakes rendered from wood, paint, and textiles. Some were sculptures made of wood, papier-mâché, or variegated cloth tubes that somehow found their way into the most unusual but highly visible locations, even on one of the concrete World War II bunkers. Others were painted onto the asphalt of streets in the different villages. A few even found their way into Switzerland, a not-so-subtle reminder of the encroaching dangers that could slip across the border, undetected, until it was too late.

On the back of the event flyer, Adam & Epfl had even created a map that transformed the sinuous flow of the valley and the Etsch (Adige) River into a serpent, its head making its way up the valley. The map demarcated each of the towns and some of the events in the Upper Vinschgau with an apple — an apple with a bite missing. Above the map was the invitation: "At various places on the 19 of May, delicacies from Paradise, along with activities and events, will be offered. All visitors are invited to participate and collectively reflect while biking, hiking, and enjoying the landscape and making a personal contribution to the Paradise of the Upper Vinschgau."

In each village, participants were greeted by various renditions of Eve in full greenery and natural regalia, complete with body paints. More than five hundred people showed up to follow the serpentine route "together with Eve." Various versions of Eve appeared near each location, painted and costumed to accompany the participants, most of whom were traveling on foot or by bicycle. The women who gave up their identities for the day to act out their own interpretations of Eve held nothing back in the artistry of their costumes, and, with theatrical allure, they readily offered passersby the temptation of an apple.

Other event hosts sported spots and sleek garments, slinking through the milling crowds as body-painted snakes, offering temptations of various sorts, while the devil herself, dressed in red and black, backed up the serpents. Were it not for her devilish horns, she might have beguiled the more unsuspecting guests. One seductive serpent created a costume to match the live boa constrictor that she carried with her throughout the day, garnering a mixture of terror and delight.

The theatrical confusion was intentional — Adam & Epfl's question for the day was, "Adam, Eve, and the Snake: Who seduces whom in the Paradise of the Upper Vinschgau?" The event organizers explained the event's intent in their brochure:

> With the spread of intense fruit cultivation in the upper Val
> Venosta, questions arise. This leads to a disagreement about
> the paradise of the Upper Vinschgau: How will we live? In
> which landscape do we want to live? From what do we want
> to subsist? Which Upper Vinschgau do we want to leave to

our grandchildren? The citizens' initiative "Adam & Epfl" is of the opinion that all of these things should be discussed in the open because this development will permanently change the Upper Vinschgau region. This change affects not only agriculture, but also all those who live or vacation here in the valley. As part of a day of action, Adam and Epfl creates places of encounter, dialogue, and enjoyment and calls people to action in diverse ways.

The weather was perfect, and people of all ages and nationalities milled through the villages with family and friends in tow. Bicycles, backpacks, and strollers interwove along the bike paths and village streets throughout the day as people pursued their interests and their gastronomic callings.

The heartiest of participants began with a naturalist's tour of the Mals Heath, the coveted location for any new apple plantations. Afterward, wise participants made their way down to Hofkäserei Englhorn where Alexander and his family served a traditional breakfast and then a variety of dishes that highlighted their cheese products throughout the day. They offered passersby cheese dumplings, a spring celery salad with hard cheese, and baked polenta with melted cheese on top. Choosing from the menu of choices after that became an exercise in self-indulgence, as many of the most intriguing restaurants and distilleries opened their doors and offered not just local foods and beverages prepared traditionally but also new delicacies — highlighting opportunities to wed entrepreneurial and culinary creativity.

In Mals's family-run Hotel Greif, known internationally for its focus on whole foods and vegetarian cuisine, Adam & Epfl supporters served pizza, breads, and pasta dishes that capitalized on the hotel's culinary themes. After visitors got a healthy taste of Paradise straight from the Garden of Eden, they were then invited to cave in to the decadence of the sweets and homemade ice cream at the café and ice cream parlor Fritz, which also offered samples of its birch sugar. A jaunt downhill to the train station in town, "The Entrance to Paradise," featured professional face painting for kids and the young at heart.

Not far from the train station is the Panorama Hotel, with an organic café and organic distillery. One of the first certified organic hotels in Italy, the Panorama featured organic seductions of all sorts, as they do on a daily basis. The organic hotel is a strong draw for tourists, but the organic distillery is popular among locals, too, featuring a visually stunning array of distilled products from heritage fruits and local herbs, all crafted according to organic standards.

Across the valley in Glurns, the Puni Whiskey Distillery opened its doors to visitors and showed how it blended old and new, all to international acclaim. Opened in 2012, Puni (named after the river flowing nearby) produces Italy's first whiskey in an ultramodern architectural wonder that seems to eschew almost all of the traditional Alpine aesthetic. Their various distillations feature local rye, along with wheat and barley, playing off local tradition while finding a new niche in the global marketplace. The distillery also found a perfect new use for some of the old World War II bunkers in the area. With their cool temperatures and high humidity, the sunken concrete structures provide the ideal aging environment for the distillery's products.

Another jaunt landed participants in the town of Prad, where local beekeepers brought hives, displays, and samples of various honeys to highlight *Evas Fleissige Bienchen*, Eve's Hardworking Little Bees. Setting up beside the bike path, beekeepers explained how they place their hives not just among different crops but also at different elevations. The various plant communities and blooming times of the different elevations create honey products from different plant species and elevations, the diversity of which is cherished by locals and tourists alike. Inevitably, some of the discussions focused on the complex relationship beekeepers have with orchardists and what it would mean to have more apples in the valley, as well as the differences between organic and conventional apple production.

Of course, any tour of the Upper Vinschgau with Eve would eventually land visitors in the closest thing the area has to a Garden of Eden, the display gardens of Edith and Robert Bernhard in Burgeis. The Bernhards offered the ultimate seduction: not just the opportunity to witness organic agriculture and biodiversity in situ, but the imperative to join the movement and take it to the next level, if only by having a home garden and relearning the skills of composting, seedsaving, and preparing raw, cooked, and conserved foods. While Robert demonstrated the virtues and how-tos of compost, Edith led visitors around the gardens, discussing the biodiversity of herbs in their collection, walking through the grove of heritage fruits, noting the stories and traits of each tree, and walking out of the orchard corridor and into the vegetable gardens, where she had a platter of colorful vegetables, edible flowers, cheeses, and rustic bread made with their own grain.

It was just another day in Paradise. But that was subject to change.

CHAPTER 10

Bedsheets to Banners

Martina Hellrigl was sitting in the styling chair of Laatsch's local beauty salon, peering into the large oval mirror in front of her. She leaned from side to side to get a better look, not at her own visage but at the early-June beauty of the gardens on the other side of the sliding glass doors behind her. Beatrice Raas's hair salon was much different from the salons she'd been going to in Zurich. Not only was it easier to get an appointment, but there was no stainless steel, no fancy lights. Its wood trim, expansive windows, gardens, and patio felt welcoming and soothing.

Born and raised in Mals, Martina had studied architecture and landed in Zurich to pursue her profession in a place where her husband, Koen Hertoge, a Belgian, also had a job. After becoming the mother of two small children, though, she felt a calling to bring her family back home. It just felt like a healthier and safer place to raise children. But she'd been gone a long time, and she was struggling a bit to find her way back into a new cast of characters in the community. She'd known Beatrice from earlier days, so she had come to her salon to seek out an old friend as much as to get her hair cut.

Beatrice appeared around the corner with a pair of scissors and began to toss Martina's straight black hair between her fingers.

"Your garden is so beautiful," Martina said, in dialect. "Your salon is a refuge from everything."

For Beatrice, it was critical to have nature close by when she worked. "It gives me inspiration," she replied, "and it's nice for me and my clients to be able to sit outside and enjoy it. We're so lucky to live in such a Paradise."

Time had quickly slipped by since the activists' brilliant guerrilla theater, but Beatrice's mere mention of Paradise turned Martina's attention to the town's plight.

"Speaking of that, I thought I saw you at the Hermann Kruse lecture a few days ago?"

"Yes. You were there?" Worried about the changes she saw coming up the valley, Beatrice had wanted to ask Martina about the information session, too. She had been keeping her concerns to herself. Like many in Mals, she wasn't quite sure if her fears and frustrations were isolated or widely shared.

"It was the first of those information sessions I'd gone to," answered Martina. "I've been worried about the pesticides and the new apple plantations, but I haven't really heard people talking about it. I was beginning to think I was the only person worried about all of it. I didn't even know about the information sessions until this one."

Beatrice sighed heavily. The session had confirmed a lot of her fears about what was coming. "As a mother, I'm worried for my kids, but I don't know much about the science of it all," she said as she snipped. "We should all be worried about living in a place covered in orchards and pesticides, like they deal with down in the valley."

Martina looked into the mirror and asked Beatrice directly, "Well, why aren't we hearing more about it? Why isn't anyone writing about it? Why haven't there been any letters to the editor? It makes me totally crazy!"

Despite the brilliant guerrilla theater and the info sessions, area activists had a long way to go before they'd secured the future of Paradise. The regional media wasn't picking up on much of the activity or helping to convey the information on pesticides and the loss of traditional agriculture in the Vinschgau. The politicians also seemed to be ignoring the calls for protecting human health in the face of such dramatic change. Even with the reassuring polling results, it wasn't clear that anything was going to change. Big Apple was still growing, and there was nothing in its way.

"What can we actually do?" asked Beatrice as she set into a fast-paced rhythm of cutting, combing, cutting.

Martina confided that she had been thinking about writing a letter to the editor, but she didn't want to do it alone and didn't know enough people to ask to join her. "I'm still feeling sort of like a newcomer here." Beatrice, on the other hand, didn't really like to write, but she did have what she called "a great *Frauennetzwerk* (women's network)!"

A coalition of Eve's successors were about to have their say.

Beatrice later described how she felt during that conversation with Martina: "My heart started racing: Finally, I felt that I wasn't alone. She gave me the strength to know that I should and had to do something. I was awakened and driven, and found the self-confidence to begin speaking about environmental issues. I was simply happy to have finally found someone with whom I could actually *do* something and not just chatter and crawl into a snail shell."

Revolutionary ideas are known for popping up in odd places. At the time, neither Martina nor Beatrice knew that that one conversation would give rise to a powerful new collection of voices — voices that had been too much in the background up to that point: those of the women of Mals. While some had graced the streets adorned as Eves for the May celebration, the committee meetings and planning had largely been the work of men. It was time to move from informing and discussing to action.

Keenly attuned to the issues of nature, nurture, and nutrition, many of the women had had deep misgivings about the transformation of their historic landscape and its accompanying arsenal of pesticides. Singly, they had been unsure about the merit of their concerns; together they would turn out to be more than just fearless — they were profoundly strategic. The press and the politicians were about to confront a body politic different from what they were used to.

This group of women — who also welcomed men but operated on their own terms — were novices in this game of social media, public relations, and politics, but it would be to their advantage: They would invent the rules as they went along.

And before it was all over, Beatrice would be operating the first certified organic hair salon in the South Tirol.

Martina went home eager to do something but second-guessing herself the whole time. Was she really ready to make such a public statement and begin stirring the pot just as she was beginning to find her way back into her hometown? What if the poll numbers didn't really reflect people's sentiments? Nevertheless, she quickly drafted a concise letter to the editor, which she sent to Beatrice to review before forwarding it any further. Once they were both satisfied with the final version, they began making the rounds to friends' houses and cafés, sticking paper copies in doors and mail slots when no one was home and sending other versions by email. They passed it on to all of their acquaintances who might be interested in signing it and sending it to the local news magazine, the *Vinschgerwind*.

On May 16, 2013, the magazine published thirteen versions of the letter, with a total of sixty-nine signatures under the various submissions. Each letter was titled *Bitte!* (Please!) and contained these two lines:

> The increasing use of pesticides and herbicides in the municipality of Mals has us highly concerned about our health and especially the health of our children. We ask our mayor, who is responsible for the health of our citizens, to ensure that our environment and our health are not endangered.

While the letter was brief and to the point, it possessed a power that stretched far beyond the boundaries of the South Tirol and all the way to Brussels, home of the European Union Parliament. By calling directly upon the mayor to act on behalf of his citizens' safety, Martina, Beatrice, and the other signers of the letter were invoking the right of mayors, designated under EU law, to take necessary measures that might exceed their usual powers, in order to assure the safety of their citizens.

They had started to change the game.

As May turned to June, things began to heat up. The letters to the editor had their intended impact: Big Apple and the provincial powers were roused from their slumber by the poke and found themselves in the midst of a game they hadn't played before. They also weren't accustomed to playing defense, since offense is the strategy of choice among giants. And the most common error among giants is to mistake beginners for buffoons.

Perhaps it was coincidence, or intuition, or just a result of the grassroots groundswell that was happening in Mals, but another Malser felt the need for a haircut, something she actually didn't enjoy and tended to avoid for as long as possible.

Pia Oswald had seen the letters to the editor in the *Vinschgerwind*, and she'd heard that Beatrice was involved. Pia had been feeling the need to get involved in tipping the apple cartel for a while, and she'd felt that women's voices and perspectives needed to be a more prominent part of the discussions and initiatives. In the end, it was worth getting a haircut.

Pia is a *Selbstvorsorgerer* — a "self-provider" — who produces an extraordinary supply of fruits, vegetables, small livestock, and honey for her family, and she is a guru among homesteader types in the South Tirol. In her orchards and gardens, tempting fruits abound, and only a few of them are apples. Most are tree fruits and berries with an origin story, a recipe, and a nutritional niche. She and her son also keep bees, and she runs a small daycare out of her home. In addition, she teaches Tirolean gardening skills to new refugees who have settled in Mals.

Pia's concerns about the influx of intensive fruit production weren't theoretical. Her homestead is situated along a fast-flowing brook up on the eastern edge of the Mals Heath; the sound of water permeates the entirety of her smallholding. As a beekeeper, she'd been worried for a while about the possibility of conventional fruit growers establishing orchards within flying distance of her hives and too close to her own orchard of heritage fruits to ensure there would be no drifting. Unfortunately, her fears materialized: One of the first apple orchards on the cherished Mals Heath had popped up right across from hedgerows on the edge of her property.

From Pia's perspective, "The bees are the first victims — they're the ones that first feel the effects of the pesticides because they take them up directly."

That's not a perspective many beekeepers in the South Tirol are willing to share publicly, simply because they are so dependent upon apple growers for hiring them to place their hives near the apple orchards to ensure good pollination. But Pia sees conventional apple orchards as a threat to the health and even the survival of her colonies. "It's always so dangerous for the bees to fly to blossoms sprayed with pesticides — sometimes so dangerous that they die on contact with these pesticides . . . or they carry the nectar or pollen that has been contaminated with these very fine pesticide particles into the colony and the young brood is fed with this contaminated pollen," she explains. "That's the danger for the development of the colonies and for the flying bees, and for that reason I avoid taking my bee colonies into these apple plantations."

Of course, as Pia points out, the honey made from bees that are exposed to conventionally managed apple plantations is also likely to be contaminated, creating a health risk to humans who savor what is often considered to be one of nature's purest gifts.

Pia would carry her philosophy of maintaining the health of her family's bees into what would soon become her newfound political calling, *Prävention*: "My interest is always in prevention." Which is what made her call Beatrice, hop in her car, and drive over to Laatsch from her home outside the tiny hamlet of Ulten for a trim and a consultation.

Pia was eager to address the business at hand. As soon as Beatrice was into the rhythm of cutting, Pia let her know that she had long wanted to pull together a group of women to advance the kind of diversified agriculture that she thought still made sense for the region, but she had never felt like it was something she could begin on her own and "give it legs." She was ready to join forces.

Beatrice was so anxious to call Martina that as soon as she was done cutting, she pulled away the barber's cape, quickly brushed a few stray clippings from Pia's collar, and picked up the phone, firing off a stream of dialect, waving her free hand for emphasis, nodding and smiling at Pia. Within what seemed no more than a minute or two, she hung up and welcomed Pia to their growing female force.

Pia's influence would be critical to the success of the entire pesticide-free campaign from that point forward — and not just because of the fruit and honey that she would bring to the long meetings that were to come.

Big Apple had finally realized there was a revolution fomenting in Mals, and they responded in kind. On June 18 the South Tirolean Farmers' Association (SBB) sponsored a public forum in the nearby town of Prad. The evening featured Hermine Reich, the EU commissioner for food safety, who spoke about the EU's role in overseeing food-safety aspects of pesticides. Two other regional experts lent their expertise on the basics of pesticides in integrated fruit production and the safety of pesticides in the fruit industry. Following the three presentations, there was a podium discussion with six experts, including Hermann Kruse. While Reich maintained the perspective that "within the set limits, there are no health dangers for consumers," Kruse again expressed his concerns about the unknowns of "poisonous cocktails," mixes that didn't fit within the paradigm of measuring the impact of single substances.

The audience lobbed challenging questions to the panelists, driving much of the focus toward the looming questions of drift. Several of the experts touted the rigors of regulations and advances in spray technology, while also decrying the "black sheep" farmers who gave other well-intentioned orchardists a bad reputation.

In the end definitive answers were in short supply that evening, at least in the eyes of the pesticide-free advocates, while questions and concerns abounded. Perhaps the biggest unanswered question came from Günther Wallnöfer, who wondered how regulations or technology were going to solve his problem. After three years of expressing concerns and dealing with pesticide residues and all of the associated costs on his farm, there was still no resolution. Everyone wondered whether Günther would be the first of many with these kinds of the problems . . . and possibly the last of many generations of dairy farmers in the Upper Vinschgau.

While the power still resided with Big Apple and friends, more than its apples were at stake; so was its reputation. Three days after the Prad info session, the Laimburg Research Center would hold a seminar on "Reputation Management as the New Challenge for the Apple Industry in the South Tirol." Ironically, it was held in the Fürstenburg School for Agriculture and Forestry, directly adjacent to and overlooking the Upper Vinschgau's biodiversity jewel, the Bernhards' display gardens. If any of the participants bothered to look out over Edith and Robert's gardens, they might have remarked that there was much more to lose than a reputation.

Had they looked just a bit farther, toward Marienberg Abbey, they might have noticed new vineyards going in. Abbot Markus is an organic gardener who also appreciates local wines, for communing and communion, so he had made arrangements to plant six thousand PIWI (fungus-resistant) vines on nearly 6 acres (2.3 ha) of the monastery's south-facing slopes. Not only would the monastery have its own label, but at a height of 4,400 feet (1,340 meters) it would also lay claim to the title of the highest vineyard on the European continent.

Big Apple needed to look out the window to understand what they still weren't seeing in the mirror: #ReputationManagement.

Meanwhile, throughout the month of June and following the success of the letter to the editor campaign, Beatrice, Martina, and Pia continued to gather a core group of women and a few men who were determined to transform all of the awareness that had built up into direct action, with tangible results. USGV, Adam & Epfl, Kornkammer, the organic certifiers, the new Advocacy Committee, and others had worked hard to gather the data, analyze the policies, bring groups together, and share the information, but the local media and politicians had barely batted an eye so far.

Soon the next group of Querdenkers-turned-activists was born. They named themselves Hollawint, an exclamation of warning in Tirolean dialect. Composed predominantly but not exclusively of women, Hollawint nonetheless became the face of the women of Mals. For Beatrice, women offered something different from the movement for a pesticide-free Mals: "I believe when one is a mother, then she simply has a completely different feel for what life is, and she is then really responsible for one's own children. She simply wants to guarantee a great, healthy future for her kids and from that simply arises a motherly sensibility."

June was a reminder that time was of the essence. With every passing summer, more apple orchards were creeping into Mals. The infrastructure for sprinkler systems was almost in place, with supporters promising that it would bring possibilities for farmers to plant crops that would earn them significantly more money than hay, grains, and vegetables.

The rapid advance lured Margit Gasser to the newly formed group. A kindergarten teacher, she had married Peter, the town veterinarian, and moved to Mals where they began to raise a family. Her hometown of Schlanders, a little farther down in the valley, had already been taken over by orchards. "Twenty years ago when I came to Mals I could never have imagined that this monoculture would arrive here, too."

The childhood she recalls before Big Apple came to her town is as idyllic as a scene from *Heidi*. "When I was three or four years old, I could run around between the meadows and orchards, where I could smell flowers that came up to my nose . . . I have these memories inside me still." Those meadows eventually vanished. "And then I realized how we lost them, step by step . . . It happened so subtly — only grass, no more flowers. They were just mowed down, with the views everywhere suddenly blocked by cement posts."

As more and more joined Hollawint, Martina had already hammered out a long list of projects to catch the attention of the media, the public, and the politicians. No media maven but one determined soul, she had gone from being *kein Facebookerin*, no Facebooker, to a reasonably competent user who knew whom to call when she needed backup. Social media, it turned out, was a critical way to engage the younger generation and get word out beyond the bounds of the group's immediate circles. It was also useful when word needed to travel fast.

Within a few short weeks Hollawint had a logo, a website, and a standing biweekly meeting open to the public. By the end of June they had more than fifty members, and a following. It was time to send a message that couldn't be ignored. They decided to recruit women and their families to turn bedsheets into banners. And once they had, they would transform the villages of Mals into a political statement, hanging the banners from balconies, windows, and cultural icons — all under cover of darkness, and all in a single night.

As the group discussed what message they wanted to send, Pia weighed in with a piece of wisdom that would become the guiding star for the rest of the campaign. Martina explained: "From the beginning, Pia saw our work as somewhat spiritual and positive." When it came time to work on the banners, she said, Pia made sure that positivity was reflected. YES was everywhere. AGAINST, ANTI, and NO were nowhere to be found. The guiding rule was simple: Focus on what you want, not what you oppose.

What could have been a campaign against pesticides became a clarion call for a pesticide-free future.

It always pays to have a journalist in one's ranks, too, and Hollawint had recruited the expertise of Katharina Hohenstein, a freelance writer and editor with a penchant for pithiness. With Pia's counsel in mind,

149

Katharina brainstormed various slogans and sent ideas to Martina via email. Suddenly the Malsers weren't calling for anything outrageous — they were simply asking for what any mother, father, or citizen might want. *Vielfalt und Gesundheit für uns alle!* Diversity and health for us all! *Für eine gesunde und vielfältige Landwirtschaft!* For a healthy and diverse agriculture! *Gesundheit und Vielfalt für unsere Kinder, Tiere und Pflanzen!* Health and diversity for our children, animals, and plants! *Pestizidfreie Gemeinde! Landschaft nützen und schützen!* Pesticide-free town! Use and protect the landscape! *Frei von Pestiziden — für uns und unsere Gäste.* Free from pesticides — for us and our guests.

Hollawint members rallied and set to work collecting bedsheets and turning them into banners over the next few weeks. They also encouraged other women to come pick up materials for their families to make their own. While everyone added their own flair to the banners and even some wooden signs, the goal was to be consistent in appearance and messaging, making it clear that there was unity across the township's villages. People traded stencils and art supplies, slowly and quietly building an arsenal of positive messages and allies willing to hang the banners and signs in prominent locations.

Martina was shocked at the enthusiastic response by women across town. When the banners were done, she said, "They were ripped out of our hands!"[1] Even women who hadn't yet joined the cause got involved. Pia went to visit the *Bäuerinnen*, the women farmers, in the small villages of Ulten and Plawenn near her home, and they surprised her with their willingness to hang banners on and around their farmhouses.

Despite the flurry of activity, the denouement was all under the radar. The night finally came when, after town lights had flickered off, the banners were unfurled. Many people didn't even realize that their neighbors were also hanging banners until the next day. It turned out to be a case of stealth solidarity.

Mother Nature was given the honors of the unveiling, and on the morning of July 31, 2013, the first rays of light began to creep over the mountains as if they were inhaling the lingering shadows of the night. Down in the valley among Mals's scattered villages, farmers pulling wheeled milk cans clanked their way toward the pickup points along the medieval labyrinth of village thoroughfares. In fact, it was probably the milk truck drivers who first realized the scope of the overnight mission as they wound their way from village to village, sucking milk from each farmer's containers and passing on news from one farmer to another of the overnight blossoming of banners and wooden signs. Undoubtedly a lot of heads were shaking around those milk cans, but there were certainly some wry smiles among that independent lot of farmers, some of whom had come in from the fields and barns to find their wives stenciling old linens for a campaign that had yet to unfold. In the end no one had more to lose than the dairy farmers. With an average of 124 acres (50 ha) around them transitioning to apples every year, almost everyone was likely to have some new neighbors soon.

By the time the sun crested the highest peaks, Mals was fully "woke." Word of the banners had spread from village to village, and townspeople were already making the rounds with their cameras and cell phones, taking photos and gathering in their usual cafés to exchange impressions. No matter what one thought about the messaging — and not everyone was happy to have the town's laundry aired in such a dramatic fashion — everyone marveled at the stealth and surprise of it all.

Banners hung from hotel balconies, farmers' fences, shop windows, village entrances, and in front of one of the more prominent World War II–era bunkers — anywhere that would attract attention or add an element of irony.

HOLLAWINT.COM was stamped, stenciled, or painted on almost every banner, leading viewers to the new website to discover that women and mothers were on the move. Hollawint's Facebook page touted a colorful statement of intent: "Everyone is talking about it. It's best if we talk TOGETHER about it: our quality of life, our habitat, our children, our local products, our health, our future, and the diversity of our landscape."

In the spirit of Pope Francis and his namesake, St. Francis of Assisi, even Abbot Markus at Marienberg agreed to having a banner hung prominently in front of the abbey, just outside its new pesticide-free vineyards.

It was a fitting precursor to yet another campaign in the works, one that would wake up people the world over. The idea of countering an insurgency through direct democracy was gaining ground.

The women of Hollawint had written their wishes across the landscape. Now it was time to find a way to post them on a ballot.

CHAPTER 11

Manifesto

"The environment is really the first factor in medicine." Elisabeth Viertler shook her head, thinking back on where she grew up. Her family's house was in the middle of apple orchards farther down in the valley, and it wasn't something that she'd really thought much about until she finished medical school and opened her pediatrics practice in Mals.

As she settled in and had the opportunity to appreciate the freshness of the air and the openness of the landscape, she began to wonder about all of the pesticides sprayed in those orchards and how it was that she and her family never really questioned the potential health impacts. Then again, few members of the medical community in South Tirol were questioning the heavy pesticide use — at least not out loud, in public — until very recently. From Elisabeth's perspective, "The agriculture and fruit industry are an important part of South Tyrol's economy, and when you grew up around it and saw it all as common practice, it takes some time until you start questioning it . . . The causalities are really only becoming clear to me now."

With her straight brown hair falling across the shoulders of her white doctor's coat and her stethoscope always at the ready, Elisabeth is a soft-spoken clinician whose entire office complex feels like a cocreation between her and her patients of the last fifteen years. The walls of every room are completely covered with children's artwork — so densely hung that it rivals the taped tapestries adorning most elementary school classroom walls and virtually disguises the primary function of the examination room. Graced with hand-drawn toothy smiles and scenes of forests and flowerscapes and imagined contraptions, her clinic is a place of wellness, complemented by the sun streaming in from the walls of windows and toys positioned strategically from the waiting room to the examination table. She even dares to open her balcony doors so that the fresh air can pour in—a rebellious medical act, but Elisabeth is interested in health and not convention.

Primum non nocere. First, do no harm. As someone who appreciates the best of Western and Eastern medicine, Elisabeth has long been in search of ways to restore balance within the human body, and she began to realize that the principles of regenerative agriculture and holistic medicine were parallel in philosophy and approach. Pesticides not only knocked agricultural and ecological systems out of whack, but also posed serious risks to humans. Suddenly what went on outside her clinic mattered as much as what she did inside her examination room.

Like Margit Gasser, Elisabeth dreaded the notion of Mals becoming a landscape like the one in which she'd grown up farther down the valley. So in doctorly fashion but with a nontraditional approach, she began to think about a prescription. This time, however, it would be a prescription for the Upper Vinschgau. And such a novel prescription warranted the expertise of a first-rate pharmacist. Fortunately, one was within easy walking distance. Elisabeth and Johannes Unterpertinger were about to conjure up the biggest remedy of their lives.

While Hollawint's supporters were stenciling the last of the banners on July 30, Elisabeth and Johannes invited all of the "doctors" of the Upper Vinschgau to pen a complementary document: a manifesto by medical doctors, dentists, veterinarians, biologists, and pharmacists calling "for the protection of health and the sustainable stewardship of soil, water and air."

People with doctoral degrees, particularly in the sciences, tend to be held in the highest regard in South Tirol and throughout Europe, and their concerns are not easily swept under the rug. So the eclectic group—bound by their education and interest in human and animal health and biological systems—gathered in Mals to fine-tune a document that politicians and lobbyists in Bozen and beyond would take seriously. It read:

Manifesto

PREMISE: We regard the property of individuals as inviolable and hold that everyone can do and allow what they wish, within the limits of the law, on their land. But this is the point: on their land! And not on the land of their neighbors, and still less on the land of an entire community. The age-old principle of law must apply to all: "The freedom of the individual is limited by the rights of our neighbors."

And the right of neighbors to unspoiled air, water and soil and to undamaged health is being endangered by synthetic chemical pesticides and massively violated as a consequence of drift.

IN VIEW OF THE FACT that large numbers of synthetic chemical pesticides and insecticides are being used in conventional and integrated fruit-growing,

IN VIEW OF THE FACT that none of these substances can be classified as "non-hazardous" and that, on the contrary, there are scientific grounds to believe that some of them are carcinogenic, while many are harmful to health, hormone-disruptive and mutagenic,

IN VIEW OF THE FACT that fruit-growing in the Upper Vinschgau Valley is increasing and that, owing to the constantly blowing wind (see for example the trees growing at a slant on the area of the "Malser Haide"), no application of pesticides is possible *without* massive drift over a range of several kilometers, meaning that the substances will be blown over every field and into every village, affecting both private and public establishments and facilities such as schools, kindergartens, playgrounds, cycle paths, and so on,

IN VIEW OF THE FACT that clean air to breathe is a necessity for life and consequently part of the human right to health, and that a large proportion of the pesticides is absorbed through the respiratory tract and the skin,

IN VIEW OF THE FACT that, owing to their physical sensitivity, the unborn and children are especially vulnerable to poisoning,

With this manifesto we are expressing our deep concerns regarding the health hazards, and with our signatures we call upon the mayor of the "Upper Vinschgau" catchment area and all those in power in South Tyrol to implement serious alternative production methods up to and including the prohibition of the use of synthetic chemical pesticides and insecticides, in particular on the Malser Haide catchment area.

It was signed by fifty-one of the most well-respected members of the Upper Vinschgau — almost every doctor of science in the region. Against the backdrop of Hollawint's banner campaign, the release and spread of the manifesto over the next few days created a frenzy in the region. If there was any doubt beforehand, it was now clear: The Malsers were taking a stand, and they were not falling for the temptation of Big Apple. "Crop protection" had somehow taken priority over the protection of humans and their environment, and the signers of the manifesto listed some of the dangers associated with pesticides below their statement.

A key element of the statement was a long-standing fundamental concept in European philosophy and law: *"The freedom of the individual is limited by the rights of our neighbors."* This concept began appearing in various forms in the late eighteenth century and was fundamental to German philosopher Immanuel Kant's thinking about an individual's rights under law.[1] Including this statement as a foundational element of the manifesto linked the basics of jurisprudence with the expert scientific opinion of the manifesto's signers.

Furthermore, their public call for the mayor to protect their health was yet another strategic move to provide the mayor with the justification to invoke his powers under European law to do what was necessary to guarantee the safety of his citizens. It wasn't that Ulrich Veith, the mayor, needed convincing. He simply needed justification and support from as many angles as possible. While the Malsers were increasingly united, they were also threatening the status quo. And the power and money behind the status quo rivaled any monetary resources the Malsers could muster. Their strength lay in pointing out the absurdity of the status quo and their right to determine their own healthy future.

The signers of the manifesto were also proponents of the precautionary principle, a concept that places the burden of proof for safety upon those who create or manufacture elements of risk, as opposed to requiring the public — citizens, NGOs, or the government — to prove the danger of a suspected risk. That question of who bears the burden of proof (the public or those who create the risks in question) is nearly as deep a divide between Europe and the United States as the Atlantic Ocean.

In Europe the precautionary principle serves as a fundamental basis for generating sound public policy; public health and safety generally trumps potential threats to it. In the United States, however, dangers have to be established through what is generally termed risk analysis, meaning that "acceptable levels of risk" are established. Any challenges to those risks have typically arisen through the slow-grinding cogs of policy and judicial action, and both avenues are highly dependent upon scientific evidence, which can be hard to pay for but easily bought. Precaution tends to be more of an afterthought than a guiding principle in the United States, and more of a guiding light in Europe.

Environmental lawyer Carolyn Raffensperger, one of the leading proponents of the precautionary principle in the United States, not only summed up its utility but also shed insight on how it was so central to the pesticide-free campaign in Mals:

> As we define it today, the precautionary principle has three core elements: the threat of harm, uncertainty, and precautionary action. I think the big surprise of the precautionary principle is the paradox of action. Taking a precautionary approach doesn't mean stopping everything or not doing anything or blocking progress. It means looking for alternatives, using democracy, and reversing the burden of proof from those who have been harmed to those who pollute.[2]

With the multitude of questions posed by pesticides, those persons impacted by their use find themselves not just caught in clouds of drift but also the fog of a cocktail of uncertainties.

Johannes has a simple way of explaining these cocktails of uncertainty, simply by going to the website for AGRIOS (*Arbeitsgruppe für den integrierten Obstanbau in Südtirol*) and downloading the PDF of their guidelines for integrated fruit production with pome fruits (such as apples and pears), available in German, Italian, and English.[3] The 2016 version of the guidelines is forty-six pages long. Johannes points out that seventeen of those pages focus solely on which chemicals are dedicated to the treatment of specific diseases, pests, and conditions and how they should be applied — all in table format.

One has to admire the extraordinary research and care put into the creation of a highly useful document. Those who work within those guidelines are farmers playing by the rules; those who work outside that framework are the so-called black sheep of the industry. However, more than seventy active ingredients are listed for use in those seventeen pages of pesticide application guidelines.

To be fair, it has to be said that *integrierte Obstanbau*, integrated fruit production — generally referred to as integrated pest management, or IPM, in English — was in many ways a positive development in the fruit industry when it first began to emerge as a guiding approach in the 1970s.[4] IPM encouraged farmers to work together with researchers to find ways to manage fruit operations more holistically, taking into account soil health, climatic conditions, disease and pest life cycles, plant nutrition, improved pruning techniques, and other elements that could minimize chemical inputs by managing the orchard ecosystem through biological and mechanical means. In addition, to combat the increasing resistance of pests, diseases, and weeds to chemical interventions, farmers were encouraged to switch from using single chemicals to utilizing and rotating multiple chemicals for those specific "problems."

IPM, therefore, tried to address the overuse of pesticides and reduce problems with pesticide resistance. However, the practice left farmers on the pesticide treadmill and introduced another complexity into the toxicological quagmire: The experts were recommending a far broader spectrum of pesticides than ever before. It was already difficult enough to ascertain the toxicological impacts of the predominantly used pesticides, but suddenly regulators were faced with even more pesticides to test for safety, simply as single substances. With the push for *integrierte Obstanbau* (doesn't "integrated fruit production" sound much better than "conventional" or "industrial" agriculture?), researchers also needed to consider the combined effects of these different pesticides, even if the doses of each are considered small. Yet that kind of comprehensive scientific testing is extremely difficult and in its early stages. Simply testing the combined effects of two pesticides in isolation is difficult enough, but it is virtually impossible to test the number of potential combinations that can actually occur.

Toxicologist Irene Witte had made it clear to her audience in Mals that those combined effects could be classified into three potential reactions: antagonistic, additive, and synergistic. Two or more pesticides could react in an immediately antagonistic fashion, creating potentially dangerous or lethal situations for humans and other organisms. Two or more substances could also have an unanticipated additive effect through their combination. Finally, they could react synergistically, creating unforeseen consequences even in relatively small doses.

The cocktails of uncertainty spark another significant concern too often overlooked in discussions of pesticides. The synthetic chemicals of concern tend to be the "active ingredients" in pesticide products. They are the chemicals whose names we've heard but can barely remember, much less spell — and also the ingredients that take care of the -*cide* part of the equation. They put an end to the target organisms.

In most pesticides the active ingredients make up only a small overall percentage of the product. The remaining ingredients are usually classified as "inert" or "inactive." They often make up as much as 95 to 99 percent of the product, so they are not insignificant. However, they often are not identified and labeled. In fact, many are considered trade secrets. Got pesticide poisoning? You better hope that the poisoning hotline you call has been given a list of the inert ingredients. However, that is not the real concern.

The inert ingredients are there for a reason. They are intended to improve the performance of the pesticide in some fashion, acting as stickers, spreaders, penetrants, or emulsifiers, or working in other ways.[5] The problem is that some adjuvants are designed to ensure that the active ingredient can penetrate cellular walls and even organelles (hardworking cell components that carry out a number of important biological tasks) in order to inflict the intended damage to the target, be it a plant, an insect, or another organism. These adjuvants can therefore do the same in nontarget organisms, such as humans or other animals. Cell walls and organelles contain critically important parts, such as DNA and other genetic material, that often have a negative charge; they are available for bonding with whatever may come their way with a positive charge, such as a pesticide's active ingredient. The result? Genotoxicity, a phenomenon only recently being explored. One researcher aptly dubbed the result, "a molecular bull in a china shop."[6]

If those AGRIOS tables are the bible for IPM, they are red flags for scientists like Johannes. According to the AGRIOS instructions, he explains, pesticides from captan and chlorpyriphos to dithianon and mancozeb can be applied from twelve to fourteen times in just one year as individual substances. "Now in the same time period, with between twenty-five and thirty different pesticides being sprayed, you get an enormous combined amount that is beyond evil. The industry has defined a toxicological value for each individual substance, so naturally the industry should also clarify the facts on how an approved value is reached." This single value is sometimes exceeded, he states, but not normally. "However, on average, in the types of fruits and vegetables that are treated, one can find eight, nine, or ten, even twelve, thirteen, or fourteen different pesticides, which, in the totality of their combined active ingredients, are still totally unexplored. Every pharmacologist, every physician, strictly warns of consuming something like this. One can see the long-term effects."

In the end, the concern expressed by the doctors of the region was not just that property lines were breached with pesticide drift: Bodies were also transgressed. The issue of "chemical trespass," the unwanted intrusion of chemical substances into a person's body, couldn't be solved with hedgerows, buffers, or new spray techniques. And no one wanted their children to be born "prepolluted" as a result of pesticide exposure. Advances in scientific research are beginning to show how pesticide exposure can potentially impact not just parents, their children, or the unborn, but also the genetics carried forward by the generation in utero.

In 1998 participants at the Wingspread Conference issued one of the best explications of the precautionary principle:

> When an activity raises threats of harm to human health or the environment, precautionary measures should be taken even if some cause and effect relationships are not fully established scientifically. In this context the proponent of an activity, rather than the public, should bear the burden of proof. The process of applying the precautionary principle must be open, informed and democratic and must include potentially affected parties. It must also involve an examination of the full range of alternatives, including no action.[7]

No one bore more responsibility than the mayor for finding a democratic path forward to protect the future of Mals.

Manifesto

When Ulrich was elected in 2009, an elderly woman came up to him and offered a single piece of advice: "*Uli, es ist schon das du Burgermeister geworden bist: schaue auf uns Kleine und habe ich keine Angst für die Großen.*" Uli, it's wonderful that you've become our mayor: Look after our little ones, and I have no fear of the Big Ones.

He graciously accepted the counsel and considered it to be the single most important piece of advice he received after his election. He had to focus on protecting the future of the children of Mals and not become paralyzed by fear of the outsiders who bore so much power and influence. Little did he suspect, however, that it was a premonition of things to come and a mantra that he would have to revisit time and again on sleepless nights.

Ulrich had run for mayor out of a desire to see Mals protect the splendor of its natural resources, its deep cultural heritage, the strength of its tourism, and the economic potential in capitalizing upon those three elements, without sacrificing any of them. "I grew up here, and I've seen how beautiful life is here," he says. "And when one observes the changes every day, then one can gather a lot of strength from that. It's never happened here that someone can destroy land and soil with poisons. That's something we've never known. But when, with an unparalleled arrogance, the entire cultural landscape is changed, the soil is destroyed, and the air is polluted, then that disturbs me extremely. And I'm charged with doing something about it as mayor; that is why I was elected. That's my role."[8]

But he also had a sense that Mals was different from the rest of the South Tirol, perhaps because it lies at the nexus of different countries, cultures, and worldviews. He himself was a product of that intersection of ideas. His time spent in Switzerland working for a manufacturing company provided him with more than just business experience. He also saw the contrasts in the Swiss political system and the South Tirolean approach to politics.

For decades following World War II, the key to survival and independence in the South Tirol was solidarity, as represented by allegiance to the one dominant political party, the Südtiroler Volkspartei (SVP). That allegiance gained the region its autonomous-province status and ensured that it had a strong, unified voice in Rome. However, the party and the approach to politics became monolithic and even stifling to the younger generation at the turn of the century. Democracy and local control began to supplant lockstep unity, and the idea of "direct democracy" began to take root, not just among millennials but also among others who felt that a democracy based solely on the votes of elected representatives risked losing sight of the people's true interests.

Das Volk ist der Souverän. The people are the sovereign. Citizens are the supreme ruler. It's a phrase Ulrich repeats over and over again, and he sees his role as an *Ausführender* — a transactor, a negotiator — who helps transform the will of the people into sensible policy and sustainable economic development.

Ulrich was a product of "political drift." His fourteen years working in Switzerland and traveling the world gave him new insights into how the political process can best represent the interests of the people, at local as well as national levels. In many ways, Switzerland is a long-standing pioneer in direct democracy, having commenced open-air assemblies of citizens debating key political issues as far back as the founding of the Old Swiss Confederacy in 1291. By the late nineteenth century, Switzerland had developed a federal government structure — sometimes referred to as a semi-direct democracy — that hybridized direct democracy at the local level with representative democracy at the national level. The people are still "the sovereign" in Switzerland by virtue of their ability to force the hand of elected representatives through popular initiatives (similar to the pesticide-free initiative in Mals) and referendums.[9]

In May 2012 Ulrich engaged several experts in direct democracy and a local working group to develop the municipal-code change that made popular initiatives — such as the referendum for a pesticide-free town — binding. This change meant that a referendum voted upon and approved by the town's citizens had to be taken up by the municipal council.

Changing the municipal code took some effort, but the subsequent challenge faced by the Mals activists was much greater: how to get the pesticide-free referendum on the ballot and in front of the voters. First they would have to run the concept of the ballot initiative by the Mals Judicial Committee. Once the committee approved the concept, they would then need to collect signatures from townspeople. The struggle to get the ballot measure approved, first by the municipal council and then by the province, would prove to be the biggest challenge of Ulrich's young political career. Even seasoned politicians with decades of experience would have failed in this endeavor, but Ulrich's fresh approach to governance allowed him the opportunity to see and do things differently from the more calcified veteran politicians.

The first attempt at securing the Mals judicial commission's approval for the pesticide-free initiative had failed in February 2013, resulting in the creation of the Advocacy Committee for a Pesticide-Free Mals. With the recent successes of the Advocacy Committee, the doctors' manifesto, Hollawint's media push, Adam & Epfl's mitreden (talk together) events, and USGV's poll results, it was time to put the call for a popular initiative back in front of the commission in August.

The judicial commission began its review of the request for the popular initiative, but it wouldn't be until December 5 that Johannes would be invited to present the formal request. He was allotted a mere twenty minutes to present and defend the proposal. Fortunately, Johannes's oral delivery is as fast as it is eloquent. With a rapid-fire oration, he succinctly and convincingly laid out the rationale for the request to put the popular initiative before the citizens of Mals. By the end of the night's meeting, the judicial commission gave the go-ahead for the required collection of at least 289 signatures in support of the popular initiative.

However, the chair of the municipal council was no fan of the request, and he and several other members did everything they could to block the ballot initiative. Finally, after they had exhausted every conceivable measure to prevent the popular initiative, they conceded. The collection of signatures was officially set to begin on February 12, 2014; the required signatures had to be collected and submitted to the town office within ninety days of that date. Within a month the Advocacy Committee would have collected more than four hundred signatures; within ninety days they had nearly eight hundred signatures. The push for more direct democracy in public affairs and the movement for a pesticide-free Mals had begun to cross-pollinate. What fruit it might bear remained to be seen. There were still some bad apples to contend with.

Despite the agonizingly slow political process, the Malsers and their allies kept up their pressure, using the warm fall weather and the harvest season to keep their message fresh and to draw in new supporters. In September, Hollawint organized a vigil and bonfire atop the Tartscher Bichl, a prominent hill in the Mals township that seems to sprout up from nowhere amid the flatness of the valley floor; it perches above the valley with a stunning vista of Mals, the entire Upper Vinschgau, and the highest of the peaks in the South Tirol. It's easy to imagine how archaeological evidence points to it as an important prehistoric cultic site, which the church later claimed with a chapel.

As they upped their game and faced ever-larger oppositional forces and the heat of controversy, the Malsers needed time to fortify their spirits and celebrate the growing solidarity they were finding in their work together. Throughout the campaign, Pia had reminded everyone that they were engaged in a spiritual quest as well as a political battle, and no matter what religious beliefs anyone had, it couldn't hurt to pray a little. A bonfire is an equal-opportunity ecumenical experience, so the blaze on the Tartscher Bichl provided everyone a chance to offer up a mix of prayers to spirits and deities of their own choosing.

While gathered around the fire, the women of Hollawint invited participants to take the time to share their visions for how Mals might become a model community in which environmental protection, tourism, and agriculture could be further integrated to create a healthy ecological and economic future. The community vision was beginning to broaden beyond the threat of pesticides and ever closer toward the idea of becoming a sustainable and resilient community that could inspire others as well.

Vigils beget vigilance, and landscapes give rise to art. So it wasn't surprising that a few weeks after the bonfire vigil, Bioland, the organic cooperative supporting Günther, worked together with the town and others to sponsor a "Cultural Landscape Days" event. In an outdoor concert, composer Gerd Hermann Ortler played his "Changing Landscapes," and to the cheers of the crowd forester Laurin Mayer gave a rousing oration, depicting Mals as a Gallic village, fiercely defending itself from outside invaders.

The sense of invasion — or at least transgression — continued to intensify, however. The USGV had received the results of pesticide residue testing from the schoolyard in Tartsch, the village just below the Tartscher Bichl, in June. Nine different pesticide residues were discovered in the analysis, and despite letters and other inquiries sent to provincial leaders, by the fall the USGV still had not received a single response, not even one from the provincial commissioner for health, Richard Theiner. USGV leaders sent out a press release expressing their astonishment at the lack of a response from any government leaders related to a request to find the means to protect the health of the region's children.

But it was an immobile flash mob orchestrated by the women of Hollawint that got the most attention. Amid the intensity of the political machinations, Margit Gasser decided that some levity was in order, so she inspired her Hollawint colleagues to take the issue to the streets at the annual Golli market in Mals, a highly celebrated farmers market that attracted large numbers of locals, tourists, and media.

The night before the market, the women gathered in the loft of a barn and, with a note of irony, stuffed white disposable pesticide suits with precious mountain hay until the Tyvek suits took on a burly human form and were able to stand on their own. They filled the hoods with hay before giving the life-sized figures cardboard faces and adorning them with respirators, signs, and placards calling for a pesticide-free future. Then they faced the logistical challenge of getting the flash mobsters set up around the market square before too many people were out and they were identified as the pranksters. Every Tirolean village has its identified pranksters, but they usually aren't kindergarten teachers, hairdressers, and architects.

The women each took a hay-filled protester or two under an arm and proceeded through the village and toward the market in the early dawn hours, strategically placing them on stairs and street corners. The farmers, shopkeepers, and municipal workers who were up and about varied in reaction: Some averted their eyes, pretending not to notice anything out of the ordinary, while others gawked or bemusedly offered greetings and guffaws. By the time the market crowd began to fill the streets, signs held by the men in white were conveying details of the health impacts of different pesticides used in intensive fruit growing, reminding passersby of the types of pesticides found in the Tartsch schoolyard and the lack of responsiveness from provincial officials who were charged with protecting public health.

Regardless of how creative and democratic the Malsers could be within their own town, they knew that they needed additional support and guidance from outside the South Tirol. One community's model town is another political party's black sheep. Neither increased democracy nor reduced pesticides were in the interests of Big Apple and its core cronies — all of whom had a lot of reach and heft far beyond the borders of South Tirol. The Malsers, still working primarily within their own small regional network, needed another infusion of wisdom and contacts from outside the provincial borders.

Realizing that the powerful international group Pesticide Action Network (PAN) did not have an Italian chapter, Martina's husband Koen Hertoge recruited another Malser, Friedrich Haring, to establish what would become a critical new ally, PAN-Italia. Koen was a native of Belgium, and his fluency in a number of languages as well as his contacts in Brussels, the heart of the EU, enabled him to put the Mals campaign in the national and international spotlight by way of the new organization, which would be based in Bologna. Interestingly, though, Koen had no political or advocacy experience whatsoever. Nor did he have any experience or expertise with agriculture and pesticides. He decided, however, that he was representing the majority of civil society: people without that kind of firsthand knowledge of food and agriculture who were, nonetheless, consumers. His role was to be their voice while also advancing the cause of his new home community. Suddenly Mals had a new mouthpiece and podium, one that would, in fact, soon help set it apart as a model community in the eyes of the world at large.

The recognition of what was happening in Mals was beginning to build. In December 2013 Hans Rudolf Herren, winner of the Right Livelihood Award, known as the Alternative Nobel Prize, wrote a letter of support to the Malsers. A Swiss entomologist and agricultural researcher, Herren designed the most comprehensive biological pest management ever implemented, in which he introduced a parasitic wasp from South America to combat the cassava mealybug in Africa, potentially helping to avert a famine that might have killed as many as twenty million people.

Then, in March 2014, Adam & Epfl was selected for the coveted Cultura Socialis jury prize, which honors an initiative that exemplifies the development of a new social and political consciousness in the South Tirol. Adam & Epfl was commended for using open dialogue and a courageous culture of discussion to help the people of the Upper Vinschgau "discover how today they — and tomorrow, the next generation — can enliven, inhabit, and cultivate this landscape."[10]

As a ballot measure for a pesticide-free Mals gained traction and recognition, not everyone admired the direction in which things were going. It was then that Johannes faced death threats, the desecration of his family grave, and, a few days later, the destruction of his gardens. Lawsuits would follow, targeting him personally for sponsoring what some persons considered to be an illegal referendum through his role as the elected spokesperson for the Advocacy Committee. According to those opponents, a referendum must come forward from the people, not through the efforts of an established advocacy committee, and Johannes was therefore liable for serving as point person for this initiative. Johannes expended countless hours and untold sums of his own money to support the initiative and defend himself, his family, and his property.

Other members of the committee also made personal and financial sacrifices while facing challenging discussions with neighbors and other acquaintances. Hinting at how difficult some aspects of the campaign were, Peter Gasser noted that many on the Advocacy Committee had the advantage of having known one another for decades. They knew one another's strengths and limitations, and they knew how to laugh together when things got particularly challenging, or even absurd. In May 2014 Johannes and the Advocacy Committee were awarded the Ilse Waldthaler Prize for Civil Courage at a ceremony in Bozen.

The world was beginning to pay attention to the small town with so many big dreams. The timing of the recognition was helpful. It wasn't an easy spring.

Some conventional apple growers, perhaps with the support of the South Tirolean Farmers' Association (SBB) and other Big Apple supporters, launched a new campaign directed explicitly at the Mals initiative. Dubbed *Bäuerliche Zukunft*, A Farmer's Future, it promoted the ballot initiative as illegal and inappropriate and touted the safety of "integrated fruit production."[11] But it was too little, too late. The Advocacy Committee and the other organizations already had a firm foothold in Mals. Nonetheless, not all the activists' battles were to be won, even when the absurdity of the opposition seemed extraordinarily high. When a legislative proposal was put forward to require the regular testing of all school grounds in the South Tirol for pesticide residues, to be followed by a report of the results and any recommended actions needed to protect the public from potential health hazards, it was defeated, seventeen to twelve, with two abstentions. Not everyone seemed to be getting the drift of the changes in the air.

In Mals, though, the spring brought a flurry of activities sponsored by the various groups. Hollawint sponsored a lecture and panel discussion focusing on the freedom of farmers to pursue organic practices in the face of intensive fruit production. In early May, Adam & Epfl recast their event from the previous May into a magical sequel on a perfect blue-sky day. Paradies Obervinschgau, the Paradise of the Upper Vinschgau, was less a guerrilla theater event this time and more of traveling culinary and infor-mational event, featuring foods from the region, hikes, wagon rides, a wine tour and tasting, and a new grain exhibit by the Bernhards, set up in the Puni Whiskey Distillery. Ägidius hosted everyone in his magnificent gar-dens, where musicians played while participants ate, drank, and learned about his permaculture-style garden methods. At the local food co-op in the nearby town of Schluderns, everyone gathered to sample treats made with traditional foods: Palabirnen, poppy seeds, heritage grains, and of course organic apples.

Glasses were raised; spirits were high. The ballot initiative was slated to take place a few weeks later, in June. But the bureaucratic shenanigans weren't over yet. Just prior to the polling, a South Tirolean government official in Bozen intervened and announced that they would not release the required voter list because the provincial government deemed the ballot initiative inadmissible. Astounded by the last-minute denial but not sur-prised by the interference from government officials, Ulrich countered that they must release the voting list, since the initiative was approved and adopted by the municipal council. At that point the commissariat suddenly discovered "an error" on the form: The updated request for the voter list must be prepared forty-five days before the vote, he declared. The vote was rescheduled for August 22 through September 5.

Officials in Bozen and the friends of Big Apple were clearly getting nervous. The train wasn't just out of the station before they'd realized it — it was almost at its destination. They hadn't taken the novices from nowhere seriously, and now the vote seemed inevitable.

In what could only be viewed as a conciliatory move, Arnold Schuler, the head of agricultural affairs in the province, made it known in June that the government would issue new regulations for pesticide applications, including new distance and buffer regulations. Schuler even proposed to impose fines between 1,000 and 10,000 euros for violations of these new rules. Months later, though, those fines would swirl down to a meager 250 euros or so per infraction — not a significant out-of-pocket expense for an apple farmer who might spend more than that on a single spraying.

The Farmer's Future campaign made one last-ditch effort to stop the voting just prior to the opening of the polls on August 22. One hundred fifty farmers signed on to a request demanding that the judicial commission's approval of the ballot initiative be deemed illegal. Unsuccessful, the last-minute appeal seemed to be the final arrow in the opponents' quiver.

The Advocacy Committee and the various groups supporting the initiative held the last of more than twenty informational sessions right before the polls opened. They invited Schuler and representatives from A Farmer's Future, but none of them showed up.

The final say was up to the Malsers themselves. At least they hoped so.

CHAPTER 12

Ja!

t was another busy evening. The weight of the August humidity let night settle a little heavier over the villages of Mals. The darkness fell first over Burgeis, Schleis, and Laatsch, the villages tucked up against the mountains on the western side of the valley floor. Then it seeped into the steep hamlets of Matsch and Planeil, and the mountains to the west cast their evening farewells to Mals, Glurns, and Tartsch. Ulten, Plawenn, and Schlinig gradually lost elevated advantage, too, until there wasn't enough light for anything except mischief.

By this point, both the town police and the Carabinieri, Italy's national gendarmerie, were used to it. They lived among artful Querdenkers. These weren't hard-core criminals they were dealing with. They weren't even seasoned troublemakers. They were novice activists with a flair for being *frech* — cheeky. They were less interested in convention than in right and wrong.

But this time, in the eyes of the commandant of the Carabinieri, they'd taken it too far. Sunflowers were everywhere. They were floating in the public fountains, placed in public doorways. Bright yellow sunflowers with a JA! in the middle — the symbol of the pesticide-free initiative — were stamped onto streets and manhole covers. Others were painted onto signs and stuck into public flower beds.

The commandant called the mayor and, with a blast of high-velocity Italian, made it clear that the sunflowers in the public spaces were to be removed. Ulrich cordially replied that he appreciated the concern, and said he would ask the town workers to remove them, which he in turn did. But he only asked the workers to remove them and set them aside. Which they did. What happened next was up to the activists. Suffice it to say, the 2014 sunflower crop in Mals from August 22 until September 5 was extraordinary.

Around the same time, the Advocacy Committee had distributed eight-page color brochures throughout the villages of Mals, spreading a blue-sky message: "Choose a healthy future, vote 'YES!' on the ballot initiative. YES to livestock. YES to field crops. YES to fruit and berry farming. YES to vegetable farming . . . without the use of very toxic, toxic, health-damaging and environment-damaging chemical-synthetic pesticides and herbicides." Inside the brochure was the wording of the ballot initiative, the manifesto, and photos and quotes by a diverse array of supporters.

The supporters of the pesticide-free initiative had campaigned diligently and respectfully all the way to the first day of polling. Town officials and advocates for the initiative were careful to design the polling process so that it could accommodate voters. The voting period was set for two weeks to ensure that as many people as possible could vote, and voters could submit their ballots in person, through the mail, or by depositing them into a twenty-four-hour voting vault outside the town hall. Yet despite their passionate advocacy, everyone — from the mayor to the municipal council to the Advocacy Committee — wanted to ensure that the voting process would be beyond reproach. The politicians and the Big Apple allies were all on the lookout for any errors or breaches of judgment that they could use to nullify the legitimacy of the vote. The mayor and other elected officials agreed not to speak publicly on the issue during the voting period.

People in Mals also had little to say about the initiative during the two weeks of voting. Margit Gasser remembers the polling period all too well: "That was such a long period of time in the village when there was such a crippling silence. It wasn't talked about anymore, not during the referendum. Nobody even looked for a conversation about it."

It was like sitting in a hospital ward, waiting on word from the doctors about whether a loved one was going to pull through or not. Talking wasn't going to change anything. There was nothing to do but wait.

Ja!

When Ulrich became mayor in 2009, Mals was on a path toward becoming an enviable model of a truly sustainable community. The villages were advancing their capacity to capture energy from area's fast-moving waters and turn it into electrical power that not only met their needs but also generated an excess that could be sold at a profit. The USGV and others had worked for years to bring back the train that took tourists, schoolchildren, and commuters back and forth between the Upper Vinschgau and the jobs and cities down in the valley. Not only did they find a way to get the rail lines functioning again, after decades of sitting idle, but they also brought in a sleek and colorful new train, designed by the Swiss, that became an attraction in and of itself. Quiet and comfortable, it featured large windows that unveiled the landscape along its serpentine path up the valley, along with bike racks, recycling bins, and compost containers. Designed to run on electricity, generated in part by the valley's hydropower systems, it ran on diesel until the necessary infrastructure was in place to convert it to electric power.

Bike paths and hiking trails were upgraded throughout the town, and Ulrich oversaw the conversion of the main thoroughfare in Mals into a pedestrian zone, creating an ambience that invited conversation and freewheeling children. He also worked with town officials and community members to increase bus services and even a car-share program for residents unable to or uninterested in owning their own cars.

In addition, the agritourism opportunities continued to grow. Food and fitness — tourists could pursue both in Mals in a way that didn't seem possible elsewhere, simply because the landscape was so unspoiled and the region's high-quality foods were so valued and celebrated.

Local businesses were creating new niches by teasing out the tensions between tradition and innovation. Food and ecotourism were fueling the Mals renaissance. Not that it was a simple equation. To the contrary, it involved building a constellation of eco-oriented goods and services, with businesses collaborating as much as competing. There was more collective success in growing a diverse and thriving economy than in building ever-bigger businesses that simply consumed one another until only a hollow shell of infrastructure remained. Mals was a network of family-scale businesses, but it took collaboration and focused leadership to maintain not only that scale but also that ethos.

For example, right along the pedestrian zone in the center of Mals sits one of the town's gems, the Hotel Greif. Run by the Sagmeister family for four generations, the hotel dates to the sixteenth century. Whitewashed gothic arches frame the ceilings of the restaurant and the bar, and tables on the terrace overlook the pedestrian thoroughfare and catch a good portion of the valley's three hundred days of sun each year. The economic dilemma for the hotel, as Robert Sagmeister describes it, is twofold: They have only twelve rooms and twenty-five beds, and they lack the typical "greenspace" that most hotels tout. After all, they are in a medieval building in the heart of the town, with no means of expansion or adding gardens or a pool.

The solution came somewhat serendipitously, when Robert's parents, Rudi and Hanni, began to specialize in vegetarian cooking, decades before it was in vogue. Rudi became a vegetarian almost four decades ago, and he brought his newfound dietary interests into the kitchen. Rudi and Hanni took many of the foods traditionally produced by local farmers and blended them with the evolving whole foods trends, creating a fare for their hotel clients that brought in more and more health-minded guests, until they also became a favorite of people suffering from cancer and other health problems. Now Sonja Sagmeister—who married Alexander Agethle and helps market their cheeses before coming to work at her family's hotel later in the day—oversees the hotel's health-oriented culinary ventures. Carefully procured grains are kept in a breathable wooden trunk—not in plastic bins—and grains are ground fresh in the restaurant's stone mill on a daily basis.

While they continue to specialize in vegetarian and whole foods cooking, they do serve meat dishes, but they are keenly focused on the local organic farms that supply their meat, and they work directly with the slaughterhouse and butcher to ensure that the meats they serve are of the highest quality possible. Robert selects the animals he deems appropriate, and he buys the entire animal, directing the butcher to provide the cuts he think will work best for their menu.

These local relationships are nothing new in Mals, but restaurant and hotel owners are refashioning these networks. In the village of Schleis, Hans Agethle manages his family's hotel and restaurant, Gasthof zum Goldenen Adler. When locals hear that you're staying at the Goldenen Adler, they almost always exclaim, "*Oh, du bist bei Hansele! Es gibt kein besser Essen in Südtirol!*" Oh, you're staying with Hans! There's no better food in

South Tirol! I know simply because I've been staying with Hans and his family for more than twenty-five years, and that's the standard response — and it's true. I'm now a *Stammgast*, literally a "rooted guest," which means more than simply being a regular.

The Stammgast tradition in Europe is a strong one. When you find your perfect vacation spot, with the ideal hosts and outstanding food, you keep coming back, and the relationships with the hotel staff are as important as the food or the surrounding recreational opportunities. So it means something when tourists are giving up their usual vacation spots in other parts of the South Tirol and coming instead to the Upper Vinschgau because of the overwhelming transition to apple plantations. Tourists complain of the trellising and hail nets that block the views, but they become really angry when they are savoring hiking and biking trails, only to find themselves surrounded by the smell of pesticides or, worse yet, caught in a drifting cloud of spray from a nearby tractor.

For now, at least, Schleis offers a reprieve from that kind of spraycation, and the Agethle family continues to manage their idyllic rural hotel as they have since 1857. With only twelve rooms in a small village, they have to differentiate what they offer. In Hans's case, the exceptional hospitality and the high quality of the food are the key to the future. There is pressure for hotels in the South Tirol to increase their number of stars — some in the region would like it to be known for the number of four- and five-star hotels it has. In fact, some loans for hotel renovations require that a hotel scale up in its ratings. Scaling up in star status can ruin the essence of what many family hotels have to offer — and the escalating prices quickly shift the clientele . . . and their expectations.

The Agethles' hotel and restaurant have never had to manufacture authenticity when it comes to local or sustainably produced food: They have long maintained a farm, and any hours Hans can spend on the farm are therapy, although it's increasingly hard for him to find the time to be in the fields instead of managing the daily operations of the hotel. However, he is keenly attuned to the fact that what happens on the farm either expands or diminishes the offerings that come out of the kitchen. The Agethles have long prided themselves on their fusion of farm and plate, and what they haven't been able to raise themselves, they've been able to procure from their neighbors and their purveyors.

Breakfast always features an extraordinary array of local honeys, cheeses, marmalades, breads, dairy products, and breads. Cheeses and cultured butter make their way down from the high pastures onto the plates, and homemade cured meats appear on special occasions. It's all a reminder that plate and palate are intricately linked to the farmer's palette. Artistry in the kitchen is dependent upon the art of farming.

One of the postcard campaigns just before the ballot initiative said it best: "Monoculture is un-culture. Culture requires a landscape with a future . . . Life is valuable."

The ballot read:

Are you in favor of implementing the following amendment to the articles of the Township of Mals?

The precautionary principle, in order to protect public health, states all measures should be taken that will help prevent harm to the health of humans and animals. The township of Mals has a particular objective of protecting the health of its citizens and guests, maintaining the sustainability of nature and waters, and making it possible for different economic models to coexist within the municipality in a fair and respectful way.

In conformance with these goals, Mals promotes the use of organic, biodegradable crop protection within its municipal boundaries. An ordinance will be issued that describes the details of this provision.

Independently from this provision, the use of highly toxic, toxic, harmful, and polluting chemical-synthetic pesticides is prohibited within its municipal boundaries. The municipal authority is responsible for monitoring the implementation and the compliance of the referendum outcome.

The polling period stretched out as long as the summer days, but even those were drawing to a close. Ulrich tried to minimize the stress with occasional mountain bike rides and hikes with his young family. The elevations provided needed perspective, and when he looked down over the Upper Vinschgau any doubts would dissipate into the thin mountain air.

Days in the office were harried, with calls coming in from Malsers, attorneys, politicians, and the media. Lunch tended to be a time when he could expect some levity, at least when he had the chance to walk up the street, just past Johannes's apothecary, and grab a bite of *bio* and *regional* — organic and local — street food at the Stroossnkuch. Advertised as "Refined Sausage Culture," the high-end hot dog stand featured products from as many local producers as possible. There still weren't enough of those producers and distributors, but it took creative enterprises like the Stroossnkuch to catalyze the needed push and pull in the regional economy.

Franz Hofer and Günther Pitscheider thought that Mals needed a different kind of *Würstelstand*, one that reflected the new food order that seemed to be building in Mals. There were great restaurants in the town — including Pizzeria Remo, which won the coveted "Pizza World Championship" — but Günther and Franz thought that the Stroossnkuch could fill another niche. Dedicated to high-quality food at a reasonable price, the Stroossnkuch is simply a retrofitted trailer in a parking lot with a few tables and stools inside and a canopy terrace with picnic tables outside. However, the two business partners are also avid proponents of *Wurstkultur*, bringing together sausage and the arts, especially music, one of Günther's many professions.

Ulrich had helped "make room" in town for this new venture — given its out-of-the-ordinary zoning status — and it had become a gathering spot for many of the pesticide-free advocates, formally appointed or not. It was as good a place as any to wait out the news.

The polls closed at noon on September 5, 2014. At 7 PM the results were announced, to the astonishment of almost everyone: 69.22 percent of the electorate had turned out for the vote, and a resounding 75.68 percent voted *Ja!* for a pesticide-free community, with 24.32 percent voting against the initiative. That three-quarter majority was no fluke. It precisely mirrored the polling done by USGV the year prior.

Mals had made its decision. It seemed like a choice worthy of a democracy.

The supporters of the ballot initiative rejoiced, but they were also careful not to flaunt the victory, realizing that not everyone was happy with the outcome and that, in the end, they all had to live and work together. It was, after all, a small town, like any other . . . except that it had chosen to be different.

The word went out far and wide, with the stunning victory being reported from the major newspapers throughout Europe to the 2014 Annual Congress of the Societas Europaea Lepidopterologica (the European Society for Butterflies and Moths). A jubilant yell went out from the podium: "The Miracle of Malles!" The ordinarily reserved gathering of scientists burst into applause, ecstatic to have one victory in a world where butterfly and moth populations were suffering the ill effects of pesticides, monocultures, and habitat loss.

Several weeks later Mals would win the prestigious European Village Renewal Award in a ceremony in Switzerland, and receive a letter of support from environmental activist Vandana Shiva, yet another winner of the Right Livelihood Award — the "Alternative" Nobel Prize — and probably the world's most recognized leader in the fight against pesticides and genetically engineered crops.

The international acclaim couldn't have been more deserved. It also made it much harder for Big Apple and the politicians to dismiss the Malsers as "green crazies." Mals had set a precedent that went well beyond the South Tirol. The good news and the bad news was that Mals was now even more of a threat. Things would not get easier.

According to the new rules for a binding initiative in Mals, any ballot initiative approved by the citizens was to be implemented within six months. However, some members of the Mals Municipal Council were not in favor of the initiative and refused to attend the council meeting in December in which the issue was to be taken up. Without a quorum, the issue was tabled.

At the same time, a group of plaintiffs filed a lawsuit against the mayor (as the representative of the municipality), the Mals Voting Commission, and the spokesperson for the Advocacy Committee. They were all required to appear in court in Bozen in January. The plaintiffs had accepted the call from the South Tirolean Farmers' Association, the SBB, to take on the supporters of the initiative, with the SBB footing any necessary legal bills. Perhaps someone forgot that some of the members of the SBB were organic farmers.

The municipal council was slated to take up the ballot initiative again in January but failed to address the issue oné more time. New elections for town officials were slated for May, so the advocates of the pesticide-free initiative rallied supporters to run for the open seats on the council. Ulrich was also up for reelection, and all of South Tirol was keenly interested in his fate, given his support of the ballot initiative.

As it turned out, supporters of the pesticide-free initiative won the majority of the seats, virtually assuring passage of the necessary amendments to the town's statutes and preparing the way for the creation of the associated ordinance that would turn the will of the people into regulations. The biggest victory, however, was Ulrich's: He won 75 percent of the popular vote, the largest win of any mayoral election in the South Tirol. It was a mandate beyond reproach.

Finally, in July, the ballot initiative was officially adopted in the town statutes, and town officials began working with expert attorneys to determine the best path forward with the ordinance. The ballot initiative was under attack, so it was obvious that the ordinance would also need to be able to withstand the inevitable litigation that was to follow.

It wouldn't be until almost eight months later, in March 2016, that the new ordinance would be released. Determining how to transform the ballot initiative into an ordinance that could withstand the legal firepower directed its way proved to be extremely challenging. In the end, and unexpectedly, the municipal council voted unanimously in favor of the ordinance.

In examining all of the relevant precedents they could find and trying to predict possible points of legal vulnerability, Ulrich, the attorneys, town officials, and advocates came to a challenging conclusion: An outright ban was legal suicide. It could and would be contested immediately in court, meaning that no ordinance would be in effect while it was in litigation. The legal stalling would not only allow the continued expansion of conventionally managed orchards but also do nothing to solve the immediate and very real problems of pesticide drift. So the Malsers chose another angle — less pure, in a sense, but still within the spirit of the ballot initiative.

A Precautionary Tale

It was left to Ulrich to present the new ordinance to the town. He knew it would come as a disappointment since it wasn't a pure ban on all pesticides, but he had faith that his fellow Malsers, with all of the cunning and creativity that they'd displayed for so long, would understand the legal cat-and-mouse game they were playing and appreciate the calculus of their unanticipated approach.

A meeting was called in the town hall at the end of March. The familiar faces of the campaign made their way in, gathering in small groups along the walls and in the back of the room to compare thoughts on what would be presented. Ulrich stood in front of the seated audience and methodically explained the necessity of a compromise. There would be no outright ban on all synthetic pesticides.

The air left the room with the audience's collective gasp. However, Ulrich continued, there was a virtual ban provided by the strict nature of the stringent new buffer requirements. Although the new buffers were still insufficient for doing the impossible — containing drift — they made pesticide spraying impractical in a town with such small and fragmented agricultural fields.

Ulrich laid out the three primary components the ordinance:

1. The two most toxic classes (known as T+ and T) of synthetic pesticides would be banned.
2. Given the demonstrated issues of drift in the Upper Vinschgau due to its windy conditions, a minimum 50-meter (164-foot) buffer would be required between the outer edge of a spray zone of other synthetic pesticides and any adjacent properties. Due to the small parcel sizes of the valley, this buffer created a de facto ban of these other synthetic pesticides.
3. Organic agriculture would be supported and advanced in the town. The town's dining facilities would be supplied with organic products, beginning with the kindergartens and progressing toward the other school facilities. Organic agriculture, including transition programs, would be financially supported.

Ulrich finished his presentation and looked at the audience. Expressions around the room varied. Some heads were nodding ever so slightly, acknowledging the wisdom of the approach. Other faces seemed cast in stone, not shifting in expression, while a few heads shook in subtle disagreement or disappointment. Everyone knew, however, that Ulrich didn't shy away from controversy or shirk his responsibility to the people who'd reelected him by such a wide margin.

Just a few weeks earlier, in February, nearly five hundred people had attended a lecture in Mals by Hans Rudolf Herren, who had followed up his letter of support with a visit to the town. The title of his talk: *Weiter wie bisher ist kein Option*, Continuing as Before Is Not an Option. That theme held true. The ordinance was a cunning compromise, and it was a game changer in a world of giants. At the end of the day, aim mattered more than the size of the stone.

Political farce would be best if it were always on stage or in print. At the very least, it might be easier to believe than when it shows up in real life.

Driven by 140 plaintiffs from Mals and perhaps other pressures or predilections, a provincial court judge in Bozen ruled in May 2016 that the ballot initiative was invalid. According to the judge, the question itself was inadmissible: Pesticide usage is under the purview of provincial, national, and EU jurisdiction. Furthermore, the referendum question should not have been posed by a group of citizens — in other words, the Advocacy Committee.

Therefore, the judge ruled, the initiative and all of the actions surrounding it were null and void. The ordinance, however, was created separately and remained valid.

While the announcement was an emotional blow at first, it was no surprise. Bureaucrats, lobbyists, and plaintiffs had been trying to sabotage the referendum process before it took place and then nullify the outcome after the vote. In these kinds of extended legal battles in which the powers that be hold on to the status quo like a scepter, to be sanguine is to be sane. Koen Hertoge, from his perspective as a Mals citizen and the cofounder of PAN-Italia, was essentially nonplussed: "It was totally irrelevant if the referendum was 'cancelled' or 'destroyed' by the judge in Bozen. For the citizens of Mals, we still have, and we will always have, the result of the referendum. And furthermore, the result of the referendum helped the Municipal Council to make their qualified decision to further implement the local rules and legislation."

A town meeting was called several days later in the Kulturhaus, and the room was filled from front to back. Johannes introduced and moderated the meeting before Ulrich took the floor and reassured the crowd that the judgment certainly flew in the face of the democratic processes that advanced the ballot initiative and the resounding will of the majority of Malsers. Nonetheless, the ordinance was still intact, and he and other town officials would continue to work diligently on implementing its various facets. Of course, other legal challenges would come, but the key was to continue moving forward, setting an example for the rest of the world while simultaneously garnering support from around the globe to expose the farce and to make it clear, as Ulrich had reiterated throughout the process, that "the people are the sovereign."

But the people of Mals were also tired. They had run the gauntlet of an initiation they'd never expected or asked for. It was time for the Malsers to shift from a defensive holding action to a strategic realignment of resources to building the future they wanted. In that vein, members of the community began gathering around the idea of a Bürgergenossenschaft Obervinschgau (BGO),[1] a Citizens' Cooperative of the Upper Vinschgau. Soon they were developing an investment model to promote economic development based on the natural resources, traditions, and competitive advantages of the region, without depleting or tainting the environment. The group is in its early stages of development, but in the search for a sustainable future, its backers want to trade the watchwords of *efficiency, competition,* and *consumption strategies* for *resilience, cooperation,* and *diversity.* The goal is to build upon the people and the resources of the region in order to strengthen the local economy and social fabric by serving as a hub, providing advice, promoting networks, supporting initiatives, and implementing the BGO's own ideas and services that promote sustainable development.

While the BGO finds its footing with staffing, a location, and additional funding, other homegrown initiatives are already in play. Martina decided to dedicate what time and energy she could muster, while also trying to raise two small children, toward the development of a distribution cooperative specializing in organic vegetables and other products related to fine food. In concert (literally sometimes) with musician-turned-sausage-culture-meister Günther Pitscheider from the Stroosnkuch, she and others have been hard at work building Vinterra, a social cooperative that functions as an economically viable distribution business. The goal of Vinterra is to help grow an economy focused on providing restaurants and shops with organic, local, and socially minded products.

When the issues of market push and pull are still being sorted out, the best business model for the entity in the middle — the distributor — is not simple to determine. And scale matters. If there isn't sufficient pull from enough consumers or adequate push from the producers, the tug-of-war ends in a draw, with both sides losing. Cooperatives work: Big Apple proved that. Now the question is whether these new cooperatives can grow based on ecological and social principles and not just on their ability to win markets for farmers and provide massive supplies of product far beyond local boundaries.

As a Querdenker among Querdenkers, Alexander Agethle has taken yet another route. He sees the future from a slightly different angle: His goal is to use his creative business model and hard-earned infrastructure to incubate other farmers and businesses. "We try to help young business-people in the realization of their ideas, to create a diversity not just in agriculture but also in the artisanal and tourism realms. That means we create a self-sustaining region and not a region that produces apples or milk for some global market."

For Alexander, it's not all about the money: "It's about creating a mood for people to realize their ideas, for cooperatives to realize their ideas, for associations to realize their ideas, and lastly, it's the humans in a place who give a region a new drive, who give a region its character, which in turn shapes the region."

Anja and Georg Theiner are a young farming couple working hard to find a way to make a living from a farm at 4,593 feet (1,400 m) near the village of Matsch. If the altitude isn't enough of a challenge, the steep slopes on which the farm sits are. Even sitting at the picnic table among their organic gardens, a case of vertigo seems to be an ever-present possibility. Georg obviously suffers from no such malady. Having grown up on the

Lechtlhof, as its been known for centuries, he leaps across pastures in pursuit of errant sheep with grace equal to theirs, barely breaking a sweat as he brings them across the pastures, perpendicular to the slope, ready for their next milking. It's a bit of a show for the guests staying in their two apartments on the farm, if they've torn themselves away from the view of Mals spread out below the balconies of their rented rooms.

The Lechtlhof's praises have been sung in poetry and prose throughout the Tirol for several hundred years. Touted as one of the most beautiful farms in all the land, it has lost none of stunning charm since then, and Anja, Georg, and their young son only add to it. Despite its beauty, however, the Lechtlhof faces the challenges of so many true mountain farms that cling with time-tested talons to the precipitous mountainsides of the region. Georg had struggled with the future of the farm he inherited — much of it in neglect in part due to the tragedy of his mother dying at a young age and leaving a family missing the guidance of that second set of vital hands and eyes to keep the farm in prime shape. Fortunately he met Anja, who was both experienced and highly educated in farming thanks to her Austrian upbringing. Together they formed a vision of a diversified income stream, with organic vegetables, a small agritourism venture with their apartments, and sheep cheese.

It is there that their relationship with Alexander proved critical. He offered to help transform their dream of raising dairy sheep — perhaps the best-adapted livestock for their high-altitude farm — into a reality. He offered to mentor them in high-quality milk production and to buy and help market their cheese. In doing so, he diversified his offerings and clientele while providing them with an immediate market, without having to set up an expensive cheesemaking facility — something they couldn't afford and, as it turned out, didn't need to replicate. Anja laughed as she explained her vision of the perfect push-and-pull scenario: "If this symbiosis with the consumer and producer or farmer would work perfectly, we probably wouldn't need politics."

Anja's point was critical. Ultimately, the story of Mals isn't so much about a referendum that was a global first or even the cunning ordinances that codify a townwide sentiment into legal protections for the most basic of human rights. The holding actions all mattered, but the holding power of it all is based in the relationships and the networks that sustain. The long-term health and the vitality of Mals are dependent upon the townspeople spinning gossamer threads and connecting anchor point to anchor point before daring to traverse the intimidatingly open spaces between.

In the year since that judgment, the political challenges within the South Tirol haven't subsided, and they probably won't. The Malsers set a precedent that exposes the dangers of self-interests gone awry, while also creating a veritable handbook for citizen-based activism and direct democracy. By trying to avoid a head-on collision with conventional agriculture, they unveiled a farce that is best left to the arts and not allowed to unfold in real life.

In the meantime, they've set an example for communities across the world. The EU has created a "Pesticide-Free Villages" initiative, modeled in large part on the Mals campaign. When pesticide policy is discussed in the European Union, Japan, Australia, and now the United States, Mals isn't just a model — it's a story, an evolving story of a small community that took on forces far bigger, won, and is still winning. When the Societas Europaea Lepidopterologica, the European butterfly and moth scientists, looked for a location to hold their annual congress in fall 2016, it only made sense to meet in that town of hope they'd heard about and applauded in 2014. They decided to hold their conference at Marienberg Abbey, from which they had a perfect view of "the Miracle of Mals."

A few months later, in spring 2017, the Umweltinstitut München, the Environmental Institute of Munich, started an online petition to the governor of South Tirol, Arno Kompatscher. Conceived as a display of solidarity for a town under duress from its own provincial officials, the initiative quickly rallied more than twenty thousand signatures stating not only their support for the Malsers but also a reticence to travel to the South Tirol if the government did not address the massive pesticide use in the region. The initiative culminated in a visit to Mals by about seventy supporters from the Munich area who joined a band of Malsers for a walk and a human chain across the coveted Mals Heath, before marching into the flag-draped town for a feast of traditional Vinschgau foods.

A few weeks later, in the auspicious days of early May when the "spray of apple blossoms" confounds the emotions of any diehard pesticide activist, the Pesticide Action Network (PAN) of Europe held its annual general assembly in Mals. Leaders of the activist community came from all over Europe to stay in Hotel Greif in the heart of the town, where they learned the story of a pesticide-free Mals from the locals and had a firsthand glimpse into the working landscape and food traditions.

I was fortunate enough to join the PAN-Europe delegates as they celebrated their thirty years of work as an organization and strategized their future endeavors. Meeting in Mals gave additional meaning to their work simply by posing the stark contrast of choices in Mals and elsewhere. Delegates alternated between local and organic dishes at the Hotel Greif, and less palatable recollections of the challenges faced by the Malsers.

On the last day of the general assembly, we left from Mals early in the morning to drive down the valley for a visit to the Gluderers' organic herb business. As our caravan exited Mals and clung tightly to the curves along the gradual descent of the serpentine highway, we found ourselves completely immersed in a sea of orchards just beginning to shed their white blossoms. It was a stunning, blue-sky morning, and the sun to the east captured the steady, linear belch of pesticides trailing tractor after tractor in the orchards that flanked us on every side, as if to highlight the dilemma one last time.

By the time that we got to the Gluderers' farm, heard their story, saw a sampling of their drift videos, and toured their farm, François Veillerette, the president of PAN-Europe, seemed caught between shock and awe. He looked around at the beauty and the absurdity of what he saw from inside the enormous translucent bubble that covered the Gluderers' crops. In all of his more than thirty years working on pesticide issues in Europe, he said, nothing rivaled the intensity of the pesticide issues and monocultural takeover that he had seen just in that morning.

Mals is becoming more than a tourist destination. To go to Mals is now an act of solidarity. It is a pilgrimage.

Meanwhile, news around the world continues to validate the concerns of the Malsers. In a report submitted to the General Assembly of the United Nations and the UN Human Rights Council on January 24, 2016, the UN Special Rapporteur for the Right to Food and the UN Special

Rapporteur on Toxics transformed the quandaries of pesticide use into an international human rights issue. Point after point, the twenty-four-page report reiterates the precise concerns the Malsers had raised throughout their initiative:

> Today's dominant agricultural model is highly problematic, not only because of damage inflicted by pesticides, but also their effects on climate change, loss of biodiversity and inability to ensure food sovereignty. These issues are intimately interlinked and must be addressed together to ensure that the right to food is achieved to its full potential. Efforts to tackle hazardous pesticides will only be successful if they address the ecological, economic and social factors that are embedded in agricultural policies, as articulated in the Sustainable Development Goals.[2]

And then the report might as well have been written with the Malsers specifically in mind:

> Political will is needed to re-evaluate and challenge the vested interests, incentives and power relations that keep industrial agrochemical-dependent farming in place. Agricultural policies, trade systems and corporate influence over public policy must all be challenged if we are to move away from pesticide-reliant industrial food systems.[3]

With more than $50 billion of pesticide products sold each year, the pesticide lobby has enormous influence worldwide.[4] If the corporate economic power were not enough to confront, the complexities of the science behind risk assessment too often give the upper hand to those who do the science, fund the science, and disseminate the results, whether they are valid or not.

As reported by the *New York Times* in March 2017 and pursued by a number of other media outlets, a US judge unsealed documents that revealed clear distortion and disruption of scientific evidence related to the health impacts of glyphosate:

The court documents included Monsanto's internal emails and email traffic between the company and federal regulators. The records suggested that Monsanto had ghostwritten research that was later attributed to academics and indicated that a senior official at the Environmental Protection Agency had worked to quash a review of Roundup's main ingredient, glyphosate, that was to have been conducted by the United States Department of Health and Human Services. The documents also revealed that there was some disagreement within the E.P.A. over its own safety assessment.[5]

Although the individual studies all have their particular complexities and true objectivity and independence are at a premium in this research arena, there is an unambiguous preponderance of evidence that pesticides are wreaking havoc upon human and ecological health. The economic costs are extraordinarily high, and the costs to economies we care about are high.

With the link between damages to human and ecological health and basic human rights, a new concept in the judicial lexicon has come to the fore: *ecocide*, the death of ecological systems. As in any murder case, intent becomes a primary consideration. In the case of multinational corporations, intent is also critical.

The activist community gathered around the issues of pesticides began to tease out whether large pesticide producers might be tried in the International Court of Justice in the Hague for ecocide. Discussions throughout the Pesticide Action Network, including Mals representative Koen Hertoge, began to focus on whether there was a judicial basis for trying Monsanto, the biggest pesticide manufacturer on the planet, for the crime of ecocide. A steering committee that included Mals supporters Vandana Shiva and entomologist Hans Herren, another leader in the fight against pesticides, along with a number of prominent activists from around the world, decided to provide a forum for a tribunal and a concurrent People's Assembly that would inform and mobilize citizens from around the world about the legal implications of the toxic legacy left in the wake of corporations such as Monsanto.

Three ICJ judges were solicited to review the presented evidence and offer a legal analysis, based both on current international law and prospective law, to determine whether Monsanto might be guilty of ecocide. The judges heard testimony from citizens around the world in the Hague on October 15 and 16, 2016, at the International Monsanto Tribunal. On April 18, 2017, they released their findings after having reviewed the case as they would any other ICJ case, based on six framing questions.[6]

The verdict? Guilty, on all six charges.

While a mock tribunal may seem to be an exercise in one-sided theatrics, in actuality the review of a case by qualified ICJ judges lays the groundwork for determining whether a future case should be officially deliberated upon by the court itself. In addition, as noted at the end of the summary of findings, it is critically important for international law to give increased primacy to human and environmental rights, and any moves in this direction will mean that deliberations such as the International Monsanto Tribunal will have more positive impacts for the people and ecosystems at risk . . . at least those that have not already succumbed to the dangers at hand.

What the Malsers have already achieved cannot be taken away by a single judicial ruling or a business move. That is the power of what they did in transforming their growing concerns into public education and then into a referendum. From the referendum, they created not only legally justified ordinances but also new networks and initiatives to support a transition toward a healthier food system and a more sustainable and resilient town.

Political activism is a tireless task: Protecting what we cherish requires constant vigilance. But political activism does have a tendency to focus on one battle at a time, whereas rebuilding a foodshed is the work of generations. What has been lost or threatened over the course of decades will likely take decades to restore, although with a strategic, collective vision, communities can move faster in rebuilding what was lost through the slow relinquishing and decay that left the destiny of the foodshed to outside forces and inner apathy.

A Precautionary Tale

After I wrote *Rebuilding the Foodshed* in 2013, I began traveling around the United States, trading ideas with people in communities who were working hard to reclaim and rebuild their food systems and local economies, often with an eye toward equity and justice. I began to wonder if a new approach to politics was emerging in the United States and abroad.

In many of the communities I was fortunate enough to visit, the idea of what I began to call *foodshed as new democracy* seemed to be taking root. However, I wasn't quite sure if the phrase was anything more than a pithy utterance and a fleeting notion. I began to share and explore the concept with audiences across the country, asking for their responses, many of which resonated deeply with me. But it wasn't until I stumbled onto the story of Mals that I truly came to understand the power and potential of *foodshed as new democracy*.

The question often tossed back to pragmatic optimists like myself is whether we are being too idealistic in our visions of healthy, sustainable, and just food systems. Harsher critics accuse us of ignoring realities like the necessity of using pesticides and genetically engineered organisms not only to grow crops successfully but for future generations to feed the world. My best response is a simple story.

When I take my family back to visit those vineyards at Brunnenburg Castle in the lower Vinschgau where I spent three summers in a rubber suit and respirator, spraying vines twelve to twenty times in a season under the watchful eye of a mischievous little Tirolean kid, I don't tell my children not to go barefoot through the vineyard or not to taste the grapes because of pesticide residues. Nik, that cunning Tirolean kid who was my frequent companion on the farm, eventually inherited those vineyards but decided to chart a different path for himself and his family.

Since taking over the vineyard operation a decade or so after I departed, Nik decided to gradually replace almost all of the standard wine grape varieties, the well-known *Vitis vinifera* options, with PIWI varieties, the newly developed fungus-resistant vines. The result? He never sprays his vines.

Of course, transitioning to organic agriculture is seldom a simple affair, nor is building an organic market, particularly when dealing with consumer taste. Perhaps no agricultural commodity carries with it as many preconceived expectations of taste as does wine, so Nik has taken on the twin challenge of determining which varieties are most successful on his farm and in his cellar.

He began experimenting with PIWI vines and wines in 2004. Unsure of whether his organic aspirations would bear fruit, he decided to use green grafting, a method by which he cut the *Vitis vinifera* vines several inches above the ground and grafted the new PIWI vines onto the well-established rootstock. Not only did he lose just a single year in production by means of green grafting, but he also had the old *Vitis vinifera* rootstock in place if the PIWI grapes didn't meet his growing or winemaking standards.

Nik planted seventeen different varieties in order to see which grew best on his site and determine which would make the best wines. Over the years, he has narrowed his choices and developed local markets for his distinctive wines. The challenge is to avoid shocking the consumer's palate with something totally new while luring it into a slightly different world of gustatory nuance.

Nik's experiments and the Mals story are both reminders that transitions take time, and they can even involve some risk. In the process of finding our way to organic or any other ideal, we confront the equivalent of a Buddhist koan: Impatience is our greatest ally, and patience is our best companion.

If I had any reservations about whether a pesticide-free future was possible, I stowed those doubts away on a hot August day in 2016, three decades after hanging up the sprayer hose for the last time at Brunnenburg. I was staying at Brunnenburg for several weeks with my family while researching the story of Mals, and I offered to help Nik for a day on the farm.

Perhaps intentionally, or maybe not, he gave me the task of cleaning out the tractor shed before he brought in some new equipment. He started the old reliable Goldoni tractor and pulled it out of the garage so that I could begin sorting through the decades of junk accumulated in the back, and I found myself throwing away old bits of blue sprayer hose, clamps, and random rubber gloves, some of which looked oddly familiar.

I took the garbage can full of old junk around back of the farmhouse, out of sight of the museum visitors, and there it was: the old sprayer machine from thirty years ago. The tank was covered with cobwebs and not as shiny as I remembered. And on the rear, that faded blue hose was coiled on its rack, cracked and unused.

Sometimes the future is dependent upon what we save from the past, and sometimes it's more about what we decide to leave behind.

ACKNOWLEDGMENTS

From the moment that I stumbled into this story with a wonderful group of Green Mountain College graduate students in 2014, I struggled with how to tell a story about a place I cared so much about — as an outsider. I invited Douglas Gayeton to come back with us to the South Tirol the following year to dig deeper into the story and try to find a way to tell it. Little did I realize that Douglas never tells a story in one way. Rather, he tells a story in as many ways as possible: information artworks, photography, video, and writing. Our digging led to yet another trip back to Mals in May of 2016 to collect additional interviews and imagery in 2016, this time with the help of Pier Giorgio Provenzano and Michael de Rachewiltz.

When we first began our collaborative journeys, I could not have imagined how much I would learn from Douglas about storytelling in multiple media. As he put it, "We're chained to the oars together on this one until we get it done." This story is far better than it would have been were it not for Douglas's mentorship on so many levels, and it would be missing a full suite of *Toppling Goliath* media to accompany it (www.topplinggoliath.org). Sorry about the chains, Douglas — looks like we can't stop now.

Michael de Rachewiltz has also been a stalwart collaborator and friend, without whom the project probably would have failed . . . or at least we would have made too many cultural and linguistic blunders. And his sidekick, Robert Delvai, isn't just an amazing mountain guide but also precisely the kind of networker one needs in order to follow the threads of such a complex story.

Pier Giorgio Provenzano is the most tireless, unflappable human being I think I have ever met — not to mention an amazing videographer, editor, animator, and translator. In addition to being one of those people you just want to have on your team in a project that transforms from a frenetic pace to the long hard work of pulling it all together into a cohesive whole, he's also a Dropbox wizard.

A Precautionary Tale

Koen Hertoge and Siegfried de Rachewiltz have been central fact checkers and proofreaders, for which I am very grateful. Koen has gone above and beyond in helping us to gather resources through his PAN-Italia and PAN-Europe networks. Any remaining errors are my fault. I am also deeply indebted to Koen and his PAN-Europe colleagues for allowing me to join them for their annual general assembly held in Mals in May 2017.

I am grateful to the Green Mountain College students who have accompanied me on this journey and hope you feel a part of this book and the accompanying *Toppling Goliath* project. I am very appreciative to Green Mountain College for the sabbatical and other resources that contributed to the success of this project and to Robin, Eleanor, and Bay for their support.

No one could ask for a better editor or friend (but she knows when to wear which hat — or sometimes both!) than Joni Praded. She was a guiding star from the moment I began thinking about this book project, and she kept me laughing through the (occasionally "stretched") deadlines.

Although I hope they didn't bear the brunt of this book project (I think I'm learning how to do this without passing on the occasional stress), I am deeply thankful to Erin, Ethan, Addy, and Asa for the needed quiet stretches. Next time we go back to Mals, I won't do any interviews, kids. We'll go play while Mama does her thing!

Deepest thanks go, too, to my Brunnenburg family, for an education that has spanned more than three decades: Mary who "gathered from the air a live tradition" and passed it on; Sizzo for sharing the warp and weft of word and work on the steep slopes; Brigitte who provided the first bread crumb that led me and my students to this story; Patrizia and Graziella for the antics and the contagious laughter that always made me feel at home; Michi for sharing his cultural knowledge, his linguistic expertise, and (begrudgingly) his Goldoni tractor; and Nik for helping me to learn German when he was barely waist-high (even though he did swipe my little yellow German-English dictionary and left me at a loss for words) and now for showing so many of us the path to a pesticide-free future through on-farm research and sheer determination.

Finally, I am extraordinarily indebted to the people of Mals and its vicinity who offered our team a window into their lives and shared food, drink, and laughter. I can only hope that I have captured their stories appropriately and accurately and that this book and the *Toppling Goliath* project help others discover "the miracle of Mals"!

How to Push Back on Pesticides at Home

The citizens of Mals followed five strategies that Johannes Unterpertinger recommends for other communities pushing back against pesticides. Here are Johannes's five succinct suggestions, followed by an explanation of how they translate to our work in the United States and beyond:

1. Always provide factual and objective information, particularly about the health risks posed by pesticides.

Gathering information that isn't oversimplified or heavily influenced by industry interests is a challenge. The information that you do find will often be focused on pesticides' active ingredients. These important active ingredients are regulated and classified, although they often make up only 1 to 5 percent of the pesticide. In contrast, the inert ingredients that constitute the rest of the substance generally are not regulated or listed, and they deserve scrutiny as well. Some of the best resources for scientific information on pesticides and policy include:

http://www.panna.org
http://www.pan-europe.info
http://www.beyondpesticides.org
http://consumersunion.org/topic/food
http://www.ewg.org

https://www.foodandwaterwatch.org
http://www.ucsusa.org/food_and_agriculture#.VyJeXD-hQqY
https://www.nrdc.org/issues/food

2. Invite the world's best experts (environment, medicine, toxicology) to give public lectures.

Bringing in experts not only serves the primary purpose of enhancing public knowledge of the issues but also brings out supporters (some of whom may surprise you), encourages public dialogue about these difficult topics, and lends credibility and networking to your efforts. Consider adding a response panel to the event so that local expertise is added to the conversation. Be sure to include one or more farmers with different perspectives on the issue.

3. Engage the best lawyers.

Policy changes may be an early or a long-term goal, but the sooner your community understands possibilities, precedents, and potential impediments, the more realistic and strategic your efforts can be. Always examine not only successful community initiatives but also failed ones. Strategize accordingly.

4. Win over the local farmers to your cause.

Polarization seldom serves a campaign or a community well, and the language you use matters. Pesticides should be labeled, not farmers. The community of Mals has kept *all* farmers' interests front and center, not only while trying to move the policy needle but also through measures of support in providing the economic and educational support necessary for transition to organic production. They also turned an "anti-pesticide" proposition into a "pesticide-free future" opportunity.

5. Present a project that is focused on health, politics, social issues, ethics, and ecology.

A strength of the Mals initiative was that activists approached their dilemmas from a variety of angles. This multipronged approach brings more players and perspectives to the table — and therefore heightened opportunities for success. The issues raised by pesticides are inherently complex, and they impact people in communities in different ways.

Applying the Five Steps in the United States

While the story of the Malsers' struggle for a pesticide-free future is a tale of local citizens protecting what they know better and cherish more than their distant political representatives, it is also a reminder that different levels of government may take significantly contrasting approaches to respecting and protecting community-level concerns.

For the Malsers, the provincial government has, up to this point, done more to protect its own interests and the interests of its political and financial backers than it has to address the concerns of the citizens of Mals. Perhaps ironically, the more distant Italian and the European Union governmental organizations have offered clear legal justification and support for local communities to protect human and ecological health, generally through the oversight of the mayor.

In the United States, thanks to the strategic if not underhanded lobbying of the chemical industry, forty-three states have some sort of law that preempts local communities from enacting ordinances that regulate pesticide use in their own localities. Only seven states — Alaska, Hawaii, Maine, Maryland, Utah, Nevada, and Vermont — still allow local communities to reduce or eliminate pesticides on their own terms!

This legislative boondoggle was no accident. In the latter decades of the twentieth century, chemical companies saw the forthcoming legal challenges associated with pesticide impacts. A Supreme Court judgment in 1991 ruled that local communities did, in fact, have the authority to create pesticide laws that were more stringent than federal laws. However, that federal judgment did not impede states from restricting local communities from writing stricter laws, leaving a door wide open for chemical industry lobbyists to peddle their influence.

In response to the looming threat to their industry, companies producing pesticides created a political advocacy group dubbed RISE — Responsible Industry for a Sound Environment. One senior official with Dow AgroSciences, who was also at one point the chair of the board for RISE, bluntly stated that RISE helped industry representatives avoid "throw(ing) somebody else under the bus to take the pressure off of themselves. We didn't want anybody to be the problem, because that meant there was a problem."[1]

RISE provided the pesticide industry in the United States with a well-funded and unified voice, and their efforts were soon bolstered by the American Legislative Exchange Council (ALEC), the powerful lobbying cartel that took advantage of state-level legislative initiatives that could protect corporate and conservative interests in ways that might be less successful at the federal level. Suffice it to say, the combined forces of RISE and ALEC, coupled with the buyout of objective research at many land-grant universities, set the stage for the industrial production of alternative facts and assembly-line legislation regarding pesticide use and safety. Unfortunately, these organizations and their allies have tried to replicate these successes and stamp out local and even state initiatives to legislate the sale and use of genetically engineered crops.[2]

All is not lost, however. Organizations such as those listed in Strategy 1 above are fighting back and training citizens and policymakers at all levels of government. They all provide an array of educational resources to inform the public of the issues as well as advocacy tool kits for tackling specific issues.

Yet, it's important to go a step beyond the review of scientific literature and advocacy tool kits. Too many well-intended movements fail due to a lack of historical understanding of the problems they face. Advocates for a pesticide-free future at local and international levels (and everywhere in between) would be wise to base future strategies on a solid understanding not just of the history of pesticides but also of the industry and advertising campaigns behind them. No resource traces this history better than Will Allen's *War on Bugs*, a brilliantly researched book, illustrated throughout with an evolution of ad campaigns for the pesticide and fertilizer industries from the 1800s forward.

However, it is the timeline that follows the development of the pesticide industry and courses its way through the pages of *War on Bugs* that provides perhaps the most important lesson for advocates. The long and painful cycle of continued pesticide rollouts, subsequent failures, documentation of harm, and ultimate abandonment is documented in detail. This timeline of repeated failures reminds us that our society is on a pesticide treadmill, fueled by a constant quest for the next best panacea, no matter how toxic or dubious.

Through this chronology of unheeded lessons, we have ample evidence that the turning point toward sane and sound agricultural production will never pivot on the introduction of the next new chemical that kills.

Rather, our advocacy for a pesticide-free future requires us to pursue an ecologically oriented democracy. And we also must remember Pia Oswald's admonition that we empower our movements with a positive perspective, always emphasizing what we are advocating for more than what we are fighting against.

It's hard to say no to yes.

NOTES

Chapter 3: Bufferless

1. Stephen Harris et al., "Genetic Clues to the Origin of the Apple," *Trends in Genetics* 18, no. 8 (August 2002): 427, https://www.ncbi.nlm.nih.gov /pubmed/12142012.

2. Ibid., 428.

3. Consortium South Tyrolean Apple, *Apple Country South Tyrol*, 4th ed., November 2013, 4.

4. Co-operative Heritage Trust, "About the Rochdale Pioneers Museum," accessed January 11, 2017, http://www.rochdalepioneersmuseum.coop.

5. "Friedrich Wilhelm Raiffeisen," *Wikipedia*, last updated October 15, 2016, accessed January 11, 2017, https://en.wikipedia.org/w/index.php?title =Friedrich_Wilhelm_Raiffeisen&oldid=744478866.

6. "History: Our Roots," VOG, accessed January 11, 2017, http://www.vog.it/en /our-company/history.html.

7. Ibid.

8. Ibid.

9. Massimo Tagliavini, "The Apple Industry in South Tyrol: An Example of Successful Agriculture in a Mountain Area," presented in Berlin on February 5, 2014.

10. Ibid.

11. Julien Meyer, ed., *Apple-Producing Family Farms in South Tyrol: An Agricultural Innovation Case Study*, United Nations Food & Agriculture Organization, 2014, 12, 16.

12. Ibid., 10.

13. Ibid.

14. Consortium South Tyrolean Apple, 10.

15. Meyer, 12.

16. Esmaeil Fallahi et al., "The Importance of Apple Rootstocks on Tree Growth, Yield, Fruit Quality, Leaf Nutrition, and Photosynthesis with an Emphasis on 'Fuji,'" *HortTechnology* 12, no. 1 (January–March 2002): 38–39, https:// www.researchgate.net/publication/265753988_The_Importance_of_Apple _Rootstocks_on_Tree_Growth_Yield_Fruit_Quality_Leaf_Nutrition_and _Photosynthesis_with_an_Emphasis_on_'Fuji'.

17. Meyer, 12, 16.
18. Martin Thomann and Jürgen Christanell, "Modern Apple Growing in South Tyrol" (South Tyrol: Beratungsring Group, 2012), 1, http://apal.org.au/wp -content/uploads/2013/07/fo-ow-09-nov-modern-apple-growing-in-south -tyrol-thomann-christanell.pdf.

Chapter 4: Frozen in Time

1. Ker Than, "Iceman's Stomach Sampled — Filled with Goat Meat," National Geographic News, posted June 23, 2011, accessed December 20, 2016, http://news.nationalgeographic.com/news/2011/06/110623-iceman -mummy-otzi-meal-goat-stomach-science.
2. Gudrun Sulzenbacher, *The Glacier Mummy: Discovering the Neolithic Age with the Iceman* (Bolzano, Italy: Folio, 2011), 61.
3. Daniella Festi et al., "Mid and Late Holocene Land-Use Changes in the Ötztal Alps, Territory of the Neolithic Iceman," *Quaternary International* 353 (December 2014): 19, doi:10.1016/j.quaint.2013.07.052.
4. South Tyrol Museum of Archaeology, "Ötzi: The Discovery," accessed December 30, 2016, http://www.iceman.it/en/the-discovery.
5. Robin McKie, "Moss 'Toilet Paper' Wipes Out Mystery of Iceman's National- ity," *Deseret News*, October 23, 1994, http://www.deseretnews.com/article /383147/MOSS-TOILET-PAPER-WIPES-OUT-MYSTERY-OF-ICE MANS-NATIONALITY.html.
6. Klaus Oeggl et al., "The Reconstruction of the Last Itinerary of 'Ötzi,' the Neolithic Iceman, by Pollen Analyses from Sequentially Sampled Gut Extracts," *Quaternary Science Reviews* 26, no. 7–8 (April 2007): 859, doi:10.1016/j.quascirev.2006.12.007.
7. Kate Ravilious, "Wounded Iceman Made Epic Final Journey, Moss Shows," National Geographic News, page 2, December 4, 2008, accessed December 20, 2016, http://news.nationalgeographic.com/news/2008/12/081204 -iceman-moss_2.html.
8. Oeggl et al., 860.
9. Heather Pringle, "The Iceman's Last Meal," *Science*, June 20, 2011, http:// www.sciencemag.org/news/2011/06/icemans-last-meal.
10. Marek Janko et al., "A5 — Ötzi Meets Nanotechnology — Skin, Wound Tissue, and Stomach Content Analysis" [Abstract], 3rd Bolzano Mummy Congress — Ötzi: 25 Years of Research, September 2016, http://www.eurac .edu/en/research/health/iceman/conferences/Documents/Abstract %20Book_%20for%20web_160926.docx.
11. Oeggl et al., 860.

12. Andreas G. Heiss and Klaus Oeggl, "The Plant Macro-Remains from the Iceman Site (Tisenjoch, Italian–Austrian Border, Eastern Alps): New Results on the Glacier Mummy's Environment," *Vegetation History and Archaeobotany* 18, no. 1 (January 2009): 32, doi:10.1007/s00334-007-0140-8.
13. Sulzenbacher, 46.
14. South Tyrol Museum of Archaeology, "Ötzi: The Mummy," accessed December 30, 2016, http://www.iceman.it/en/the-mummy.
15. South Tyrol Museum of Archaeology, "Ötzi: Equipment," accessed December 27, 2016, http://www.iceman.it/en/equipment.
16. Ibid.
17. Stephen S. Hall, "Last Hours of the Iceman," National Geographic, page 2, posted July 2007, last updated September, 2007, accessed December 30, 2016, http://ngm.nationalgeographic.com/2007/07/iceman /hall-text/2.
18. Daniela Festi et al., "The Late Neolithic Settlement of Latsch, Vinschgau, Northern Italy: Subsistence of a Settlement Contemporary with the Alpine Iceman, and Located in His Valley of Origin," *Vegetation History and Archaeobotany* 20, no. 5 (September 2011): 367–79, doi:10.1007 /s00334-011-0308-0.
19. Ibid., 377.
20. South Tyrol Museum of Archaeology, "Ötzi: Clothing," accessed December 29, 2016, http://www.iceman.it/en/clothing.
21. Festi et al., 377.
22. Stefanie Jacomet, "Plant Economy and Village Life in Neolithic Lake Dwellings at the Time of the Alpine Iceman," *Vegetation History and Archaeobotany* 18, no. 1 (January 2009): 53, doi:10.1007/s00334-007-0138-2.
23. Ibid., 56.
24. Ibid., 55.

Chapter 5: Seeds

1. "The Benedictine Monastery of Marienberg in Burgeis," Stiegen Zum Himmel, accessed January 3, 2017, http://www.stiegenzumhimmel.it/en /sites/17-the-benedictine-monastery-of-marienberg-in-burgeis.html.
2. "Fürstenburg bei Burgeis im Vinschgau," Castleside of South Tyrol, accessed January 4, 2017, http://www.burgen-adi.at/burg_furstenburg.
3. "Fürstenburg," Vinschgau, accessed January 4, 2017, http://www.vinschgau .net/de/kultur-kunst/sehenswuerdigkeiten/burgen-schloesser/10 -fuerstenburg.html.
4. P.I. Robert and Edith Berhard, September 5, 2015.

Chapter 6: Seduction

1. Christian Riedl, "Potential des Obervinschgaus nachhaltig nutzen," posted May 17, 2011, accessed January 14, 2017, http://www.vinschgerwind.it/archiv-beitraege-vinschgau/2011/ausgabe-10-11/567-schleis-obervinschgau-landwirtschaft-alexander-agethle.

Chapter 7: Organic Uprising

1. "Biozide — Krebserkrankung durch gemischte Expositionen und Schadstoffe: Laudatio für Prof. Dr. Irene Witte anlässlich der Verleihung der Rachel-Carson Medaille von Prof. Dr. med. Rainer Frentzel-Beyme, Bremen," Umwelt-schutzgruppe Vinschgau, https://umweltvinschgau.files.wordpress.com/2011/10/laudatio-witte-fb.pdf.
2. Josef Laner, "Nicht verboten, aber bedenklich," *Der Vinschger*, accessed January 14, 2017, http://www.dervinschger.it/artikel.phtml?id_artikel=17225.
3. "Umweltschutzgruppe Vinschgau," YouTube video, 5:01, posted by "initiativesuedtirol," November 14, 2011, https://www.youtube.com/watch?v=S6RADsqsHBs&html5=1.
4. Ibid.
5. "Großes Interesse unter den Zuhören: Reaktionen — Viele Fragen rund um die Lebensmittelsicherheit und die gesundheitlichen Auswirkungen von Spritzmittel im Obstbau." *Tageszeitung Dolomiten,* November 5, 2011.

Chapter 8: Rallying Cry

1. "Bauernbund Vinschgau: Ja zu Versuchsfeld Laatsch," Südtiroler Bauernbund, posted April 16, 2012, accessed March 5, 2017, http://www.sbb.it/home/news-detail/index/2012/04/16/bauernbund-vinschgau-ja-zu-versuchsfeld-laatsch.

Chapter 9: A Precautionary Tale

1. "Tavola 07: Principi attivi contenuti nei prodotti fitosanitari per ettaro di superficie trattabile (in chilogrammi). Dettaglio per regione — Anno 2014—," accessed March 9, 2017, http://agri.istat.it/jsp/dawinci.jsp?q=pl07a000001 0000012000&an=2014&ig=1&ct=428&id=3A%7C45A%7C66A%7C67A.
2. Christine Helfer, "Volksabstimmung wird stattfinden — Mals pestizidefrei?," posted July 12, 2013, accessed December 5, 2015, https://www.salto.bz/article/07122013/volksabstimmung-wird-stattfinden-mals-pestizidefrei.
3. "Travola 07."
4. "Südtiroler wehren sich gegen die Vergiftung ihrer Heimat," Südostschweiz, posted April 26, 2013, accessed March 10, 2017, http://www.suedostschweiz.ch/vermischtes/suedtiroler-wehren-sich-gegen-die-vergiftung-ihrer-heimat.

5. "Eine Schweinerei," *Der Vinschgerwind* 10–13, no. 417 (May 13, 2013).

6. "Zeitung Vinschgerwind 10-13 Vinschgau Suedtirol," *Issuu*, posted May 14, 2013, accessed March 12, 2017, https://issuu.com/vinschgerwind/docs /zeitung_vinschgerwind_10-13_vinschgau?reader3=1.

Chapter 10: Bedsheets to Banners

1. Madlen Ottenschläger, "Umweltgifte: Aufstand unter Apfelbäumen (Reportage, Brigitte Woman 4/2015)," posted April 2, 2015, accessed October 2, 2015, http://www.madlenottenschlaeger.de/umweltgifte -aufstand-unter-apfelbaeumen-reportage-brigitte-woman-42015.

Chapter 11: Manifesto

1. Immanuel Kant, *Die Metaphysik der Sitten* (1797), "Erster Teil. Metaphysische Anfangsgründe der Rechtslehre: Einleitung in die Rechtslehre," B. Was ist Recht?, C. Allgemeines Prinzip des Rechts, http://www.zeno.org /Philosophie/M/Kant,+Immanuel/Die+Metaphysik+der+Sitten/Erster +Teil.+Metaphysische+Anfangsgr%C3%BCnde+der+Rechtslehre /Einleitung+in+die+Rechtslehre.

2. Nancy Myers, "Debating the Precautionary Principle," Science and Environmental Health Network, posted March 2000, accessed May 23, 2016, http:// www.sehn.org/ppdebate.html.

3. AGRIOS, "Guidelines for Integrated Pome Cultivation 2017," accessed March 19, 2017, http://www.agrios.it/guidelines.html.

4. AGRIOS, "History," accessed March 19, 2017, http://www.agrios.it /history.html.

5. James M. Witt, "Agricultural Spray Adjuvants," accessed March 7, 2017, http://psep.cce.cornell.edu/facts-slides-self/facts/gen-peapp-adjuvants.aspx.

6. Melinda Hemmelgarn, "Food Sleuth Radio, Warren Porter Interview," produced by Dan Hemmelgarn, PRX, posted February 16, 2017, accessed March 19, 2017, https://beta.prx.org/stories/198129. This interview with Dr. Warren Porter is an exceptionally concise scientific overview of how pesticides and herbicides can impact the human endocrine, nervous, and immune systems while also creating issues of genotoxicity.

7. Maria Mergel, "Precautionary Principle," Toxipedia, posted May 11, 2016, accessed March 30, 2016, http://www.toxipedia.org/display/toxipedia /Precautionary+Principle.

8. Alexander Schiebel, "Pestizid-Abwehrkampf und Demokratie," Salto, March 16, 2017, https://www.salto.bz/de/article/16032017/pestizid-abwehrkampf -und-demokratie.

9. Robert Nef, "Direct Democracy: What Does It Mean and How Does It Work?," *IDDE*, May 3, 2016, http://iddeurope.org/direct-democracy-what-does-it-mean-and-how-does-it-work/1210.
10. "'Cultura Socialis': Jury-und Publikumspreis vergeben," Landesverwaltung, posted March 24, 2014, accessed March 19, 2017, http://www.provinz.bz.it/news/de/news.asp?news_action=4&news_article_id=454052.
11. "Bäuerliche Zukunft," Bäuerliche Zukunft, accessed March 19, 2017, http://www.baeuerlichezukunftmals.com/baeuerliche-zukunft.

Chapter 12: *Ja!*

1. "Bereiche und Projekte," DA, accessed April 29, 2017, http://da.bz.it/bereiche-und-projekte.html.
2. Report of the Special Rapporteur on the Right to Food, Human Rights Council, 34th Session (27 Feburary–24 March, 2017), Agenda Item 3 (United Nations, January 24, 2017), http://reliefweb.int/report/world/report-special-rapporteur-right-food-ahrc3448, 22.
3. Ibid.
4. Damian Carrington, "UN Experts Denounce 'Myth' Pesticides Are Necessary to Feed the World," Environment, *Guardian*, March 7, 2017, https://www.theguardian.com/environment/2017/mar/07/un-experts-denounce-myth-pesticides-are-necessary-to-feed-the-world.
5. Danny Hakim, "Monsanto Weed Killer Roundup Faces New Doubts on Safety in Unsealed Documents," *New York Times*, posted March 14, 2017, accessed April 30, 2017, https://www.nytimes.com/2017/03/14/business/monsanto-roundup-safety-lawsuit.html.
6. "International Monsanto Tribunal – April 18, 2017," accessed April 30, 2017, http://www.monsanto-tribunal.org/Conclusions.

An Activist's Primer

1. Anne Nagro, "[RISE 25th Anniversary] Looking Back: The Rise of RISE," October 19, 2015, PCT: Pest Control Technology, http://www.pctonline.com/article/pct1015-responsible-industry-sound-environment-rise.
2. Matthew Porter, "State Preemption Law: The Battle for Local Control of Democracy," Beyond Pesticides, from *Pesticides and You* 33, no. 3 (Fall 2013), https://www.beyondpesticides.org/assets/media/documents/lawn/activist/documents/StatePreemption.pdf.

INDEX

Index

Index

Index

Index

Index

Index

Index

TOPPLING GOLIATH

WWW.TOPPLINGGOLIATH.ORG

Toppling Goliath is a multimedia project depicting how a group of citizens in the South Tirolean town of Mals banded together to pursue a pesticide-free future, ultimately becoming the first town in the world to use democratic methods to ban all pesticides. Comprised of a traveling pop-up show, short films, a website, and the book *A Precautionary Tale: How One Small Town Banned Pesticides, Preserved Its Food Heritage, and Inspired a Movement* (Chelsea Green Publishing), the project is a multilingual — English, German, and Italian — exploration of the dangers of pesticides, alternative models of sustainable agriculture, the conservation of traditional foodways and landscapes, direct democracy, and successful strategies for activists.

The project offers a portable pop-up show of twenty "information artworks" — by internationally acclaimed multimedia artist, author, and filmmaker Douglas Gayeton, a cofounder of the Lexicon of Sustainability — for use by groups throughout the world. Short films, photos, interviews, and an "activist toolkit" are available to international audiences at www .topplinggoliath.org, thanks to the support of the Lexicon of Sustainability.

Toppling Goliath is a two-year collaborative effort between the Lexicon of Sustainability, Brunnenburg Agricultural Museum & International Study Center, ididthisfilm.com, and Green Mountain College.

For more information and to contact the Toppling Goliath team, visit the website at www.topplinggoliath.org or send an email to ja@toppling goliath.org.

ABOUT THE AUTHOR

Eric Hudiburg

PHILIP ACKERMAN-LEIST, author of *Rebuilding the Foodshed* and *Up Tunket Road*, is a professor at Green Mountain College, where he established the college's farm and sustainable agriculture curriculum, directs its Farm & Food Project, and founded its Master of Science in Sustainable Food Systems, the nation's first online graduate program in food systems, featuring applied comparative research of students' home bioregions. He and his wife, Erin, farmed in the South Tirol region of the Alps and North Carolina before beginning their twenty-year homesteading and farming venture in Pawlet, Vermont. With more than two decades of field experience working on farms, in the classroom, and with regional food systems collaborators, Philip focuses on examining and reshaping local and regional food systems from the ground up.

ABOUT THE FOREWORD AUTHOR

VANDANA SHIVA is a world-renowned environmental leader and recipient of the 1993 Right Livelihood Award (the "Alternative" Nobel Peace Prize) as well as the United Nations Environment Programme's Global 500 Award and the Earth Day International Award of the United Nations. She has authored several bestselling books, including *Earth Democracy*, *Who Really Feeds the World*, *Water Wars*, and *Soil Not Oil*. Activist and scientist, Shiva leads, with Ralph Nader and Jeremy Rifkin, the International Forum on Globalization. Before becoming an activist, Shiva was one of India's leading physicists.

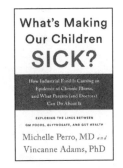
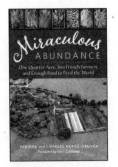